TO:

_____

FROM:

_____

MESSAGE:

_____
_____
_____
_____
_____
_____

DATE:

_____

This book is for every person who has, at one time or another, doubted themselves and the grace of a living God.

Published by First Media and Events © 2016
First Edition 2023

Cover and content layout by Johan Kok, IseeCreative
Photo credits: Steve Haag | Cricket South Africa | Gallo Images
David van der Sandt | Salomien Smal | Outsider Media
Translated by Lourieke Haller
Edited by Gillian Fraser

Unless otherwise stated, photos have been used with permission.
We have made special efforts to trace ownership and copyright details of all photographs in this book. Where questions arise regarding the use of a photograph, we apologise for any error on our part and are prepared to rectify the matter.

All video footage is recorded and used with the permission
of each sportsperson in the book.

Scripture quotations have been taken from the English Standard Version,
unless otherwise stated.
All rights reserved. Used with permission.

Typeset and printed by Print on Demand
ISBN 978-0-6397-7120-5

© All rights reserved. No part of this book or video may be reproduced by any means, mechanical or electronic, including laser disc or tape recordings and photocopying without the written permission of the publisher, except citations for research and reviews.

Bibliography:
wikipedia.org

LISTEN
God's voice
in my life

Karien Basson
in collaboration with Tanya Powell

Foreword: Allister Coetzee

Proverbs 3:5-6, NKJV
"Trust in the Lord with all your heart, and lean not on your own understanding; in all your ways acknowledge Him, and He shall direct your paths."

It is indeed a great honour and privilege to be part of this book! It is a precious source of hope, love, and encouragement, and it also serves as a moral guideline in our lives.

I met Karien Basson in 2010 – of course during the rugby season – while she was working as an announcer for Radio Tygerberg. What struck me immediately was her humanity, how she interacts with people – sharing in their joy and engaging with their sadness with love and empathy. The listeners could always identify with the players' and coaches' frustrations and emotions. She is sincere, objective about her opinions, and has always used the truth as her guideline – a God-fearing person!

This book will definitely take readers to greater heights, with the help of our Master's game plan! With so much negativity in our society these days, we sometimes get tired and feel like we have run out of answers. These 41 stories teach us to trust in God, regardless of circumstances and challenges! Just listen...

Just like a compass accurately indicates direction, so do the Scriptures in this book. The Bible is our moral compass for our life's journey. Our true North is reliable and constant – our Heavenly Father, the Alpha and the Omega.

Proverbs 3:1-10 depicts the value of following the Bible – so simple. Just do it and strive to live according to it! Every story in this book reflects this and refers to God's presence in every person's life. God is the anchor in my life and, therefore, I consider Proverbs 3 as my bread and butter, food for my soul!

"Trust in the Lord with all your heart, and lean not on your own understanding; in all your ways acknowledge Him, and He shall direct your paths." – Proverbs 3:5-6, NKJV

Foreword: Johan Ackermann

Romans 8:28,
"And we know that all things work together for good to those who love God, to those who are the called according to His purpose."

I believe that God shapes and guides us through everything, and especially when we do not understand everything; His presence is always there. Our character is shaped and our testimony built; we just have to trust and believe (Heb 11:1).

In every struggle or situation, His voice is there, and He will make all things work together for good (Rom 8:28). This book shares inspiring testimonies about challenges that people have had to overcome; they testify about the influence and hope of God's voice. I pray that those who read this will find new hope in God and realise that He is with each one of us, regardless of our mistakes and our past.

Our happiness, peace, and how we feel should not be linked to success or other people's opinions, because then we are on an emotional seesaw. They must be anchored in who you are in God (a child of God) – He is with you, He created you, and His time and plans are perfect. Even if we make a choice that sometimes takes us on a detour, He stays with us and His voice is always there. May we make a difference when and where we are in that situation. Sometimes when we look back at a certain time in our lives, we only later see how God's voice was always there – even if we did not realise it at the time.

You do not have to be a Springbok rugby player or a famous athlete to make a difference. No, make a difference where you are – at school, your workplace, next to the sports field, and at home. God wants to let His voice testify through you where you are – where sports stars may never get to.

My favourite Bible verse is Joshua 1:9, this is my prayer for everyone.

Congratulations to Karien and Tanya on compiling this book and may everyone who reads it realise that God's voice is true, that Jesus Christ is taking their life's journey with them, and that God always receives all the glory.

Foreword: Toks van der Linde

1 Corinthians 13:4,
"Love is patient and kind; love does not envy or boast; it is not arrogant or rude."

I page through the stories in this book and realise one thing: God is good, in the midst of and despite the circumstances in our past, present, and future! These stories make me reflect on my own story – I see God's grace in everything.

Toks – a name that needs an explanation.

Albert-dingetjie-toksie-skat (Albert-little-thing-toks-darling). This was my older matric brother's attempt at name-calling after some merciless teasing by me, his annoying younger brother, about the appearance of his girlfriend. I was in standard five and had a lot to say about how his girlfriend looked. This strange combination, *Albert-dingetjie-toksie-skat*, was the best he could come up with as a counterattack! Nevertheless, the nickname stuck and "Toks" van der Linde was born.

It was the descriptive name and passion for the game that would only make my baptism of fire and storm, at the age of 22, that much worse. I was the first choice for the Springboks when, unfortunately, a tackle with a knock on my neck announced the end of my rugby career. My broken neck halted a dream that had lived in my heart for eighteen years. Question upon question sounded in my head. Why now, Lord? Why me, Lord? Why did You allow this?

Just like many of the sports stars throughout the pages of this book, one meets God in the darkest places of your life. Today I look back on a rich rugby career. The Lord was gracious and I will forever be grateful that I was able to realise my dream. I underwent three neck surgeries and was able to enjoy years of good rugby. I know that I should have actually died – because of my injury and because I wanted to take my own life one night – but God had other plans for me. I am incredibly grateful for that...

Today I know that when one door closes, fifty other doors open. Even if things do not always turn out the way we planned them, God is still in control. At the age of 53, this book has taught me one more thing: You must listen to God's voice and have Him by your side.

I know how it feels when you let go of God. You feel it in your deepest, innermost being. When you leave Him, you lose everything. That is why our world looks the way it does. It is time for us to ask for forgiveness and to turn back to God, because He is the only true Saviour for every person and for our country.

Foreword: Johan Beukes

Romans 12:2, TMT
"Don't become so well-adjusted to your culture that you fit into it without even thinking. Instead, fix your attention on God. You'll be changed from the inside out."

Listening – one of the hardest things to do. That is why this book is special to me.

It contains stories of high achievers who have listened and are still listening:
- to Jesus' invitation: "Follow Me ... You are made in My image ... You are more than what you do."
- to their innate passion for sports.
- to their bodies' limits – when to exert themselves, when to rest, and when to recover.
- to coaches who guide them to reach their full potential as individuals.
- to team members who help them perform in good times and in bad times.
- to family that creates a safe space of unconditional love.
- to the beginning seasons and the end seasons.

If I could extend an invitation to all who read this book, it would be this:

Place your life before God
"So here's what I want you to do, God helping you: Take your everyday, ordinary life—your sleeping, eating, going-to-work, and walking-around life—and place it before God as an offering. Embracing what God does for you is the best thing that you can do for Him. Don't become so well-adjusted to your culture that you fit into it without even thinking. Instead, fix your attention on God. You'll be changed from the inside out. Readily recognise what He wants from you, and quickly respond to it. Unlike the culture around you, always dragging you down to its level of immaturity, God brings the best out of you, develops well-formed maturity in you." – Romans 12:1-2 (TMT)

Listen...
He loves you...
He knows you...
He calls you...

FOREWORD

Tanya Powell

In Psalm 37:23 (RSV) David says,

"The steps of a man are from the Lord, and He establishes him in whose way he delights."

When I look back on my life, this verse has a deeper meaning now. As a young, little blonde girl, the smells, colours, and sounds of rugby matches were much more familiar and safe to me than the so-called "normal" environment of a primary school girl. Weekends were spent next to sports fields, in the company of those who love rugby – and there my passion for the sport of rugby began.

When I say passion, it was never a desire to play or just to be a supporter, but rather a deep appreciation for what it truly entails to be a professional rugby player, as well as the challenges that come with it. It is, therefore, no surprise that I qualified as a biokineticist – specialising in rugby rehabilitation. I wanted to make a difference and play a part in the rugby environment that I respect so much, rehabilitation was the most sensible choice. Little did I know that the Lord had already started preparing me, from the age of five, for the life He had planned for me.

The words of many who warned me to "never marry a rugby player, because you are only looking for trouble" ensured that I made the walls around my heart even higher and thicker against any possible relationship with a rugby player. But see, God does not listen to the opinions of the world; He has His own plans for your life. And so, a wonderful man walked into my life. One who radiates respect, integrity, and morals – and God smiled, because this man is a rugby player. For the past 13 years, I have journeyed as a rugby wife (sometimes "widow"), walking a road with a man who has an incredible love for the young men who play rugby. Out of those special relationships and connections, we share the stories of rugby players' lives that have changed and touched my own life. Stories that deserve to be told – not because they come from the mouths of famous people, but because God uses broken people to testify to His goodness.

Everyone's story is a delicate thread that connects people from different places, backgrounds, and preferences on a spiritual level – it is a thread that has been dyed red with Jesus' Blood and His grace. It was a privilege to be able to work on this project with a precious friend. I trust that this is a project that will change hearts, as it has already done with mine.

Karien Basson

We love an all-powerful, all-knowing, omnipresent, and indescribable God who controls the universe. The One who always had time to answer me in a way that I could understand.

I was only eight years old when I came to know God. As a logical thinker, I wanted clear answers from Him; precisely because everything around me could be explained biologically or scientifically. I never questioned the reality of a living God, but His character traits, as seen through the eyes of others, were always contrary to how I experienced Him personally. With the desperate pleas of a mother's prayers addressed to a heavenly Father, my mother asked Him to meet her constantly-searching daughter in a very personal way. I was given my own little yellow box of "Bread on the Water" Bible promises. I would ponder and pray about a specific topic, and then ask God to answer me through one of the scripture cards that I would draw. I then read the entire chapter and trusted God to answer me in this way. It was certainly not like a Lotto machine, full of luck and potential answers. I only used the box when I had big questions to make. That box of Bible cards carried me through the toughest choices in my life ... to this day. God met me at my level of faith again and again – it was logical, black and white, but it still required faith and a relationship with Him to hear His voice. Not because I am special, but because I had established a non-negotiable principle of seeking guidance through His Word.

In October 2022, it was a Bible card and the words of Psalm 9, dotted with sports terminology, that led me to start writing this sports book.

*Psalm 9 (TMT), "I'm thanking you, God, from a full heart, **I'm writing the book on your wonders**. I'm **whistling**, laughing, and **jumping** for joy; I'm singing your song, High God. The day my enemies turned tail and ran; they **stumbled** on you and fell on their faces. You took over and set everything right; when I needed you, you were there, taking charge. You **blow the whistle** on godless nations; you **throw dirty players out of the game, wipe their names right off the roster**. Enemies disappear from the **sidelines**, their reputation **trashed**, their names erased from the **halls of fame**. God holds the high **centre**, he sees and sets the world's mess right. He decides what is right for us earthlings, gives people their just deserts. God's a safe house for the battered, a sanctuary during bad times. The moment you arrive, you relax; you're never sorry you **knocked**. Sing your songs to Zion-dwelling God, **tell his stories to everyone you meet**: How he tracks down killers yet keeps his eye on us, registers every whimper and moan. Be kind to me, God; I've been **kicked** around long enough. Once you've pulled me back from the gates of death, I'll **write the book on Hallelujahs**; on the corner of Main and First I'll hold a street meeting; I'll be the song leader; we'll fill the air with salvation songs."*

I am grateful that God entrusts us with something as precious as this. My prayer is that you will meet God in a new way through the pages of this book; may you LISTEN when He speaks and may He be a reality to you, forever.

Table of Contents

Neil Powell	1
Duane Vermeulen	7
Mignon du Preez	13
Joey Mongalo	19
Schalk Brits	27
Swys de Bruin	33
Victor Matfield	41
Isabella Kruger	47
Theuns Stofberg	53
Thomas du Toit	61
Reinardt Janse van Rensburg	69
Ine-Marí Venter	75
Sandile "Stix" Ngcobo	81
Ivan van Rooyen	87
Jannie Putter	95
Ruhan Nel	105
Vernon Philander	111
Philip Snyman	117
Cameron Wright	123
Brok Harris	129
Adele Broodryk	135

"Be still, and know that I am God!"
Psalm 46:10, NLT

Arnold Geerdts	143
Muller du Plessis	149
Anruné Weyers	155
James Murphy	161
Angelo Davids	169
Willem Alberts	175
Grant Lottering	181
Dr Eduard Coetzee	187
Pierre Coetzer	195
Rocco van Rooyen	203
Zoë Kruger	209
Impi Visser	215
Hennie Koortzen	221
Ronald Brown	229
Henco Venter	235
Warren Whiteley	241
Theo Bierman	247
Wenda Nel	255
Marco Labuschagne	263
Leon Schuster	269

> *"Live carefree before God;*
> *he is most careful with you."*
> 1 Peter 5:7, TMT

Neil Powell

Johannes Daniel (Neil) Powell, born on the 28th of June 1978 and better known to some as "Coach Neil", is a former South African rugby player and head coach of the national sevens rugby team (the Blitzboks). He is currently the director of rugby for the Sharks. This golden boy from Namibia and denizen of Bloemfontein looks back on an illustrious rugby career that began in 1993 at Hoërskool Sentraal in Bloemfontein. Neil's rugby career as a student and provincial player includes matches as a player for Free State u21 and UFS Shimlas (1998), Toyota Cheetahs (2000-2003 and 2008), Sharks (2003), Cats (2004-2005), Griquas (2005), and Blue Bulls (2006-2007) in the Currie Cup series and Vodacom Super Rugby competition.

Neil donned the green and gold for the first time in 1999 when he played for the South African u21 team. He also represented South Africa as a Blitzbok and later as captain in 32 tournaments and 91 matches as part of the HSBC Sevens World Series (2001-2003 and 2007-2012).

Under Paul Treu's coaching, the Blitzboks won a bronze medal at the Commonwealth Games in Delhi in 2010 – Neil participated as a player. In 2013 he took over the title and responsibility as head coach of his beloved Blitzboks and fulfilled that role until 2022. During this nine-year period, the Blitzboks experienced unprecedented victories, achieved and maintained records, and, among other things, won a gold medal at the 2014 Commonwealth Games in Glasgow, a bronze medal at the 2016 Olympic Games in Rio de Janeiro, and a gold medal at the 2022 Commonwealth Games in Birmingham. Under Neil's golden reign as Springbok sevens coach, the Blitzboks became the holders of three World Rugby Sevens Series titles. Of the 75 World Series tournaments under his leadership, the team played in 37 finals and won 22 of them.

Neil is the only person in rugby sevens who has a gold medal as a player and coach in the World Series to his name.

He is married to Tanya, and they have two sons, Joshua and Caleb.

My love for sport began... *with my brothers. I was the youngest of three and my older brothers started playing rugby before me. I later had big dreams of becoming a Springbok, especially after I watched the 'Springbok-sage 1891-1976' (Afrikaans videotape).*

If I was not a sports star, I would... *have become a farmer or would have liked to have my own restaurant or maybe just be the chef of a restaurant.*

I am incredibly grateful for... *my family. I married a God-fearing woman and have two young men with hearts for Jesus.*

If I could edit my life, I would... *have liked to do better academically in school. I was not very fond of sitting behind the books. I would also have taken a few more chances, as I was far too exemplary.*

One of the biggest lessons I learnt this year... *Maybe not this year, but a few years ago: The only opinion that matters about me is God's opinion. The Lord wants us to love the people who judge us and it is not always easy.*

My biggest achievement was... *when one of my former players said that he is raising his children differently because of my involvement in his life. I feel my greatest work and purpose is to raise up a new generation of fathers who are faithful and who will raise the next generation of children according to God's Word.*

The best decision I ever made... *was not going to Saracens in 2009. I would never have met my wife.*

The Bible verse that carries me...

2 Corinthians 12:9,
"But he said to me, 'My grace is sufficient for you, for my power is made perfect in weakness.' Therefore, I will boast all the more gladly about my weaknesses, so that Christ's power may rest on me."

Neil with Seabelo Senatla, Ruhan Nel, Werner Kok, and Angelo Davids

Neil and Siya Kolisi congratulating each other

MY STORY
Neil Powell

One of the first newspaper headlines about the Powells was in the Namibian newspaper, *Die Republikein*. It read: "There is rugby blood in the Powell brothers' sporting veins." Neil, the youngest of the three Powell brothers, stood proudly alongside his brothers as they received their rugby awards. Like little organ pipes they stood there, from the oldest to youngest. This is where the love for the sport began. There was constant competition amongst the three, and teasing back and forth, but also an unstoppable support for each other and a passion for the oval ball.

According to psychology research, birth order has a significant influence on behaviour as an adult, with the last-born often described as sociable, charming, loving, and open, but also temperamental, irresponsible, and self-centred. The negative qualities of this description could be written on a cricket ball and hit for a six, because young Neil Powell would break this stereotype and do everything differently, as he did not run with the herd. No, even from a young age he would not play for the pavilion or bow the knee to expectations. He would follow the rules and respect leadership but would politely stand his man when he disagreed with someone. *"I had four strong older examples in my life. All I had to do was to pay attention and listen, follow in their footsteps, and do what they did, because all of them were hardworking, honourable people in their own right. My father was a strict man who did not tolerate any shortcuts in life. My mother put in extra work to make sure that all three of us, her sons, had ironed clothes to wear, a good breakfast in our bellies, and money in the bank to get us through university."* The Powells were indeed a formidable team, but when they left the vast expanse of Namibia for a plot in the Free State, the boys had to go to boarding school, and with it, Neil had to face the challenge of following in his brothers' wake. *"My brothers were brilliant in everything they did. They performed well academically and, more often than not, they were the captains or leaders of their sports teams and in their boarding schools."* Neil would never shake off the underlying expectations of teachers and fellow students because he was a Powell. He had to perform even better, or at least be up to Jimmy and Corné's standards. The persistent, underlying pressure built up and gnawed away at him. Before Neil could protect his heart, the fear of self-doubt took hold.

> *"I am not good enough.*
> *Will I ever be good enough?"*

These words ran through his thoughts like a refrain. No one but Neil and God could sort it out, because the train of thought and nagging identity crisis hounded Neil, keeping him from a powerful calling on his life and preventing him from developing into the man God intended him to be. He could prove himself on the rugby field, but in the daily course of life, there were more questions than answers in young Neil's heart.

"I had to sit at the feet of the Lord for months, because after a while I could no longer put up a front anymore. I did not know who I was when I took off that rugby jersey. I knew I was Neil Powell, the scrum half and rugby player on the field, but off the field, I searched for who I really was, full of uncertainty."

As a famous American author wrote, "The reward for conformity is that everyone likes you but yourself." Neil had to press the stop button. He had to take hold of 2 Corinthians 12:9 with both hands, start believing it, and then start living it, *"My grace is sufficient for you, for my power is made perfect in weakness. Therefore, I will boast all the more gladly about my weaknesses, so that Christ's power may rest on me."*

Neil would come to know God. A God of mercy and honesty; of integrity and respect; of love and compassion. The One who had him in mind in his mother's womb and the One who would shape him into the man he was supposed to be. Neil could anchor himself in this knowledge, never to doubt again.

"I cannot imagine achieving everything I have done without God. I do not know how one deals with failure and even success, without God."

"How do you deal with absolute failure? How do you stay humble in great success? I do not think it is possible." Neil started and established a non-negotiable relationship with God. During his sports and coaching career, he would gain fame for his "poker face" that shows little to no emotion. He could do this because achievement – winning or losing – was no longer what the game of rugby was about. No, there is no price that could be placed on the hearts of young men and no rand value could be attached to relationships. Neil was aware of the privilege and opportunity he was given, to lead the future husbands, fathers, and leaders of our country. *"God still deemed it a good idea to entrust the hearts, lives, and identities of a bunch of young men to me, even after all my own fears and questions. It is my responsibility to, together with God, establish their identities in Him. I choose relationships first, over the game."*

Time and time again, Neil has to remind himself of his own words when the pressure of negative media and opinions on social media comes knocking at his door. That is when it matters, in the dark times when there is no celebrating on mountaintops. It is then when you should guard against setting up camp in the valley of the shadow of death;

you must keep moving, pushing on, and seeking God's voice amidst the noise. *"There have been several times where I cried out to God because I could no longer see the light; a time when I sat alone in a hotel room in Vancouver and really wrestled with the Lord. It felt like He abandoned me. However, God never leaves us, and suddenly His peace came over me, because He wanted to impress the message on me, 'I've got you, My child.'"*

Neil stands firm in his living relationship with God and considers the affirming Bible verses that people have sent him, or prophecies about his life that have come true, as confirmation that God will always carry him and never leave him. Even in his weakness, his inabilities, or doubts about the things that are not his strengths, Neil knows – God is there! *"I think the price I pay for being in the public eye and playing this role has taken away my privacy and time with my family. But I also know that God knows my heart. I was like Moses. I had a fear of public speaking, but He prepared me step by step, and day by day for the work He wanted me to do now."*

Rugby has long ceased to be Neil's identity. In reality, he is just a man who wants to spend enough time with his family and does not want to get stuck in the rush of society's ideas. He is a man with an extraordinary talent for leadership and mentorship; a coach with a passion for players and sport and is one who does not concern himself too much with achievements. What does carry weight for him is what God says, as well as the opinions of the men he works with daily. *"Because, without me having to tell them, they must see respect, honesty, and sincerity in my actions. That is all that matters, and that is all that really counts."*

What do you think is the biggest obstacle in men's lives?

I think that it is different for each man. There are many common obstacles that can be highlighted: money, gambling, pride, complacency, drinking, drugs, women and pornography, among other things. The list goes on and on because there are too many things to mention. However, it depends on each man. Will it forever be his obstacle that will hold him back from reaching his full potential – from what the Lord has planned for him? Or, is he willing to get over it, lay it down, ask for forgiveness, be healed, and move on in his life? God cannot make that choice for a man. The person must make that decision in their own heart, soul, and mind.

How would you like to be remembered?

I would like to be remembered as someone who helped raise the next generation of fathers and husbands. I really think that is what is needed – a new generation of men who are reliable husbands and loving fathers.

Neil with wife, Tanya, and sons Joshua and Caleb

Photographer: Abri Kruger

Your message to South Africa

There is room for all of us in South Africa. We must be more tolerant of each other and operate out of love. If everyone just takes the time to sit and listen to each other, learn together, and look at each other through the eyes of love, then unity in our country is not too far-fetched. We should strive to become a country where we not only tolerate each other, but also love each other, regardless of colour, race, or gender.

Neil Powell
Exclusive interview
Scan the code to watch

Neil with his father Johan, mother Linda, and older brothers Jimmy and Corné

Duane Vermeulen

Daniel Johannes "Duane" Vermeulen is a South African professional rugby player. His nickname, given to him by fans, is "Thor" – the Norse god of thunder. He currently dons the green and gold for the South African national team and has been playing for Ulster in the United Rugby Championship since 2021. Duane, a child of the Lowveld, born in Nelspruit on the 3rd of July 1986, is a former learner of Nelspruit High School. His illustrious rugby career includes playing 26 games for the Pumas (2005-2006), 28 for the Free State and 20 for the Cheetahs (2007-2008), 38 games for the Western Province (2009-2015), 89 games for the Stormers (2009-2015), 68 for Toulon (2015-2018), 13 for the Kubota Sears (2018-2020), 6 for the Blue Bulls, and 23 games for the Bulls in Super Rugby (2019-2021).

Duane made his international debut for the Springboks on the 8th of September 2012 as part of the starting team that would face off against Australia. In the subsequent tests, he showed his mettle against New Zealand, and, on the 29th of September 2012, he was part of the team that tasted victory with a final score of 31-8 against Australia. He has played 63 games for the Springboks since 2012.

His honour roll and awards include: SARU Rugby Player of the Year 2014, Super Rugby Player of the Year 2014, Super Rugby "Unlocked" Player of the Year 2020, SA Rugby Player of the Year for 2020, and Currie Cup winner.

As a key player for the victorious Springbok team in the 2019 Rugby World Cup final against England in Yokohama Stadium, Japan, Duane helped ensure that the Webb-Ellis Trophy returned to South Africa for the third time. This eighth man, who is equally skilled at playing blindside and openside flanker, was named man of the match.

My love for sports began... *from a young age. I was interested in any and all sports and looked up to my father who was a talented sportsman. At school I was very interested in athletics, especially field events such as high jump, discus, and javelin. My father also passed on his love for pole vaulting to me; sport has always been in my blood. I played my first rugby match barefoot in the snow at De Doorns and, from then on, it was just love for this sport.*

If I was not a sports star, I would... *want to be a chef or a farmer! Fortunately, I can still chase those dreams...*

I am incredibly grateful for... *my family – without their support I would not be where I am today. I am grateful for good coaches who have believed in me and for opportunities that have come my way. I am grateful for the talents that the Lord has blessed me with. I have the privilege of doing what I love every day and making it my career.*

If I could edit my life, I would... *not change anything. I do not think one should ever try to edit the past, because one learns important lessons for the future. Every day is a new step and every choice you make – good or bad – determines how you approach the future. Are you going to do it in the same manner, or are you going to make adjustments and improve? Enjoy every day to the fullest. Dwelling on the past and what you could have changed prevents you from moving forward.*

If I had to change something, it would be to have my father in my life for a little while longer. I would have liked to get to know him better. And I would have liked it if he could also have been a part of my wife and children's lives.

One of the biggest lessons I learnt this year... *is that your family, relatives, and friends are one of the most precious gifts you can receive. Time is a gift from above – you must spend it well and with the people you love the most.*

My biggest achievement is... *being a part of the World Cup team in 2019 and being a dad to two incredible boys.*

The Bible verse that carries me... *I actually have two that are very special to me.*

Lamentations 3:24-26,
"I say to myself, 'The Lord is my portion; therefore, I will wait for him.' The Lord is good to those whose hope is in him, to the one who seeks him; it is good to wait quietly for the salvation of the Lord."

The other verse is **1 Corinthians 13:4 and 13,**
"Love is patient, love is kind. It does not envy, it does not boast, it is not proud ... And now these three remain: faith, hope, and love. But the greatest of these is love."
This was a part of the sermon on our wedding day.

MY STORY
Duane Vermeulen

It was a very special day in Duane's life – the day he confessed his faith during his confirmation. It happened late in his life, in 2011, the year before he was to marry Ezél. *"What is your testimony, Duane?"* the reverend asked him. *"Today I am here to testify and tell my story. I can declare:*

'I am Duane Vermeulen, and I am a child of God. Without Him, nothing is possible.'"

It was the hard Lowveld soil of Mbombela and the tough snow-covered grass in Touwsrivier, De Doorns, that shaped the young Duane Vermeulen from a rough diamond into South Africa's own "Thor" in green and gold. He plays his heart out, leaves everything behind on the field, and never holds back, because that is what he saw in his father during the eight short years of life with him. His dad, André, played club rugby in his younger days and also played for Boland. He always tackled a task with vigour. This inspired the young Duane – a spitting image of his dad – to follow in his father's footsteps. Duane inherited his dad's athletic talent, and, like his mother, wears his heart on his sleeve. He has never seen the point of holding back and not showing how he feels or being who he truly is. He is passionate in everything that he does, always! After his dad's death, Estelien, his mom, took on the dual roles of both mother and father. There was nothing that she could not do and, with the extra work she took on, she raised Duane and his little sister in a safe family environment. She leaned on a young Duane who had to grow up fast, who had to learn to endure, persist, and push through. He learnt about working hard and doing extra chores: from how to make his sister's ponytails to cooking and doing housekeeping. Because that is what it takes and that is what a family does in difficult times. They stand together, work together, and play together.

It is also this character development that made Duane a perfectionist from childhood. *"I am a little OCD. I choose my roommates on tour because I do not tolerate a messy room. I cannot function in such an environment."*

It is the fundamental things in life that are non-negotiable for him: his faith in God, his relationship with the Lord (on and off the field), and the responsibility of the Springbok on his chest – for him, these carry weight. From the age of 19, God entrusted Duane with a definite role as a sports person for South Africa. The Lord entrusted him with prestige, but the pruning process would be hard and continuous. *"A great responsibility comes with the role you receive. I think that was the most important process I had to go through, to know who I am and what I stand for. One cannot make a difference and carry responsibility if you cannot answer these questions honestly. It took me a while. The Lord and I had to work together in faith and trust, letting Him chisel away at my rough edges!"*

Duane recalls two distinct experiences in his life where he felt God's presence. Both times the Lord put strong male figures as role models in Duane's life, even if it was only for a moment. *"The first time was when I was sitting in a shopping centre drinking coffee after an operation. A man, whom I did not know at all, walked up to me, and told me that the Lord had told him to come and pray for me for complete healing after my operation. The second time it happened again, in another shopping centre, also after my knee surgery. An elderly man stopped me and said, 'I just want to pray for you today.' After he prayed, I took his phone number. His name is Uncle Theuns Rossouw and, to this day, we still keep in touch. He is a very inspirational man."*

Every challenge leads to an opportunity. And even when the COVID storm played havoc with the planned calendars, it gave the Vermeulens a chance to regroup and to re-evaluate their dreams and ideas. *"Every person experiences a stormy season in their life. For a long time, injury after injury was that season in my life – until I realised that every injury taught me more about myself and strengthened my relationships on all levels."*

Daddy Duane with his young men, Anru and Zian

COVID affected everyone, forcing introspection, and asking hard questions. It forced Duane to ask, "Who am I, in character and as a human being, away from the sports field?" To the world, he is the most sought-after rugby player, with a string of achievements and awards, but to Ezél he is a husband and to his two sons, just their daddy. *"I read wise words and it made me realise once again where I am currently in my life and where I would like to be. It says: 'If you die tonight, your employer will advertise to fill your position by the end of the month, but your loved ones, family, and friends would miss you forever. Do not get so busy making a living that you forget to make a life.'"*

The giant in front of this young David was defeated. The burden on his shoulders was less. After the World Cup final in 2019, Matthew Proudfoot pulled him closer, hugged him, and whispered these words. Duane no longer needed to impress, he is everything a sportsman, father, husband, friend, and son could dream to be.

His father would have been proud. His heavenly Father is proud. And now he knows, that is enough.

Duane, Ezél, and the boys

What do you think is the biggest obstacle in men's lives?

To show feelings and talk about what their biggest fears are. There are fears on different levels: faith, finances, love, are they good enough, and where are they in their lives? Most men have these fears and if they cannot talk about them, they play a big role in their lives.

How would you like to be remembered?

I would like to be remembered for my humility – I think that as long as you stay humble and trust in the Lord, your actions that follow will speak volumes. My wife always says that as long as your feet stay firmly on the ground and your eyes are fixed on high, you can overcome any obstacle.

Your message to South Africa

Regardless of how big or how small the battle ahead of you is; you and the One who made you, can make a difference. Believe in yourself and trust in your Creator. There are valuable words that I read one day, and they stay with me, "Your magnificence is your light, the light that you were born into this life to shine. It is uniquely yours and you are here to express the magnificence that is uniquely you; to be powerful beyond measure."

Duane Vermeulen
Exclusive interview
Scan the code to watch

Mignon du Preez

Mignon du Preez, born on the 13th of June 1989, is a South African cricketer who was the women's team captain in all three forms of cricket – test matches, ODIs, and T20 matches (2011-2016). Minx, her teammates' nickname for her, is a former learner of Doringkloof Primary School and later of Hoërskool Zwartkop and was a promising player from a young age. At 12 years' old she played in a provincial u13 match between Gauteng and North Gauteng. She scored 258 runs with a strike rate of more than 200, hitting a double century with 16 sixes and 25 fours in the match of 40 overs. Mignon made her debut in the green and gold in January 2007, at 17 years' old, when she stepped onto the pitch as a right-handed batsman and wicket keeper in a match against Pakistan. She holds the record as the South African player with the most matches as captain in ODIs, as well as T20 matches. She is also one of the highest run-scorers for South African women's cricket in ODIs and T20 matches. On the 21st of February 2016, she became the first South African woman to score 1000 career runs in T20Is against England. Mignon's cricket career includes playing for Northerns (2003/2004 to present), Melbourne Stars (2015 and 2017-2020), Sussex (2017), Loughborough Lightning (2019), Manchester Originals (2021), Hobart Hurricanes (2021/2022 to date) and Trent Rockets (2022).

On the 21st of June 2016, Mignon handed over her captaincy after leading the team for almost five years (since 2011) in one test match, 46 ODIs, and 50 T20 matches. In March 2022, she also announced her retirement from test cricket, ODI, and T20 matches, but confirmed her continued availability for domestic T20 leagues.

Mignon's list of awards includes 2010 SA Woman Cricketer of the Year and Cricket South Africa's Sportswoman of the Year for 2011.

My love for sport began... *at the age of four. I actually started playing by accident. My brother played in a mini cricket tournament and my father was the coach of that u7 team. I went to support my brother at one of the matches. When I went to cheer him on, I always made sure I was dressed in a team shirt and shorts. One of the players did not pitch up and my dad asked me to replace him. In the end, I was crowned best female batsman of the day. I fell in love with the sport there and then.*

My parents exposed me to all types of sports. In primary school I did tumbling, played netball, hockey, chess, badminton, tennis, and participated in athletics – you name it, I was there!

If I was not a sports star, I would... *have liked to work in the medical field. I am afraid of blood, so being a doctor is out of the question, but because I have my honours in marketing, there could have been an option to become a medical rep! I would have also liked to work at a school – not necessarily as a teacher, because standing in front of a class and teaching is far too challenging for my personality. However, I would like to work as a sports coordinator. The thought of school holidays is also a great incentive for me.*

I am incredibly grateful for... *my support structure. My husband is cricket crazy and his support means everything to me. We were high school sweethearts, he saw me take my first step into professional cricket and, fifteen years later, he is still by my side. My parents supported my career with so much passion – in those times when it was difficult, it was them, my friends and family, who carried me through. Because they believed in me, I could believe in myself.*

If I could edit my life, I would... *not change anything. It is one's past that makes you who you are today. I do not want to mess with it. The only adjustment I would perhaps make is to give advice to a younger Mignon on how to be more daring. I was a real goody two shoes! I was very careful about taking any chances and was the one who always followed the rules. Looking back, I wish I was a little bit more relaxed ... and took more chances in a good, responsible way.*

One of the biggest lessons I learnt this year... *you cannot always keep everyone around you happy. Especially not at the expense of yourself.*

My greatest achievement... *was being named captain of South Africa's women's cricket team. The Protea on my cricket shirt has always been something to be proud of.*

The Bible verse that carries me through...

Jeremiah 29:11,
"For I know the thoughts that I think towards you, says the Lord, thoughts of peace and not of evil, to give you a future and a hope."

"My support system." Mignon together with her husband, Tony, and her parents

"The sea where our souls find rest"

MY STORY
Mignon du Preez

Mignon found herself on the sidelines. A place she was not used to; one she did not like at all. She represented South Africa for more than ten years, played more than 100 matches in the green and gold, and was one of the most celebrated captains with a string of awards and records to her name. But still she was not good enough.

In that moment, Mignon's world came crashing down. Disappointment cloaked her, her game was not up to scratch and, therefore, she was not selected for the team.

Never did she think that this would hit her so late in her career.

Every team meeting became a personal torment of questions and self-doubt. *"Each time the doubt gnawed at me: Am I still good enough? Will I ever play again? Should I still be here?"*

As a child, Mignon's talent for cricket was discovered by chance one afternoon. She was only four years old when the opportunity presented itself, but she was ready for action, almost as if she always knew that a special moment could arise at any time. Her love for the sport ignited and when she stepped onto the cricket pitch, it was always with an expectation that something wonderful was going to happen. It was her gift from God – what she did with it was her gift back to Him. But somewhere along the way, Mignon lost her first love for the sport and found herself at a sports psychologist with more questions than answers. *"I had to answer certain questions for myself and address two hindering facts:*

1. *I failed to live up to what I firmly believed in all these years. 'My talent is a gift from God to me and what I do with it is my gift back to Him.' My own motto in life evaporated. I believed that I was returning a poor gift.*
2. *I was in a danger zone; I realised that my self-worth was linked to my sporting achievements, to the cricket scoreboard, and not to God."*

With a pen and paper in hand, big Minx wrote a personal letter of apology to little Minx. *"There is a saying among us sports people that the sports psychologists drill into us:*

> *'Behind every successful sportswoman there
> is a little girl who fell in love with the sport.
> Play for her and not for the pavilion.'*

Mignon felt guilty that she had allowed the professional era to rob her of her happiness – and the real reason why she started playing cricket in the first place. The pruning process involved forgiving herself. *"The privilege to play for your country, the love of the sport, the privilege to shine God's light on a sports field, and the love must always be preserved."*

Little did Mignon realise the importance and true value of this experience, as COVID-19 and the lockdown followed shortly on the heels of this learning process. *"COVID awakened the fear in my mind that I would lose my sports career and end on a low. Retiring from cricket was around the corner and I was running out of time! COVID stole the time that was left, one day at a time!"* Actually, she was not on the losing side, on the contrary, Mignon gained time – she regained years and months of lost time with her family. She was able to catch up and make up for the big celebrations she had missed due to years of tournaments away from home. She could re-evaluate her priorities and make the necessary adjustments. Mignon was ready for the final phase of her 15-year career.

The 2022 twelfth ICC Women's Cricket World Cup in New Zealand would include Mignon's 150th match for South Africa. As the women's cricketer with the most ODIs to her name, Mignon was geared for the game. It should have been the fairy tale ending with a heroine winning the game for her team or scoring another record number of runs, but on that day, Mignon only scored one run for her team. *"Things did not go as I expected, at all... so much so that after all these years I began to doubt my own abilities. I was angry and discouraged. Why did God just leave me alone; allowing me*

Mignon and Tony, together with close friends Johan and Anneke

to be humiliated on my big day?" They were going to celebrate her big game as a team, but instead of popping champagne corks, it was a night of wiping away tears. *"I wanted to put my bat down and encourage the coaches to select someone else in my place. I was humiliated…"*

It was the advice, prayers, and love from her support system that kept Mignon going that week.

She had to keep silent and spend time with the Lord.

She had to declare Jeremiah 29:11 over her career, let go, and allow God to intervene. South Africa's fairy tale led to a final group match against a strong Indian team – the one country that eats, sleeps, and lives cricket. South Africa qualified for the semi-finals, but for India, everything was on the line. If they won, they would also qualify for the semi-finals, but should they lose, they would go home. This match would also determine in which semi-final match the Protea team would play – whether they would compete against England or Australia. South Africa wanted to win against India, because then they would play England in the semi-final, rather than Australia (Australia was the favourite team to win the tournament by far, therefore South Africa only wanted to face them in the final).

Mignon remembers the match as "the day when God intervened". It was a titanic struggle that gave her the platform to let His light shine that day, and not her own. With her hands in a familiar grip on the bat she loves so much, Mignon hit the winning runs against the dreaded India team and won the match for her team and South Africa. *"In my TV interview I thanked God for His faithfulness, only to later receive messages via Twitter saying: 'Your God was so busy watching cricket that He forgot about the war in Ukraine!'"* But Mignon shrugged it off, she was bigger than the match and God was bigger than her will. In her mind's eye she could see Him rejoicing with the words: "You see, I've got you and I am proud of you."

In 2022, Mignon announced her retirement from test cricket and one-day cricket as well as T20Is but confirmed her continued availability for domestic T20 leagues. When she puts on her helmet, dons her gloves, and picks up her bat, it feels like she is putting on the armour God gave her. *"Every time, just before I step onto the pitch, I kneel and pray: 'Jesus, You died for me and now I have the opportunity to play for You.'"* Every game was, is, and will always be an opportunity for her to honour and worship the Lord. *"I give God all the credit, because He granted me the favour and opportunity to be able to do what I love so much."*

What do you think is the biggest obstacle in women's lives?

We tend to compare ourselves with others, who we are, what we do, and what we own. We become dissatisfied with what God entrusts to us. We get caught up in other people's lives and are not grateful for what we have in our own lives.

How would you like to be remembered?

I would like to be remembered as a God-fearing woman who let my light shine so that people could see God's goodness and favour in my life. I want to be remembered as the person I was and not just as a cricketer. I want people to remember how they felt when they encountered me and remember me as someone who put God and my family first.

Your message to South Africa

A small act of kindness can have an enduring ripple effect. Make a point of leaving your surroundings better than you find them.

Mignon du Preez
Exclusive interview
Scan the code to watch ◄◄◄

Mignon and her sister making soup during lockdown

Mignon after she hit the winning runs against India

Mignon and Phoenix

Joey Mongalo

Joey Mongalo was born on the 6th of January 1985 and grew up in Brits, a small town in the North-West Province. He matriculated in 2003 as a learner at Pretoria Boys High, and in the same year made his mark in rugby as a full back against Afrikaans Hoër Seunskool. Joey scored 18 points and broke the drought of any wins for his school, in this league, over the previous 18 years. He is a versatile sportsman and also enjoyed football and cricket until he made the choice to play rugby. During Craven week he ran onto the field for the Blue Bulls as a scrum half. Joey played for the South African junior team from 2004-2007 and represented South Africa in the Junior World Championships in 2006. He also donned the Tukkies' Varsity Cup rugby jersey in 2008. He played in the Vodacom Cup and one Currie Cup game for the Blue Bulls. However, in 2011, after a few years in the labour market, Joey seized the opportunity to become team manager for the Lions u19 team. This is where his future as a coach began and was confirmed. Among others, he shared in the successes of Wits, King Edward VII School, Parktown Boys High, and St Stithians College. His professional coaching career as head and defence coach includes a position with the Emirates Lions (2011-2019), the Vodacom Bulls (2020-2022), and the Cell C Sharks (2022 to date).

My love for sport began... *with my parents. My late father was a very good football player, and my mother is an ardent football supporter of Chelsea F.C. and Kaizer Chiefs! My brother played for his university football team and my younger sister played netball. As the middle child of a sports-crazy family, sport played an integral role in my life. My father died when I was only seven years old; my brother was fourteen and my sister only two years old. We had to find other role models. At Thornhill Primary School, the coach, Marius van Heerden, played a big role in my interest in cricket and rugby. The team element has always been the biggest attraction for me. Working together as a team, learning, and enjoying something together taught me that you can halve your worries and double your happiness when you support and carry one another. The team element changed my life, as well as the other players' lives. Sport and coaching gave me the platform to have a positive say in other people's lives and for that, I am infinitely grateful.*

If I was not a sports coach and involved in management, I would... *have liked to be a sports psychologist for a test cricket team. My love for test cricket stems from the respect I have for the players who can stay focused for such a long period of time, maintain a team culture, and support each other in the highs and lows of the game.*

I am incredibly grateful for... *a man by the name of Cory Thompson. He taught me what discipleship looks like. We were both boarders at university and it was the example of his life that taught me what purposefulness is and how to really love God and other people.*

If I could edit my life, I would... *have studied sports psychology. I would be able to apply the theory practically in my own career and further my own sports career. I also wish I had taken my relationship with God seriously earlier in my life. This would have prevented the bad habits I picked up in my teenage years.*

One of the biggest lessons I learnt this year... *is to be really grateful and live with gratitude. 1 Thessalonians 5:16-18 says, "Rejoice always, pray without ceasing, in everything give thanks; for this is the will of God in Christ Jesus for you." When I am grateful from the start, my attitude is better, and things go better.*

My greatest achievement is... *that I could have the privilege and responsibility of coaching in the United Rugby Championships (URC) and Super Rugby Final. But the constant privilege is knowing that God can use someone like me, with all my faults, to have an effect in other people's lives, who in turn influence their circles.*

The best advice I ever received was... *in 2021. The manager of Vovo Telo told me that enthusiasm is contagious! When you are passionate about what you do, it will inspire others to do better.*

The best advice I ever gave was... *that one should find out what your calling, passion, and talents are and pursue them with everything in your heart.*

The best decision I ever made was... *marrying Zinzi! She is everything that is good in my life. She is a mother to our little girls, a wonderful spiritual partner, and the perfect life partner. I would choose her every day, again and again.*

The Bible verse that carries me...

Isaiah 26:3-4,
"You will keep him in perfect peace, whose mind is stayed on You, because he trusts in You. Trust in the Lord forever, for in the Lord, is everlasting strength."

MY STORY
Joey Mongalo

It was in the prayers to God from the heart of a mother of three children – ages two, seven, and fourteen – where the foundation of a household and its prayer life was cemented. When a mother put aside the pain in her heart after the death of her husband and prostrated herself before God, bringing the fears of raising her children on a nurse's salary to Him, that was when God's character as Provider and Father came to the fore. It was in those early years of stormy seasons that Joey saw the hand of God and experienced the faithfulness of God to his mother.

> **Joey had never needed to prostrate himself before God, until one day...**

When God chooses you as a role model for others, He entrusts you with prestige, and together with that, there always is a price to pay. The price? A pruning process where you have to lay down your own will and choices. There are parallels in the story of Joseph in Genesis 39 and what happened to Joey. Joseph found favour in the eyes of Potiphar and became his servant. Potiphar put Joseph in charge of his household and entrusted everything he owned to him. At that time, the Lord blessed the house of the Egyptian for the sake of Joseph. However, there was a twist in the tale, Joseph ended up in prison after Potiphar's wife tried to seduce him and he rejected her sexual advances by fleeing from her, whereupon she falsely accused him of rape and his punishment was life imprisonment. It was only when God stepped in that justice was done and Joseph's reputation and honour was fully restored.

For Joey, it played out as follows: The Lions and his coaching team experienced a glorious season in 2018 with a place in the Super Rugby final against the Crusaders in Christchurch. Joey, a young 34-year-old defence coach with big dreams in his heart, learnt a life-changing lesson that year. A lesson that prepared him to be able to speak authoritatively about the danger of soul ties with someone other than your spouse. "A soul tie is an intense emotional bond between two people. A soul tie is not necessarily sexual in nature, but within the covenant of a marriage it is dangerous to develop a bond of this nature with a third party," is the experts' opinion.

Joey's friendship with a woman – with no immoral behaviour, but nevertheless without the knowledge of his wife – led to a yearlong court case after a false accusation was made. It almost derailed the young star's coaching career and marriage. It was an expensive price to pay personally, emotionally, and financially. Just like in Joseph's story, Joey learnt the value of honesty and righteousness. When God intervened and His voice became clearer than the false accusations, and the dust of the court case settled, He could heal the disappointment and pain. When reputations were damaged, He saw to it that the heartfelt remorse stood out – head and shoulders above everything else. Restoration and second chances could then begin.

Genesis 50:20, "But as for you, you meant evil against me; but God meant it for good…" This is the promise that Joey held onto for 15 months. Soon after, God opened the door for him at the Vodacom Bulls, with successful seasons that followed.

Our Father's focus is not perfect Christians,

He uses the mistakes and experiences of His children to demonstrate that He is a living God who forgives and makes everything work together for good for those who are willing to repent.

There is no mistake for which there is no forgiveness. It is precisely our imperfection as His children that demonstrates the almighty God's forgiveness and help. His Spirit guides us daily to become more like Him and to extend forgiveness, as He did to us.

Joey as coach

What are the words and message from God's heart to you over the past two years? What has He shared with you about your life, character, and being, away from the sports field?

1. Almighty! God is almighty. These are the words that come to mind when I think of the past two years. Nothing has or will ever catch God off guard. He is, was, and always will be in control of everything around us. The certainty that I am a son of this God has brought unprecedented peace in my heart. My safety, my future, and my family's lives are in His hands. And yes, in any situation there are consequences for decisions that are sometimes beyond our control, whether financial or personal, but despite everything, He remains the God of every animal of the forest, and the cattle on a thousand hills (Psalm 50:10). He remains omnipotent.

2. The lockdown led to the rise of the online church. It was a period where we could praise and worship together, nationally and internationally, but it was also during that time when I came to realise the value of community and church community; that we are not made to function independently. Iron sharpens iron, friends shape each other! Ecclesiastes 4:9-10 says it so beautifully: "Two are better than one, because they have a good reward for their labour. For if they fall, one will lift up his companion. But woe to him who is alone when he falls, for he has no one to help him up." Verse 12 overwhelms me with the message that a threefold cord is not easily broken! This is a clear sign that God made us to function in community with others and that we need each other. We all have a responsibility towards each other. We must be held accountable and serve each other as Jesus served the people.

3. After the incident in 2018, where I could have potentially lost everything and my coaching career hung by a thread, God stepped in and won the court case for me. Through His love and forgiveness, I could learn to live in His faithfulness and grace. Exodus 14:14 reads: "The Lord will fight for you; you need only to be still."

Joey, his wife, Zinzi, Zinani, and older sister, Ziayna

How did you keep the players under your care standing when it sometimes felt like you could not keep standing yourself?

In the words of my friend, Herkie Kruger, and my own life motto: Rugby is what we do, not who we are. It is not your identity, and although you do it for several hours of the day every week, it does not encompass all of who you are. On the contrary – you are much more.

There is a physical and spiritual element to this question. When we, as coaches, do our job right, we will empower players to handle any situation, be it scoreboard pressure or physically challenging situations. These are the principles that must be so deeply ingrained that they can fall back on them.

The spiritual element goes even deeper, precisely because each player has to believe that us coaches believe in them. Just as our identity in Christ can never change, these young men need to know that we always consider them worthy – even when they have a weaker match, regardless of highs or lows. Every player needs to know that we are there to support them, that they are seen and appreciated for who they are and what they bring to the game. The pressure of the media and public opinion should never overshadow the truth, and that is that the players are worthy, both on and off the field.

What do you think is the biggest obstacle in men's lives?

There are four important focal points:

1. *Our responsibility as men has been questioned and challenged from the very beginning. A clear sign of that is the ingenuity of the enemy who ignored Adam and spoke directly to Eve. It is in these times when my masculinity as a spiritual*

covering must come to the fore, when I take authority in the spiritual realm and forbid anything challenging God's authority to speak to my wife.

2. As men, we have Godly principles to live by. It is easy to push the responsibility away. When the troubles come, we tend to blame one another in the marriage. These principles include respecting our wives and children, standing strong, being the head of our homes, and loving our wives as God loves the Church.

3. We must lay down our pride. When money, titles, and status become the main focus, we easily forget who the Giver of those gifts is.

4. Finally, sex and sexuality are important points that must be addressed. Some of the most famous men in the Bible succumbed to lust. Solomon, David, and Samson are clear examples to us that this is not a new challenge. Men need the support of discipleship groups that hold them accountable for their decisions and choices; groups where the problem of pornography or flirting can be openly discussed, precisely because everyone is susceptible to these temptations. No man should face this alone, and no man should be caught in a web of lies that keeps him away from the promises God has for him.

How would you like to be remembered?

I would like to be remembered as a man of God, a good husband to my wife, and a good father to my children. It is a challenge that I choose to take seriously every day – specifically because I lost my father at a young age, and my wife comes from a family with a history of men who did not take their responsibilities seriously.

I would also like to be remembered as a coach who cared, who was first of all interested in the rugby player as a person and then transferred some skills of the game in a unique way.

I would want to be remembered as someone who had my eye on eternity, not just an earthly goal, but also someone who invested in the Kingdom of God by being involved in discipleship that had an impact in more than one person's life.

Behind the scenes with the players

Your message to South Africa

I am the biggest advocate of the "growth mindset":

- When you keep trying, you will eventually master it.
- You can be excited about any challenge, because when you persevere, a good reward awaits you on the other side. Do not avoid challenges.
- Learn from your mistakes.
- Criticism is something we can learn from.

South Africans! We have an incredible country with natural diversity in 11 cultures and national languages and this depicts something of God's Kingdom. Learn from each other about your cultures and overcome judgemental opinions. Where there is unity, there is strength.

Our country needs leaders who will stand up for justice and the law. It is the responsibility of each of us to fight on our knees in prayer; to proclaim the following in our homes and offices, "If my people, who are called by my name, will humble themselves and pray and seek my face and turn from their wicked ways, then I will hear from heaven, and I will forgive their sin and will heal their land." – 2 Chronicles 7:14

South Africa can be a beacon of light to the rest of the word, a witness to God's goodness.

Joey Mongalo
Exclusive interview ▶▶▶
Scan the code to watch

Schalk Brits

Schalk Burger Brits, born on the 16th of May 1981 in KwaZulu-Natal, is a former South African professional rugby player, and two-time Rugby World Cup player. The former Paul Roos learner's provincial career kicked off in 2002 when he put on the striped WP jersey as a 21-year-old and played for the Western Province for two years. Schalk's career as a powerful hooker includes contracts with teams such as the Golden Lions and Cats (2004-2005) as well as four seasons with the Stormers playing 51 games (2006-2009). He also rejoined this Cape franchise from 2006-2009 as part of the WP team before accepting a contract overseas and becoming a member of the elite Saracens club (2009-2018) for 216 games. Schalk realised his big dream in 2008 when he donned the green and gold and made his debut in the Springboks match against Italy. He subsequently maintained an international, provincial, and national career with a short-term loan agreement between Saracens and South Africa (2011-2018). During his time at Saracens, he was part of a team that won four Premier League titles in 2011, 2015, 2016, and 2018. He also helped Saracens win the European Champions Cup in 2016 and 2017.

Schalk returned as a Springbok and, after a test series, was included in the South African squad that participated in the 2015 Rugby World Cup, returning with a bronze medal. Schalk, a son of Empangeni and a former Maties student, played 11 matches for the "Blue Train" in 2019 as a hooker before he was selected for the South African national team and Rugby World Cup team – a second time – at the age of 38! Not only did he run onto the field as captain in the match against Namibia, but he also played as eighth man, not his usual position, and even scored a try! South Africa won the 2019 Rugby World Cup by defeating England in the final.

Schalk announced his retirement from rugby in 2019. He is an ambassador, expert, and works for an investment holding company. He is married to Colinda and is the father of three sons. As a legend in South Africa and friend to many, Schalk was named the Player of the Year in the 2009/2010 season. He was also inducted into the RugbyPass Hall of Fame in 2021.

My love for sport began... *when I was a child! I was a hyperactive boy and young man; my only outlet was sport! My parents encouraged me to participate in every sport, because as an only child it gave me the opportunity to make friends and be part of a team. It became the way in which I could express myself as a person.*

If I was not a sports star, I would... *probably have studied something in the medical field or would have gotten involved in golf. My uncle is a doctor, and his stories were always very interesting. I also believe there was room for growth in golf for me, as a sportsman who enjoyed the game with a handicap of 1. But instead, I studied managerial accounting, as my interest lies in private fund management, private equity and property management, as well as venture capital investments. I enjoy data analysis, although I am not analytical by nature, rather more people oriented. That is why I am now spreading my wings and exploring all the different options.*

I am incredibly grateful for... *my support network. I was an only child, and all I know is my parents' love and support. They put their careers and time on the line so that I could achieve my dreams. To this day, they always answer when I phone; they never miss one of my calls. It was thanks to their support that I ended up at Paul Roos Gymnasium. I have the greatest respect for the teachers and coaches there, such as Mr Hanekom and Mr Van Niekerk who both invested in me. I met some of my best friends in high school and I am grateful for those who walked the road with me and kept me humble. Sometimes my alma mater still sees me as Schalkie who started my schooling there in standard 6! But my greatest gratitude in this season of my life is for my wife and children. Colinda is a wonderful person who, as a working mother of three sons (six, eight, and ten), keeps our whole life together. Often, I learn more from my family than they learn from me.*

Finally, I am grateful to the Lord. Without grace, nothing would have been possible. I am also grateful for my health. It gives me the privilege to live life to the fullest.

If I could edit my life, I would... *learn a higher work ethic earlier in my life and train harder. When you hear from an early age on that you have a talent, you tend to focus more on that, leading to a mindset that leads to a lower work ethic. If I had worked harder as a young player, I could have done much better in my rugby career and therefore have been more successful. Unfortunately, I only realised later in life that the recipe for success lies in discipline and hard work. One enjoys the benefit of good sports genes, but if hard work does not become part of your routine, your age and the success of others will catch up with you and, before you know it, you will be competing with people who were willing to put in the hours of hard work. Today I know that both a continuous sound ethic and good personal relationships in a team context keep you relevant. The people in your team are the ones who walk the road with you – it is essential that everyone functions at one hundred percent capacity. So, acknowledge the value in others.*

One of the biggest lessons I learnt this year... *was realising that no transition from one season to another is easy. For the first time in my adult life, I had to shift my focus away from rugby. One then tends to only focus your shortcomings. Stay true to your principles, no matter where you find yourself. Be sure to do a SWOT analysis (strengths, weaknesses, opportunities, threats) and implement it. Sometimes it takes a while but make time for it.*

My biggest achievement is... *I always try to treat everyone in the same way, and I try to be a people's person consistently. My biggest investment right now is the time I spend* with my wife and children. No one can outsource the role of being a father and being a man. It is more important to me to be present in every family moment; it carries more weight than anything else at this time. Yes, rugby was a good phase of my life with many highlights, but the memories I made away from the rugby field, with my wife and children, are much more valuable to me.

The Bible verse that carries me...

*I do not just have one specific verse.
Today I still do exactly what I did as a young boy ...
I open the Bible and read. God has always met and
answered me in this way – in His time!*

MY STORY
Schalk Brits

Schalk's father used to say, *"Everyone knows success in their own way. Some people's success is in the public eye, and is noticed, others' not. That is why it is important to treat everyone the same, show respect, afford everyone enough time, and not be judgemental."*

It is only when these words take root in your life and become a reality that you can bear fruit at the right time, because everyone experiences change and different seasons – whether it is expected or unexpected. And these changes can make or break you.

Schalk finished his rugby career, retired from the game, and closed the door behind him. Until one evening...

It was one o'clock in the morning, while Colinda and he were still talking, when the WhatsApp messages arrived. *"You are the best hooker I know. Your game on the field is still as good as it was ten years ago. We want to involve you. We need your muscle and ingenuity, your spirit, experience, and heart in the team. Greetings, Rassie."* Schalk chuckled and dismissed the message as a joke from his teammate, Malcolm Marx. But after the third message and a confirming phone call, he mulled over the words and invitation of the Springbok coach, Rassie Erasmus.

"Just be yourself, because there is only one Schalk. Do not try to be someone else," was the best advice he would ever receive as a young man. It was this advice, and the support of Colinda that night, that made Schalk realise that his time in rugby was not over yet! The 37-year-old Schalk Brits would be included in the Springboks team after an absence of two years. As one of the more senior players, he played for South Africa in a world cup for the second time.

As the wife of a professional rugby player who knows what it feels like to have her husband at home only fifteen days out of eight months, Colinda did not hesitate or doubt this decision for a moment. Schalk had to live his dream to the fullest, because playing rugby was what God called him to do … in that season of his life. Within one month, she packed up their house and moved from England back to South Africa, got their three boys into schools, and managed her own professional career to support the dream.

It was the years in England that taught Schalk and Colinda to recognise God's voice for themselves and not via a preacher or parent. No, there in England there was no other support to lean on. If you wanted to pray, you had to choose to pray. If you wanted to seek God's face, you had to carve out a quiet time because no one was going to force, encourage, or prompt you to do so. In each season of his life, Schalk learnt to quieten his heart and see the truth for what it is. *"Just like Job and the disciples in the Bible, not everyone always goes through good times. They were also in a constant struggle for survival or in search of answers. I cannot be hypocritical; my actions will reflect my relationship with God. I am a warrior in spirit; living a principled life speaks volumes. This is how I influence people's lives, in my own way."*

After his official retirement in 2019, Schalk had to learn to trust God, and, just like in the days of injuries and not having a player's contract, he had to believe that God would be there in the next phase as well. Every season has highs and lows, and no one can afford to stagnate. However, the pruning process in this new season was more painful than he had anticipated.

Schalk, Colinda, and their three men

For any sports person, the transition from a routine according to a sports calendar to a professional corporate environment is a huge adjustment. Schalk, who for most of his adult life was part of the top 1% of the world's sports elite as a professional rugby player, had to make the transition in mind, soul, and body in the blink of an eye. *"All of a sudden, you are part of something that is the reality for 99% of the people around you and you may not even be half as good at something as the people around you."*

Reality hits hard and unless your identity is established in the message God is declaring over your life, you are going to falter. A performance driven Schalk walked into his house late one night after a long day, week, and month. The serious faces of his three sons in their pyjamas greeted him. It was the harsh words from the mouth of his ten-year-old, his eldest, that startled Schalk. *"We want our dad back,"* was the request. The words from the heart of a little boy cut deep. *"Rather go and play rugby again. You are not home in any case, and your work, daddy, does not make you happy. You are not around anymore, and you do not play with us anymore."*

What makes you re-evaluate your life? The right situation, an undesirable result?

Schalk's balance sheet did not add up, even though he wanted it to so badly.

His childhood as an only child was a happy one. Today, Schalk's father is still a family man with non-negotiable principled standards. Schalk's mother contracted an illness that halted her life as a businesswoman and made her dependent on the care of Schalk's father. There was not a hint of a question or argument about it, only unity in spirit and heart.

This led Schalk and Colinda to decide that he was going to take "sabbatical leave". He would be the proverbial stay-at-home dad, away from any corporate commitments, spending time with the children and investing in them as a family. The competitive go-getter struggled at first with society's perception that the man should be the breadwinner in the house, but then quieted his heart and began to listen to what God wanted to say about the new role he had to play.

"This chapter in my life is something completely unfamiliar to me. Every day is a new day. An opportunity to influence the people around me and leave them with something of value. People do not always remember what you say, but they remember how you made them feel. I now have to make a new list of non-negotiable values for me, my family, and new job."

The concern is a reality, but as a young boy Schalk opened the Bible with the expectation of hearing God's voice and guidance, and today it is no different, because we serve a God of faithfulness who is the same yesterday, today, and tomorrow. *"Ask your questions but wait on God. He will reveal the answers to you at the right time. We are used to an instant society, but this is not how God works. Quieten your inner being, evaluate, work hard, and do what your hand finds to do, but wait on God for His guidance."*

What do you think is the biggest obstacle in men's lives?

Money, women, and booze. Every man has his own cross to bear. The perception of a man's role sometimes hangs over his head like a sword, but the relationship between a man and a woman is what is of importance. I would say, "Men, stop competing with the woman in your life. Support your wife and see the value she adds. A relationship has two parties. And then – balance your books and see what you come up with. Make sacrifices and look at your heart. Follow God's voice and be yourself."

How would you like to be remembered?

I would like to be remembered as a good husband to my wife and a good father to my children. A man whose word was his honour and who lived what he preached.

Your message to South Africa

Do not lose heart. See the light.

Don't be focused on what we don't have, but live in gratitude for what we do have. Look forward, but also look around you and live every day in the moment.

Swys de Bruin

Zacharia Francois de Bruin – better known as Swys – was born in Ficksburg on the 18th of February 1960. He is married to Marilize, and is the father of Neil, Francois, and Jamie, and friend to many. As a South African rugby coach, former head coach of the Lions Super Rugby and Currie Cup teams, and attack coach of the South African national team, he has had the privilege of making an impact on many young men's lives. His coaching career began at Durban North College, formerly known as Afrikaans Hoër Durban-Noord. He was the head coach of the Sharks u21 team in 1997 (winners of the national under 21 competition). In the 1998 Vodacom Cup series, he took charge of the Natal Wildebeest team to lead them to the semi-finals. Swys' era as a coach includes time with the Griquas (1999-2003), South Africa's u21 team (2001), as well as head coach and high-performance coach of the Sharks Academy (2004-2012). After a total of ten seasons in Durban, Swys moved to Johannesburg to join Johan Ackermann and the Golden Lions as assistant coach (2013-2017). Under their leadership, the team set unprecedented records in rugby circles, achieving the most victories during the Super Rugby tournament and finished at the top of the South African conference for the first time since 2001. The Lions won the Vodacom Cup in 2014, the Currie Cup in 2015, and played in three Super Rugby finals from 2016-2018. Swys was head coach of the Lions from the end of 2017 to 2019 and formed part of the Springboks' coaching team in 2018 and 2019. He was also assistant coach of the World Barbarians team in 2018. He was appointed as director of coaching of Shimla rugby for the 2022 and 2023 rugby seasons. Nowadays he is a familiar face as a presenter and sports analyst on SuperSport. He also hosts coaching clinics and is a motivational speaker in his spare time.

My love for sport began... *as a young boy. In Ficksburg, where I was born and grew up, I played with one or the other type of ball all day every day, ever since I can remember. I always loved playing rugby, cricket, tennis, golf, and even football. When I was a little boy, my father called me one evening and said that Uncle Schalk, the chairman of the town's rugby club, had dropped in with an envelope for me. In the envelope was free entry as "honorary member of the Ficksburg Rugby Club". This was because I was at the team's practice every night to kick the balls back to the team's kickers. When our u11 team finished training, I stayed behind at the village rugby field to wait for all the other school teams who took turns training, and for the village team that would later come to practice.*

If I was not a sports coach manager, I would be... *a sports commentator! From a young age I wanted to be a rugby commentator like the famous Gerhard Viviers (Spiekeries). As a boy, I often entertained our family with my "broadcasting skills". Ironically enough, now, at the end of my career, I got the opportunity to work at SuperSport in the broadcasting industry.*

I am incredibly grateful for... *an experience that confirmed my calling. When I was 14, we went on a road trip in my father's Volkswagen Kombi, and I was privileged to watch all four tests against Willie-John McBride's British Lions with my father. That experience made me realise that rugby was my great love. I am eternally grateful to my father for giving me such opportunities. I will always be grateful to my incredible mother too, because I know that she prayed for me every day.*

I am so grateful to each of the coaches who made a difference in my life, and that I was given so many opportunities to live out my passion. We should never underestimate the influence that teachers and coaches have in the lives of children and young people.

I thank God that I was able to meet my wife at university, because she is the rock and pillar for me and our three sons.

I am grateful that the Lord was able to use me as a teacher to live out my passion and work with children, after my own rugby career was cut short at a young age due to a serious ankle injury.

I will always be grateful to Brian van Zyl and Garth Giles, who gave me the opportunity to start coaching rugby full time at the Sharks. I am also thankful to Hans Scriba at the Sharks Academy. He was my spiritual mentor and is still a precious friend. If it were not for Johan Ackermann (Lions) and Rassie Erasmus (Springboks), I might never have had all the incredible opportunities that I now look back on with so much gratitude.

If I could edit my life, I would... *change absolutely nothing. I believe that everything that happens to a person – good or bad, happiness or hardship – is part of the Lord's plan for your life, if you know Him.*

Swys with Rassie Erasmus

One of the biggest lessons I learnt this year... *Due to my work with coaches and players in the training courses that I present, I noticed that there is a greater need than ever before for mentors, guardians, father figures, and leadership – especially on a spiritual level. The world has become an exceptionally uncertain place, especially after COVID, with many people feeling directionless and overwhelmed. Despondency and depression are the order of the day. One of the other big lessons I learnt is that social media, with everyone's access and use of it, has the power to destroy people's lives. I learnt to not attach too much importance to the comments and opinions of others.*

My greatest achievement is... *not any trophy, medal, award, or jacket that I have received – this is simply the Lord's grace; His gifts to me – but I believe my greatest achievement is to possibly make a difference in the life of even just one player or coach.*

When I look at my own three sons – the incredible young men they are (warriors for the Lord) – I want to believe that this is my greatest achievement, even if it is not mine to lay claim to (it is actually thanks to their mother – and the Lord's grace).

The achievement that I am most proud of... *I was privileged to be the attack coach for the Springboks when we won 36–34 against the All Blacks in Wellington in 2018. The team scored five tries that day and that was certainly the achievement that I am most proud of.*

The best advice I ever got was... *the words of Jannie Putter, the Lions' former sports psychologist: "Everything that happens to us, happens for us!"*

Former Springbok forward Julian Redelinghuys also inspired me with his personal testimony and advice: "Play for an audience of One." I think if we can apply this perspective to all aspects of our lives, we will save ourselves a lot of stress and heartache.

The best advice I ever gave was... *"Go and make a difference!"*

The best decision I ever made was... *Apart from asking my wife to marry me, the best decision I made was to leave the comfort of our lives – in Durban and at the Sharks Academy – behind, to move to Johannesburg and assist Johan Ackermann with the Lions team.*

The Bible verse that carries me...

Jeremiah 29:11,
"For I know the thoughts that I think toward you,
says the Lord, thoughts of peace and not of evil,
to give you a future and a hope."

MY STORY
Swys de Bruin

It was a day of rain showers, lightning, and thunderstorms; a sad day for eleven-year-old Swys de Bruin. He arrived at the front door of his vice-principal and coach, Mr Slang Fouché, and knocked on the door to find out when they were going to train. Rain was pouring down, forming drops on the glass of his spectacles. There would not be a rugby practice, but Mr Fouché invited the ever-eager Swys inside and offered him a warm cup of soup in the hope that it would at least make it a more cheerful day for the youngster.

Swys' passion for rugby was obvious. He ate, lived, and slept rugby. Yet his own rugby career was cut short at a young age because of a serious ankle injury. It taught Swys two lessons: the first, that rugby is a physical, unforgiving contact sport. He later learnt something else: that on the surface, rugby is not always synonymous with Christianity. One can easily scare the players and the public off by trying to appear too "holy".

The solution? It was important to always be sincere, honest, and as fair as possible, so that people could see God reflected in his life, rather than by Swys telling them about his faith. His experience of God's goodness was as genuine and tangible as his love for the sport.

He was a third-year student at Kovsies when, one holiday, he drove to Pietermaritzburg to visit his girlfriend, Marilize, who would later become his wife. A man had picked him up and, as Swys got in, he spotted the words of the well-known song, "Amazing Grace", on a pamphlet on the seat. A meaningful, deep conversation about the meaning of grace followed.

The conversation on the short journey to Harrismith touched Swys' heart so deeply that he went down on his knees right there on the side of the road and asked the Lord to have mercy on him.

Never would that driver, a pastor, realise that the short lift was a Damascus moment for this young man. Although his final surrender would only take place more than a decade later...

In Swys' first year with the Sharks, his main focus was training the coaches. The inspiration to put together a manual that would help coaches was exciting. Swys experienced the overwhelming feeling that it was not him who did the writing. When finalising the text, he thanked his Creator in the preface for the wisdom in compiling the book. This was a controversial step and the mood of his colleagues, sobering. Apparently, a preface of this nature was not really suitable within the rugby culture. However, it was at that moment that the still, soft voice of the Holy Spirit gave Swys peace about his decision. *"The foreword remains the same or the manual does not get printed,"* he stuck to his guns.

The manual was printed as it was and, after that experience, Swys would always give the Lord the glory in his rugby career, under all circumstances, and experience many miracles on and off the field.

However, pruning processes would be ongoing because one's ego gets the better of you sometimes. It is the prestige that players and coaches experience, as well as the pressure of coaching at a high level, that often makes leaders forget how dependent they are on the Lord.

> ***"You get carried away by achievements and the praise of others."***

"I believed I could handle everything; and when I finally cracked under the pressure of two demanding roles over the course of almost two years – first with the Lions as head coach of the Super Rugby team, as well as the role as attack coach with the Springboks – I realised that I wanted to do too much. I forgot how dependent I really am on the Lord."

Swys with his wife, Marilize, and eldest son, Neil, soon after the Lions qualified for the Super Rugby final in 2018

Burnout in 2019, at the peak of his career, brought Swys to a standstill. He was away from home for 25 weeks of the year, one rugby season after the other. A few months before the World Cup, the constant pressure of the two roles took its toll and he had to make the drastic decision to give up his role with the Springboks. It was the professional help of Prof. Gerhard Schwär, a psychologist, who guided him on the first steps of his recovery.

"When such a storm rages in and around you, you often doubt your decisions, but for me it was the only way out. I now realise that, with God's help, I made the right choices for my self-preservation, even if it was very difficult for others to accept."

"I now know that the Lord allowed the burnout to happen so that I could learn valuable lessons. He was, as always, there to catch me."

One of the most important lessons that Swys would learn from this is that you should not leave your wellbeing up to other people's opinions: There are, were, and always will be those who criticise in difficult times, do not believe in you, or stand with you. After seven wonderful years, Swys had to walk away from his beloved Lions, only to find himself stuck in two years of COVID, yet still believing that God was always there.

What were the words and message from God's heart for you these past two years? What has He shared with you about your life, character, and being, away from the sports field?

COVID has touched every single one of our lives in one way or another. My family has been so blessed that no one got seriously ill or died as a result of it. It was a time in which my family and I were forced to stop and to experience each day as precious and God-given. We grew closer to each other and to the Lord, and it gave me a totally new, fresh outlook on life.

The Lord made me realise one thing clearly: Do not worry about tomorrow, especially because at that time we literally did not know what the next day would bring. It was actually also a time of healing for me, where I was no longer trapped in the rat race of work and of winning or losing. I realised anew that the Lord, even in our isolation from each other as people, was still as close to us as ever. We might not have been able to go to church, but we could still call on Him, praise and worship Him, and strengthen our personal relationship with Him.

How did you keep the players under your care standing when sometimes it felt like you could not stay standing yourself?

As a coach at the Lions, I was very blessed to be surrounded by an excellent management team and players. The culture that Ackers established is one that I still follow today: If someone was struggling mentally, the others were there to lift him up, reassure him, and strengthen him. Our doors were always open to any player and our brotherhood was one of our greatest values. We always played to glorify the Lord and to entertain our fans.

What do you think is the biggest obstacle in men's lives?

The first obstacle is often our egos. In my work, the media and social media definitely play a big role regarding this. Guys are easily exalted as idols, and you even begin to believe you are invincible. You often lose perspective and contact with reality and then struggle to deal with any criticism or failure.

We also come from a culture that prescribes that men should be tough ("cowboys don't cry"). I believe this is a huge obstacle, because the more you are in touch with your own emotions, the better you can understand and empathise with those of others.

Another obstacle is that men often struggle (or refuse) to speak about their inner worries. The steam in the pressure cooker builds up and, if it is not released little by little in one way or another, an explosion becomes inevitable.

How would you like to be remembered?

I would like to be remembered as someone who was sincere, who made a difference in other people's lives, and in whom one could see the light of God.

Swys with the Springbok backs

Father and sons on the Hartebeespoort Dam

Your message to South Africa

South Africans are unique, truly a rainbow nation. We are resilient and our power lies precisely in our diversity. My prayer for our country is that there will be a unifying campaign, from the highest levels of government, that will bring us all back to God and bind us together stronger than ever. Soli Deo Gloria.

And of course, I always wish that the Springboks would play more running rugby!

Swys de Bruin
Exclusive interview
Scan the code to watch

Victor Matfield

Victor Matfield, born on the 11th of May 1977, is a former South African professional rugby player. The pride of Polokwane was a versatile cricket and rugby player from a young age and participated in the Far North Schools Cricket tournament. An injury that hampered his batting and bowling gave him enough reason to focus solely on rugby. He was selected for the Far North's Junior Craven Week team before playing lock for Hoërskool Pietersburg. Victor qualified to go to the Craven Week competition for high schools two years in a row. As a former student of the University of Pretoria, he played for the u21 team and, soon after, was selected to play for the Blue Bulls u21 team. Victor donned the green and gold for the first time in 1995 as part of the SA Academy team. In 1997, he played in the u21 Springbok team under the captaincy of Bobby Skinstad and made the team again in 1998. In 2000, he played for the SA u23 team. His provincial career includes various years with the Blue Bulls, Griquas (1999-2000), Cats (1999-2000), Bulls, Toulon (2007-2008), and 17 games for Northampton Saints (2015-2016). He is, however, most famous for his success in disrupting opposition lineouts together with teammate, Bakkies Botha. This skill became the cornerstone of his Springbok career as a senior player (2001-2015). Victor made his debut in the senior Springbok team on the 30th of June 2001 in a match against Italy. He is widely regarded as one of the best locks to ever play for South Africa. He initially retired after the 2011 World Cup. However, he made his comeback to rugby in 2014 and was the first choice for the Springbok World Cup team in 2015. After this match, he was also the person with the record for the most Springbok caps.

His achievements include the International Rugby Board (IRB) Player of the Rugby World Cup 2007. In 2008, he was captain of the first team to beat the All Blacks in New Zealand at the "House of Pain" (Dunedin Rugby Stadium) since England in 2003. Victor and his team won the Currie Cup final three times (2002, 2004, and 2009), the Super 14 title in 2007, 2009, and 2010, as well as the Tri Nations series in 2004 and 2009, and the Rugby World Cup in 2007. In 2008, he was inducted into the University of Pretoria's Hall of Fame.

Victor's coaching and consulting career includes time with the Australian NSW Waratahs and Blue Bulls (2013).

He is currently part of SuperSport as a television presenter and is a businessman.

My love for sport began... *as a young boy. My parents were both teachers, which meant that I grew up next to the sports field with a ball in my hand. My entire school career revolved around sports – mostly cricket and rugby. I never wanted presents for my birthday, but rugby and cricket balls or a bat or racket were always welcome.*

If I was not a sports star / TV presenter, I would... *have a job in the field of BCom. I studied BCom accounting at the University of Pretoria, but I am currently involved with mines and the wholesale of diesel. I am an entrepreneur.*

I am incredibly grateful for... *first, my incredible parents. I grew up in a wonderful home where they raised me with a lot of love and a good value system. My parents did everything to give me the best opportunities in life. They also raised me with the most important focus on earth: being a Christian. Second, I am grateful for my wife and children in my life. We are an extremely close family. I would not have been able to reach the heights I did if it was not for my wife's support.*

If I could edit my life, I would... *not change anything. I am very happy with most of the decisions I have made in my life.*

One of the biggest lessons I learnt this year... *I think it would be forgiveness. We are so caught up in our own lives that we care too much about our own interests, and not those of others.*

My greatest achievement is... *My family. I have a wonderful family and we are very close.*

The Bible verse that carries me...

I am not a specific Bible verse person, but the most important thing is our love for our fellow man and that we know the only way that we can be saved is through the grace of Jesus Christ.

Victor Matfield and Bakkies Botha

Victor, Monja, and their two oldest daughters

MY STORY
Victor Matfield

He is 2.01 m tall, the son of Fai and Hettie Matfield. He is a tower of a man and a rugby genius whose work ethic and leadership skills have been apparent from a young age. He was praised for his mobility and speed, his temperament on and off the field. He became synonymous with the number 5. Victor's blood was blue, yet also green, and if he could sleep on a rugby field, he would! Sports commentators loved talking about his game. With 127 games for the Springboks, Victor will forever be regarded as one of the best locks in the history of South African rugby.

God entrusted Victor with a role as a sports hero for South Africa, and He still entrusts him with the accompanying esteem. However, the pruning processes Victor had to go through, time and again, was something that helped to shape his character. He never shied away from the pruning process.

"The love for sport in South Africa gives me the opportunity to touch people's lives. I think my biggest impact is telling people about my mindset. I always see life as being positive – I always look for the positive side in everything."

"I take every challenge as a goal and the vision to overcome it drives me so hard that nothing I have to sacrifice feels like a sacrifice to me."

"I just focus on the dream and enjoy the journey with all its obstacles."

However, there was one day that underscored this mindset; a watershed moment in Victor's life that he can always refer to. At the time, he was wrestling with big decisions. He was playing with his little daughter in the park in the estate where they lived. *"The next moment, an unfamiliar car stopped next to the park and an unknown man got out to hand me a note. On the note was my answer to what decision I had to take – I still do not know who the man was and how he reached me..."*

Since then, faith has played a big role in his sports career, and his relationship with God has been non-negotiable. The experience would be a puzzle piece in a bigger picture, because Victor no longer only knew God via his parents – no, he now had a direct relationship with God himself, because God knew his name and Victor was His.

"As a sportsman, I based all my principles on Biblical values, and I think that kept me humble and hardworking. In marriage and in the business world, all that keeps you on the straight and narrow path is your values that are rooted in God."

When the world around them wants to make everything acceptable – even unethical business and family values – the Matfields look for true North and use God as a compass to guide them.

> **"The world has made everything so acceptable that we cannot afford to not read the Bible and stand on our relationship with Jesus."**

The world will go through transformations, and yes, change is good, but Victor refuses to bow the knee to an imaginary giant and make issues bigger than they need to be. *"My wife says I might be too unemotional, but I have not experienced many storms yet. Perhaps I simply do not experience most difficult times as storms; even during COVID, that was the case. Yes, there were difficult times in our business, and we had to make hard decisions, but I grew so much during that time. I know I did the best for everyone in my company, and, in the end, I did not have to lay anyone off. So, was it difficult? Yes. Do I feel positive about how we handled it? Yes. We once again made the best of it."*

One of Victor's favourite memories is the day Jake White walked into the team room on his first day as Springbok coach and wrote the words "World Cup Champions 2007" on the whiteboard. It was never wiped off and, for four years, everyone worked together on this dream. If you ask Victor today if this is still the way he functions, he gives an affirmative nod, because he lives what he believes and speaks. As the title of his biography, *Journey*, suggests, he realises that success does not come overnight and that no one can stay standing on their own. God is our foundation, and He is an integral part of a team and an important link – or key – to the end result.

Monja, Tasmin, Giselle, Victor, and Jamie

What do you think is the biggest obstacle in men's lives?

I think our egos. We are very proud, and we convince ourselves about what gives us identity. It is rare that we ask for help and, many times, men bury things deep in themselves until it is too late and then they explode. Sometimes it is then too late to get help.

How would you like to be remembered?

I would like to be remembered as a humble person who always had time for other people and who had even more time for his family. I love to be there for my children.

Your message to South Africa

I have been in many teams and each individual must have their own dream and vision, but the team's vision/dream must always outweigh the individual's dream. We are a diverse group of people in South Africa and each person and each language group must have their own vision. However, it is important that our vision as South Africans must always carry the most weight. Our vision for South Africa must be based on our Christian principles, of which love and tolerance for each other must be the most important.

Victor and Monja

Victor with two of his daughters

Isabella Kruger

Isabella Kruger, born on the 30th of March 2005, is a right-handed South African tennis sensation. She is currently 336th on the Women's Tennis Association (WTA) ranking and 155th on the International Tennis Federation (ITF) ranking. As the daughter of the former Springbok rugby player, Ruben Kruger, she has sporting talent in her veins. Isabella made her Grand Slam debut at the junior Wimbledon Championship in 2022.

My love for sport began... *from a young age. I grew up in a family that loves sports. My father played rugby and my uncle is a tennis coach. Therefore, I was interested in sports from very young. I have been playing tennis since I was three years old, because my older sister also played tennis and I always wanted to do what she did! At primary school, I participated in all kinds of sports, but tennis has always been my favourite, my first love!*

If I was not a sports star... *I am still young and can still make many decisions about my future, but if tennis did not take up so much time, I would have liked to study psychology. I am interested in how the brain functions in different circumstances and situations; how people, words and an environment can affect you positively or negatively. I glean from psychology books how to improve my mindset and thinking on the tennis court. The value lies in applying this advice, and allowing it to guide me. I experience the power it has and the difference it makes in my own life and game plan.*

I am incredibly grateful for... *so many things in my life. The one big change I have made over the past two years is to live in gratitude. Life is more enjoyable when you focus on gratitude, rather than on the shortcomings and the absence of things. In every situation, there is something to be thankful for. I am so grateful for the people who the Lord has placed in my life: my family, friends, and team. Everyone in my life adds value. My family and friends bring me closer to the Lord; they are people who care about me and with whom I can share both the good and bad moments. I am also very fortunate that sport allows me to travel to other parts of the world, experiencing different things. I follow a profession that can teach me so much wisdom about life. Since a young age, I often toured alone to tennis competitions – there were numerous times where I had to solve problems alone in a foreign country. These experiences make me grateful for the people around me.*

If I could edit my life, I would... *not change anything. This is a very difficult question to answer because there have been so many "bad" moments, but I think that those times have made me wiser and have taught me the most. Without the bad moments in one's life, you cannot understand the value of a "good" moment. The bad moments taught me that I cannot function without the Lord. Every decision and every season I had to go through is part of the Lord's plan for me.*

One of the biggest lessons I learnt this year... *is that my identity does not lie in my sport, but in the Lord. Everything I do, I do to honour Him, not to make my name great. I also realised the power of prayer.*

My greatest achievement is... *that I have changed my mindset over the past few years. I always had a lot of trouble seeing the positive in bad situations and learning something from it, but during the lockdown I had a lot of time to reflect on what is important to me and how I can change my life. The change in my mindset helped me win some of the biggest matches of my career so far! The opportunity to represent our country at Wimbledon was an incredible experience.*

The Bible verse that carries me...
is one that my mother always repeats to me.

Psalm 23:3-4,
"He restores my soul; He leads me in the paths of righteousness for His name's sake. Though I walk through the valley of the shadow of death, I will fear no evil; for You are with me; Your rod and Your staff, they comfort me." *This Bible verse means a lot to me because it reminds me that the Lord is always with me. This goes hand in hand with* ***2 Corinthians 5:7,***
"... for we live by faith, not by sight."

Isabella with her father, Ruben

MY STORY
Isabella Kruger

"Faith in the Lord is very important. It is to live with an unwavering expectation that the Lord will make His plan for your life come to pass, because faith is a firm trust in the Lord and the confidence in what we pray and hope for. It is an assurance about the things we do not see."

Isabella is only 18 years old, but the lessons she has had to learn, voluntarily and involuntarily, have been life changing.

Faith in an invisible God and believing that He has the best in mind for them, as a family in the unknown, was all that young Isabella Kruger had to hold on to.

She was only nine years old when her mother made the big decision to settle in America. *"We did not know anyone there. It was a total change of environment and even though it offered the best opportunity for a successful sports career for my sister and me, it was the hardest thing to get used to. The adjustment was enormous, the foreign country and unusual culture sometimes became so challenging, but we had each other and that was enough."* With the security of a protective mother who gave guidance while being her daughters' biggest fan, Lize taught Isabella and her sister how to make the right choices and overcome difficult situations. After the death of their father, Ruben, they had to leave the familiar sunny South Africa and the Afrikaans culture behind, as well as the safety net of an extended family. Florida became their new home and they soon got to know the airports between Madrid and America very well. Zoë, Isabella's older sister, moved to Spain in order to focus on and advance her career there.

Isabella no longer had small dreams. She had to obey the driving force of the sporting blood in her veins. *"I was about seven years old when I first set foot on Wimbledon. I just remember meeting Roger Federer and that he was so kind – his mother is also a South African. I was so small, but that memory spurred me on to make a success of my career. I remember watching Serena Williams, while Maria Sharapova was also playing at that stage. From that moment on it was my dream to one day play at Wimbledon too."*

Hours of practice, patience, and hard work lay ahead for Isabella. But she would first have an encounter with the Lord, because she had to learn to do everything for His glory and not for her own gain. Therein lies the joy, otherwise the opinions and criticism of people would have consumed her. Isabella realised that she was taking up the tennis racket for a greater purpose than just sport. She had to look beyond the comments of the public on social media and shoulder the responsibility of a calling in the spotlight. Because whatever sits on the throne of your heart will dictate to you who you are and what your value is. *"When I understood that I must put the Lord first in every aspect of my life, I experienced a sense of peace that I never had before. Knowing and believing in a living God and putting all my faith in the Him, was my salvation. To know that He had a plan for my life changed everything. I realised that anything I do, regardless of whether I play tennis or not, must be to magnify His Name."*

> **"When I changed my approach and realised that I play for the Lord; whether I win or lose it is part of His plan for my life – it immediately relieved so much of the pressure on the court."**

God definitely entrusted Isabella with a role as a sports person for South Africa. He trusted her with a title and prestige, but there was a lengthy pruning process that she had to go through. Her calling to play tennis became her new reality and it was accompanied by a few changes. Her routine away from the court had to change. Small things like what time she went to bed, what she ate, and how often she talked to the Lord throughout the day, all played a role. For the first time, Isabella would understand the extent of her responsibility and the magnitude of the opportunity.

"I realised that the Lord could give me a great opportunity, but if I did not do my part to prepare well, I could not take advantage of the opportunity." Her character on the court also had to change. *"I began to understand that it does not matter if you win or lose, the impression that your character made is what people will remember. I also asked the Lord to make love the true motive of my heart, and to help me to be more patient with myself and others."*

She adjusted her attitude towards other people; how she reacted when she was angered. She had to ask the Lord to remove people from her life who enticed her away from Him. The changes that followed were not at all what she had planned. *"It was not part of 'my plan', but it was part of the Lord's plan. God's opinion about me matters much more than people's opinion about me."*

Then, shortly after COVID and a challenging lockdown period, Wimbledon knocked on her door. Isabella's dream as a little girl became a reality at the age of 17.

"The whole thing was just so unreal."

"Previously I had been to Wimbledon as a fan and to enjoy the atmosphere, but let me tell you, it is very different to step out there as a player on the court!"

The uncertainty of unanswered questions, the bumps, knocks, and bruises of growing up, learning new habits and getting rid of bad old ones, together with all the other changes in her life, strengthened Isabella to stand strong. It was the power of prayer that kept her going. *"The realisation that I have the privilege of being able to talk to the Creator of the universe and that He knows my name, kept me going."*

Isabella could look back in gratitude and see her whole life in a new light. Her identity is in Him. She could play tennis for Him and leave her whole life in His hands. *"I no longer compare myself to people around me and therefore I can rejoice with them when there is a highlight in their life; really celebrate it with them, because we all have different seasons in our lives."*

What do you think is the biggest obstacle in women's lives?

We tend to think and react more emotionally, and sometimes too quickly, but this is why the Bible's truth is so important. We must also always refer back to the facts first, especially in a difficult time, because they can teach us how to handle situations and how to respond out of God's love. However, in my opinion, being emotional is not a bad quality. God made men and women different for a reason. We can empathise with people and really understand when someone is voicing their emotions.

How would you like to be remembered?

For me, it is not so important how I am remembered, but rather what impact I could make in the world and on other people's lives while I was here. I want to show the Lord's love. If I were to be remembered for something, I would like it to be how I witnessed to His Name and that I am someone who did everything out of God's love. Part of that involves showing that I am not perfect and that everyone makes mistakes; that only speaks of the infinite love the Lord has for us and that He will always forgive us and love us.

Isabella (centre) with her mother, Lize, and sister, Zoë

Your message to South Africa

The phrase, "The man who loves walking will walk further than the man who loves the destination", means a lot to me. It is important to enjoy the process and journey. This means that there will be many "ups and downs" in your life. Things are not always going to go your way, but that is part of your learning experience. Learn how to enjoy your journey and live each day in confident expectation and faith in the Lord.

Isabella Kruger
Exclusive interview
Scan the code to watch

The two Kruger sisters with Roger Federer

Theuns Stofberg

Marthinus Theunis Steyn 'Theuns' Stofberg was born on the 6th of June 1955 in Villiers, a small town in the Free State on the banks of the Vaal River. He is named after the former president of the Orange Free State and, with leadership in his blood, his future was paved to the top with a string of leadership titles to his name. Theuns is one of the 64 captains who have led the South African national rugby team. His rugby career began at Dirkie Uys Primary School and continued at Gray College in Bloemfontein. His provincial career began as a student at the University of the Free State (1976-1980). During his conscription in Pretoria, he donned the light blue rugby jersey with the well-known red daisy on the chest (1980-1982). Theuns left Northern Transvaal in 1982 and moved to their arch-enemies, the Western Province Rugby Union, where he played for WP for four years (1982-1985). On the 14th of August 1976 he made his debut in the Free State Stadium as a young 21-year-old flanker for the Springbok team against New Zealand. He took over from Jan Ellis, his childhood hero, who is remembered for his speed and size – both remarkable for a flanker at that time. His first test as captain took place on the 18th of October 1980 against the South American Jaguars in Montevideo, where the Springboks won 22–13. Between 1980 and 1984, he led the team in four tests and, during this time, scored six tries for South Africa. Theuns fulfilled the role as captain in one of the most important tours in New Zealand, and also in rugby history – the infamous 1981 Springbok tour. It was disrupted by protesters. During the third test, a low-flying plane bombarded the field with leaflets, smoke, and flour bombs. Theuns played 21 tests in the green and gold and played his last two international tests against England in 1984; they won both and he scored a try in the second test. Due to a knee injury, he retired from the sport in that same year, as a 31-year-old at the peak of his rugby career. Until 2021, he was the only player in history to have won the Currie Cup with three different teams. He won titles with the Free State (1976), Northern Transvaal (1979 and 1980), and Western Province (1982 and 1983). In total, he played in seven finals, winning four (1976, 1980, 1982, and 1983) and drawing one (1980).

Today Theuns is a husband, father, and grandfather and manages a small wine farm, Rouana, and the Rouana guest farm, together with his wife Martie. He also runs his family mediation and marriage therapy practice in the Western Cape.

My love for sport began... *at my parental home. It was a privilege to grow up in a wonderfully happy parsonage where sport played a rather important role. The upbringing of us six children was based on my parents' motto that a healthy body houses a healthy* mind, and this was how we also lived as a family. Some of my earliest memories were those of my parents on the tennis court on Saturdays. My mother swam and played tennis for the University of Stellenbosch. My siblings and I were all sporty. My sisters played hockey, while us four boys were mostly busy on the rugby field. We spent hours each day playing rugby against each other on the lawn at home. It was especially fun for me to grow up with my brothers and I believe this is where my love for sports was born. Athletics also played an important role in my sports world as a child.

If I was not a sports star, I would... Sport was part of my whole life, and I participated for the pleasure of it. I took part in sports as an amateur and, at school, had already decided to go into a medical qualification. With physiotherapy combining sports, treatment of sports injuries, and medical care, my career choice was to qualify myself as a physiotherapist. Later, in my own practice, I focused on orthopaedic and sports injuries. I was, however, forced to make a career change, and qualified as a marriage counsellor and family mediator to help people alleviate the emotional pain in their relationships and also to act as a mediator in family conflict situations. I would have liked to do this earlier in my life.

I am incredibly grateful for... the Christian education I had as a child and for the example set in my parents' home. I could not have asked for a more emotionally safe world, and it played a role in many of the decisions I made throughout my life. I am grateful for a full life. I am married and in a happy and safe relationship with Martie, I have children of whom I can be very proud, and I have a quiver full of grandchildren who give us great pleasure. I am grateful for the opportunities I now have to make a positive contribution to other people's lives.

If I could edit my life, I would... change very little of it, because I have learnt a lot from the negative and positive events in my life, they shaped me into who I am today. The choices and decisions I made; I always did for the right reasons. However, one only learns later on in life that those choices do not always yield the results that you had in mind.

21-year-old Springbok

Theuns and his wife, Martie

One of the biggest lessons I learnt this year... *is as Psalm 90 clearly teaches us. The life that we have been given, regardless of the time period, is very short if we see it in perspective and consider that the years we are given are only a very small portion with an eternity ahead of us. We must live in gratitude, that is our greatest responsibility.*

My greatest achievement is... *To me, the definition of achievement is something that has been successfully achieved with effort, skill, and courage. In light of that, I can probably consider my rugby career as an achievement. Today, however, I am a family counsellor and mediator. It is now the greatest achievement for me to help two people who are in a relationship to use the tools that are available, and to realise the uniqueness of each person. For me, it is an infinite reward to be of help to others in that way, to families who are falling apart, so that there is a turnaround that has eternal value.*

The Bible verse that carries me...
The entire chapter of Psalm 90.

"So, teach us to number our days, that we may gain a heart of wisdom" (verse 12). This Psalm of Moses plays an extremely important role for me, where he confirms the transience of man and compares us to grass that withers (verses 5-6).

In this part of the Psalm, the psalmist confesses that the secret of life depends on God's gifts, on His mercy (verse 14), His love (verse 14), and the years He gives us (verse 15). It is when we realise that He gives His love in abundance every day (verse 14) and He makes sure that His work and greatness becomes clear to our children (verse 16) that life begins to make sense and we can experience joy (verse 15).

That is why the psalmist asks that we will experience the goodness of the Lord our God in such a way that He will establish the work of our hands. What incredible insight into how life works and what an important prayer to pray!

Match against France

Tour in New Zealand

MY STORY
Theuns Stofberg

Theuns Stofberg will always be proud of the fact that he is a reverend's son and the fourth of six children. Yes, everyone always joked that the reverend's children were the naughtiest, but in the same breath they also confirmed that Theuns had a calling as a leader. He had a strong focus on ministry, to lead and make sure that his words carried weight. Theuns always had a love for people of different cultures and respect, honesty, and fairness was and still is important to him. Even though he was young, it was these principles that he exhibited on and off the field. It was the year of 1981, during a rugby tour – better known as the rebel tour – where he would run out onto the field as captain for the Springbok team and had to make very important decisions.

In 1981, the South African rugby tour to New Zealand polarised opinions and resulted in widespread protests in New Zealand. The controversy followed the South African rugby team to the United States, where they continued their tour after their departure from New Zealand. Apartheid made South Africa an international pariah and other countries were strongly discouraged from signing sports contracts with South Africa. However, the New Zealand Rugby Union would break all the rules by inviting the South Africans to their home ground so that the All Blacks could compete against their strongest opponents, the formidable Springboks. A huge furore erupted over the heads of the New Zealand management over the question of whether politics should influence sport in this way and whether the Springboks should be allowed to tour. The matches were played in secret and some matches were boycotted, with Springbok players having to be escorted under police guard in convoy.

> **It was in situations like these where the young Theuns had to discern the difference between his talents and his calling.**

God blessed him with both; the skill of the game came naturally, here he could rely on his brute strength and size. However, it was the development of his calling – to understand stewardship, to trust one hundred percent in God for guidance and wisdom – which would later make him a brilliant mentor. *"In the Christian home where I grew up, to live by faith was a daily way of life. The experience of God's presence came during the times when you called upon Him and asked for His help regarding choices you had to make. Where everything seemed hopeless and with no solution ... that is where I learnt: God can help."*

Years of character building and this awareness of God's voice in his life carried Theuns through the biggest storms. He survived it knowing that God always stands with him in the midst of a storm. *"Like the time when I was rescued from the crashing waves deep at sea in Stilbaai, when I no longer had any hope left. Also, when I sought His comfort at the death of my first grandchild."*

> **"I knew God was the only One who could console."**

"And when I was diagnosed with a serious illness, it was one of the times I had a very personal experience with God."

Theuns was diagnosed with an autoimmune disease in 2008 after he temporarily lost the use of his hands and feet. His nerves were affected, and he had to make big changes in his life. However, this unlocked his calling, and he began working as a counsellor and mediator. *"I had to go through an illness to discover my calling to help other people with their relationships! It is experiences like these that brought me closer to God and gave me a personal experience with Him that I cannot walk away from."*

It is more than 40 years on, and God still entrusts Theuns with a role as a sports person – someone who contributes to other people's lives. *"My sports career ended many years ago, but it cultivated in me a lifestyle of gratitude for the gifts I received. Since I am still considered a sportsman, it gives me a platform to play a role in mediating family relationships, in various businesses, as well as in disputes between ethnic groups in our country."*

Theuns and the legendary Frik du Preez

The seed of leadership was sown in a household in Villiers. That seed germinated under pressure and difficult conditions on the rugby field in the 1980s and, today, Theuns still bears the fruit of the Spirit. *"I live what I learnt from my parents, that a healthy body with a healthy mind will put you in a position to bear the fruit of the Spirit."*

God could trust Theuns Stofberg with a definite role as sports man in South Africa and, today, He still trusts him as a relationship mediator with people's lives.

> *"Knowing that God trusted me to play a role in South Africa, is the greatest honour."*

"The price for that privilege is to sacrifice time. Time – which we actually receive from God for free – is life, and life is time."

"I have been a therapist for more than 45 years. It is the most amazing job in the world. I care for people in their darkest times. I hear touching, often heartbreaking, stories about people's journeys, and marvel at their perseverance. I have the privilege of offering compassion, direction, insight, inspiration, and profound care to others. I am humbled by the countless lessons I have learnt from clients about the richness of the human spirit."

Today, Theuns Stofberg is still the leader who is willing to learn.

What were the words and message from God's heart for you over these past two years? What did He share with you about your life, character, and being, during COVID?

COVID was a unique and also terrifying period where almost everyone had to make adjustments because we were threatened by the unknown. Many of us lost family or friends and we have been brought closer to the reality that there is an end to life on earth; we are reminded of the transience of man. This made me realise again that it is not about how much time we have at our disposal, but what we do with the time we are given.

What do you think is the biggest obstacle in men's lives?

Men's unconscious and primary function is to provide. As men, we believe that we are measured by it. In our pursuit of being the provider, many men do not realise how they harm others in the process of attaining that highest goal. The time and attention given to achieving it can cause so much damage, and harm relationships with friends and family if you do not have insight.

I believe the biggest obstacle in men's lives is not getting to the point of knowing that life is not really about yourself and your success. Most of us go through a stage between 20 and 35 when we believe that life revolves around us, and that success is measured by our status and achievements. Living egocentrically, I believe, is one of the biggest obstacles in many men.

How would you like to be remembered?

Each of us had our childhood heroes, mostly sports heroes. We wanted to be like them. We wanted to be remembered as such a hero, but as we got older, we realised there are other heroes. I call them the "unknown heroes" who actually each deserve a statue. I know that each one of us can be such a hero on a daily basis in our actions towards others. To do the right thing at the right time without thinking of the consequences or the sacrifice, and to do it without being noticed. Like those times when a wife looks up to her husband to make the right financial decisions, then he is her hero. When you help a hungry person who pleadingly looks at everyone walking by, when you give to satisfy a child's hunger. What about when a son or daughter looks to their father or mother to set an example of how to resolve conflict in a relationship. There are so many such opportunities for us to be heroes.

I would like to be remembered as someone who played a positive role in other people's lives and their relationships.

Stofberg family, 1967

Theuns as a young 20-year-old Free State player

Your message to South Africa

Almost daily we receive foreign tourists here with us in Stellenbosch and, almost without exception, everyone who visits us cannot stop talking about the wonderful country that we live in. It is not only the breathtaking beauty of nature, but also the exceptionally hospitable and friendly people of South Africa. We are so inclined to focus on the negative in our country that we miss the beautiful things that we do have.

I have learnt a great life lesson: By paying less attention to the negative and focusing on the positive things in life, your life can change. Many of the things that make you depressed and rob you of hope disappear when you change your outlook and focus on what is going well and what you have to be thankful for.

Be grateful and fix your eyes on the positive. I have; it has changed my life.

Theuns Stofberg
Exclusive interview
Scan the code to watch

Thomas du Toit

Thomas Joubert du Toit, born on the 5th of May 1995, is a South African rugby player who played for the Sharks in the United Rugby Championship, as well as for the Springboks. This son of Moorreesburg laced up his rugby boots early in his life and represented Boland in 2008 in the u13 Craven Week competition. In 2011 he played for the Western Province in the u16 Grant Khomo week, and in 2013 in the u18 Craven Week competition. The former Paarl Boys' High School student played for the school's first team in 2012 and 2013, captaining the team in 2013. In the same year, Thomas was included in the South African Schools team, which played three matches that August. In 2014 he was selected to join the Sharks Academy. As a 19-year-old, he moved to Durban. It was in that year, during the 2014 IRB Junior World Championship and the subsequent 2015 tour of Argentina, when Thomas was afforded the opportunity to join the South African u20 team. For the first time in his life, he would sing the national anthem with his hand on the Springbok emblem on his chest.

Even though he had no previous senior rugby experience, Thomas was surprisingly included in the Sharks squad for the 2014 Super Rugby season. He made his debut for the Sharks on the 7th of March 2014 against the Border Bulldogs in East London. He came on the field as a half time substitute and scored his first senior try within 15 minutes of play. Thomas' other professional contracts include a three-month stint with the Irish Pro14 team, Munster, and the South African A rugby team, which, in 2022, played a two-match series against the Saxons, a touring team from England.

Thomas, who was initially not included in South Africa's squad for the 2019 Rugby World Cup, made his debut as a senior Springbok prop on the 23rd of September 2019 when he was called to replace the injured Trevor Nyakane in South Africa's playoffs. As a result, Thomas became part of the South African team that won the Rugby World Cup by defeating England in the final.

The intimidating physique of this 1.89 m tall, 128 kg front row giant is perfectly captured by his nickname, "The Tank". He has perfected the transition from loosehead to tighthead prop, meaning that he can pack on both sides of the scrum with equal destructive force.

Thomas left South Africa at the end of 2023 to settle in Bath, England.

My love for sport began... as a 7-year-old boy at Dirkie Uys Primary School in Moorreesburg. It was a very small school, and I was the biggest boy! Therefore, I participated in everything the largest boy had to do. In athletics, I participated in javelin, discus, and shot put. I also played a bit of rugby as a loosehead prop and eighth man – actually every position as a ball carrier. Although I loved sports, it was not until high school that I actually realised I had a talent for rugby, and then I became more interested in it. I played rugby just because I enjoyed it and never thought that I would make a career out of it. My passion for rugby only took hold much later in my life.

If I was not a sports star, I would... definitely have taken up farming. I was on my way to Elsenburg to study and then would have returned to our family farm. At one stage, I also considered athletics as a career because I enjoyed it and excelled in it, but rugby was my calling and the Lord decided to use me in this capacity!

I am incredibly grateful for... my wife! She is an amazing person, and I would never want to be married to anyone else or share my life with anyone else. I need her in my life, and I know that we make a good team. We are accountability partners who keep each other on the right path. We can handle anything together: from raising our children to making big decisions and moving to another country.

I am also very grateful for my family. I have the best and most loving family in the world!

Last, but not least, I am so thankful for my children. They are the most precious possessions God has entrusted to us. It is sometimes a merry challenge, because it feels like we are "outnumbered", but they are the greatest reward.

If I could edit my life, I would... probably not change anything. I do not know if earlier in my life I would have focused more on rugby, because I feel I had a good balance between sport, friends, academia, family time, and alone time. I would never change my choice to join the Sharks, because then I would never have met my wife and had my children or the life I am so grateful for. I am thankful to the Lord for how He made my life turn out.

One of the biggest lessons I learnt this year... be resolute in your decisions – regardless of whether they were wrong or right decisions. Go for it one hundred percent! Go "flat box" for it, not half-hearted, and apply this principle to everything in your life. This is

Thomas receiving a trophy in grade 7

Thomas and his wife, Elaine, and their son, Ruben

exactly how I live – it was what we did when we decided to get married, and also when we wanted to start a family. It is also how we make career choices and decisions about contracts. It is also important to complete things in your life. Finish the season and do not walk away from something halfway through the process.

My biggest achievement... *has everything to do with my personal life: Finding my wife was my biggest achievement! If I did not have her, I would not have my two children or the life I love so much.*

The Bible verse that carries me...

**John 3:16,
"For God so loved the world that He gave His only begotten Son, that whoever believes in Him should not perish but have everlasting life."**

Thomas with Ruben after his last game at Kings Park Stadium

MY STORY
Thomas du Toit

Thomas du Toit was 12 years old when the Springboks took part in the sixth Rugby World Cup in France with 20 countries that, for four years, had worked hard to compete – not just for the title and trophy, but for the honour that came with it. On the 20th of October 2007 the Springboks, led by coach Jake White and Captain John Smit, beat England with a score of 15—6, jubilantly lifting the William Webb Ellis trophy for the second time! South Africa erupted in a frenzy of joy. Somewhere in a farmhouse in Moorreesburg, the Du Toit family, together with family and friends of the farming community in the area, also cheered in exuberant joy over the victory and then stepped outside, lit the fire for the braai, and continued with life as normal. *"I remember that day so well, because in our house sport was not a 'big deal'. We have always been very patriotic about our country, but never too focused on sports. No one in my immediate family, my uncles and aunts, or my grandfathers and grandmothers, ever participated in sports. We always simply focused on people and friendships. Real people, farming, food, visiting, laughter, love, and good stories were what we were about. Not sports!"*

However, God had a different plan, and this was totally contrary to what Thomas thought. Thomas "The Tank" du Toit's life was already planned and laid out for him in his mother's womb, and rugby was his calling. Though it was not the little boy's dream, and even when he kicked against the idea, God's hand in his life and rugby became visible, time and time again. *"I was firmly convinced that I would study agriculture and be involved in the business of our family farm."*

> *"Never did I think that I would excel in rugby. A life as a professional rugby player was never an option, not to mention a dream to become a Springbok!"*

"Sport was just a fun pastime. I was the biggest boy in my primary school and, therefore, I participated in everything that a big boy in his age group does. Rugby was only one of the options and the fact that I played it well, I attributed to my size."

The God-given talent was in Thomas' blood. It would awaken in his heart at the right time – in God's timing – and develop into a great passion, but only much later in his life. He would first get to know God, build a steadfast relationship with Him, and later let His light shine in rugby circles.

Thomas grew up in a loving family where he was allowed freedom of choice and open conversations were welcomed. It is precisely that approach to life that gave Thomas the freedom to make Paarl Boys' High his choice for high school and thus shape the path of his life. Rugby legends such as Mannetjies Roux, Corné Krige, Gurthrö Steenkamp, and Frans Malherbe all wore the school's blue and white striped jersey. He followed in the footsteps of these famous rugby players. Thomas not only developed his rugby talent year after year, but the passion for rugby ignited in his heart, to such an extent that he captained the first team as an 18-year-old matric pupil.

"I look back on my school years and am so grateful for my support systems. My father, Jacobus, my mother, Adele, and the circle of friends I surrounded myself with all anchored me firmly in God. I remember going to Shofar church with my friends as a young boy; how I chose to allow pastors and leaders to have a positive say in my life. The same friends who played a tough game of rugby with me were also the guys who loved God and influenced me to grow in my faith. It was a priority for me to get to know God and to learn more about Him and our Christian faith."

"I wanted to know and understand why I called myself a Christian. I wanted to know who Jesus is and what the purpose of the Holy Spirit is."

"Those growing up years gave me a firm foundation in my faith. It is of immense value, and I will always be grateful for it…"

After the day of his encounter with God, Thomas stopped looking for answers about faith and his vocation, he cherishes that day as the most important of his life. *"I found steadfastness in Him, even though I was only a young man. The importance of my relationship with God lay in the things it prevented me from engaging in. I knew God did not want to withhold things from me; He just wanted to protect me from bad consequences. So, I only engaged in things I was sure about. He gave me confidence in my choices because I knew that at the end of that road, the Lord would be there. I recognised His voice in my life and listened to it."*

The black rubber band with the white lettering around his wrist reads, *"I am second."* It is a sign and reminder of his decision about his faith in God. Thomas is a practical person – he wants to know what it is he is holding on to and why he believes it. That is why he stands on the one fundamental scripture in the Bible: John 3:16, "For God so loved the world that He gave His only begotten Son, that whoever believes in Him should not perish but have everlasting life."

He does not hesitate to admit that other people will be able to quote more passages of scripture in the Bible, but he knows what he believes in! *"This scripture is not about the death of Jesus, but His love, resurrection, and victory. If Jesus had not risen from the* dead, He would have been just another Bible character, but He is not. He is the Son of our almighty God and therefore I know that I can trust Him with everything!"

Thomas is steadfast at heart – he does not waver. When tumultuous seasons full of injuries or big decisions come knocking, he knows what to do. He turns to his support system, they talk it over, pray together, and trust together, because God is real and He always answers at the right time. *"Two years ago, I was baptised in front of a group of people in a friend's swimming pool. Yes, I was christened as a baby and I always heard about the value of being baptised as an adult, but I first had to find out for myself what it meant and what the importance of the decision was. On the day of my baptism, I pushed aside my own will and being, as well as my image as the 'tough guy', and I knelt before God in vulnerability, because this is what our faith requires. God wants us to experience our dependence on Him and it is an honour to bow the knee before Him. I trust God with everything within me for myself, my family, and the people I love."*

Thomas' name means "twin" in Hebrew and, as if God Himself had planned it that way, there are indeed two sides to Thomas du Toit! On the field he is the strong, fearless rugby player known as "The Tank", and at home, among his own, he is the gentle son, husband, and father who is everybody's friend. He is comfortable with both these sides of himself. He knows exactly who he is, what God expects of him, and where he is going, because he knows God knows his name.

Two signs hang like standards in his house. The one expresses the clear message of Joshua 24:14, "But as for me and my house, we will serve the Lord." The second hangs over the braai area and reads: *"In hierdie huis is daar nie dingetjies nie"* (In this house, we don't sweat the small stuff). "Tx4" aka Thomas "The Tank" du Toit is not fussy and does not give himself airs and graces. He keeps things simple and fun and makes sure that everyone he meets can just be themselves.

"God knew why He made me this way. He uses me just as I am. He wanted me here in rugby among the men and this is where I now live out my passion – for Him and for rugby."

*December holiday in Mossel Bay with Thomas' family.
Marzet, Danie, FG, Elaine, Adele and Jacobus*

What do you think is the biggest obstacle in men's lives?

We are too proud, and we refuse to appear fragile. We also do not always want to accept that our views and opinions can be wrong, and then we argue, even though we are very aware of our mistakes or shortcomings. Sometimes it requires you to put your pride in your pocket and admit that you are wrong.

How would you like to be remembered?

As a man who had a positive influence on people spiritually. As a plain person who liked simple things. A man who could be himself and talk to anyone – someone who valued open, honest, and straightforward conversations.

I hope the Sharks remember me every time they drink good coffee, light a fire, or talk about a 4x4 "bakkie"! May we remember the lovely, easy-flowing conversations about everything.

Daddy Thomas with Ruben and Leah

Leah's dedication

Your message to South Africa

I am coming back!

We live in the most beautiful and best country. Jan Braai always says: "To all my friends abroad ... we are still okay here in SA." And that's what I always want to be able to say. Our country is special and there is no place like home. I know we all go through seasons of being fed up, but when you feel like it, light a fire, have a braai, and crack a beer... live in the moment and know that there is no other country like South Africa. Our people and the cultural differences make South Africa unique!

Reinardt Janse van Rensburg

Reinardt Janse van Rensburg, born on the 3rd of February 1989, is a South African professional road racing cyclist and six-time Tour de France participant. Reinardt, the 1.81 m tall speedster, was born in Virginia, a small town in the Free State. As part of the Denver Disruptors team in the American NCL (National Cycling League), he is the hero of many a young South African cyclist. The teams that Reinardt has ridden for in his professional cycling career include: MTN Energade (2010-2012), the Dutch UCI ProTeam Argos-Shimano (2013-2014), South African MTN Qhubeka team (2015-2021), and the UCI WorldTeam Lotto Dstny (2021-2022).

He made his debut in the world-famous Tour de France in 2015 and represented South Africa for a second time in 2016. The Tour de France is an annual multiple-stage cycling race that mainly takes place in France, but the route sometimes also passes through nearby countries such as Belgium, Spain, Italy, and Germany. Like the other Grand Tours (the Giro d'Italia and the Vuelta a España) it consists of 21 stages, each a day long, over the course of 23 days. The tour usually consists of 20 professional teams of eight riders each and covers around 3600 km. It is the oldest of the Grand Tours and is widely regarded as the most prestigious. In 2022, South Africa's Reinardt held the multi-coloured flag aloft for the sixth time in this race as part of the UCI WorldTeam Lotto Dstny.

My love for sport began... *as a child. From childhood I really enjoyed playing and watching rugby and cricket. My sporting heroes were all the South African rugby and cricket players. I remember crying in the bathroom as a seven-year-old boy after Wales beat the Springboks in a test match! I have always loved sports. My father started cycling when I was ten years old, he took us to road races. It was not until the year after I got my first proper bike for Christmas – an upgraded version of the Pick n Pay bike I used to ride – that my interest in cycling took off.*

If I was not a sports star, I would... *work in sports administration or biokinetics. I studied sports science at the University of Pretoria and am currently studying managerial accounting. A future with my own business may therefore just be a good option.*

I am incredibly grateful for... *the people who have supported me in my career. I would never have achieved all the highlights without them. I am grateful to my family and especially my wife who had to make many sacrifices to support me.*

If I could edit my life, I would... *There will always be things that we would want to change because we think the result would have been different. There are things here and there that one regrets, but I would actually not change anything. You have to live with your decisions and accept that you will make mistakes. That it how you find your way.*

One of the biggest lessons I learnt this year... *is to realise that you are not always in control of everything. Do your best and pull your weight, but also know that it does not always produce the results you expected. In 2021 and 2022 I was without a contract. During this time, God taught me patience, peace, acceptance, and trust. I had to trust Him for a way out and I experienced how He opened doors for me in His time.*

My biggest achievement is... *After not having a team in the beginning for 2022, it was a massive achievement to get a contract to ride for a professional team in May, and then be selected by the team as part of the eight riders of the Tour de France.*

The Bible verse that carries me...

Isaiah 40:29-31, NIV,
"He gives strength to the weary and increases the power of the weak. Even youths grow tired and weary, and young men stumble and fall; but those who hope in the Lord will renew their strength. They will soar on wings like eagles; they will run and not grow weary, they will walk and not be faint."

Reinardt and his brother, Lean, visiting Irish castles on their bikes

MY STORY
Reinardt Janse van Rensburg

It was Reinardt's father who introduced him to cycling, and it was his father who proudly stood and waited at the finish line of every junior competition. It was in 2012 – only two months before Reinardt would have started his professional cycling career in Europe – that his father passed away. Never would his dad see his son's achievements and sporting highlights, and never would he know that the dreams he had for Reinardt to become a Tour de France rider would come true – not just once, but six times!

Reinardt was 24 years old when his father and biggest supporter died. He had to pick up the pieces and focus on the task ahead.

He lived the words of Isaiah 40:29-31, "He gives strength to the weary and increases the power of the weak. Even youths grow tired and weary, and young men stumble and fall; but those who hope in the Lord will renew their strength. They will soar on wings like eagles; they will run and not grow weary, they will walk and not be faint."

"These are the words that carried me through some of the most difficult circumstances in my life. In this case, I was in another country, surrounded by another culture. I wanted to make things work and do well to encourage everyone back home and to give them hope."

It is characteristic of him as a sprinter to work hard, chin to his chest, head down. Reinardt knows all about gritting his teeth and pushing on, but when the news of his wife's kidney failure came in 2014, the doctor's unexpected diagnosis caught him completely off guard. His wife's condition was already advanced, and dialysis had to begin immediately. It took six months before a suitable organ donor was found and she underwent a kidney transplant. *"It is in times like these that one realises the value of family. Cycling is just a sport, a facet of your life, something that provides entertainment to people. It is only one small aspect of your life and not your whole life. Those close to you, your loved ones, are your heart and they must be cherished."*

It was with this mindset that Reinardt approached the races that followed – and even the prestigious Tour de France. He had to learn early on that faith and Christian values were the foundation upon which he must build. It was also this realisation that kept him humble. And when prestige came, especially with children who revered him, he took this responsibility seriously and re-evaluated and adjusted his behaviour.

"Every action and every decision you take affects other people."

"They mimic your behaviour and the decisions you make – good or bad. I wanted to use my Christian values and faith in God to keep myself stable, despite bad things happening."

Reinardt's professional sports career was also not without its challenges. When it was the beginning of 2022, as a husband and breadwinner of a family without a fixed contract and without any stable income, his heart was torn. He was faithful to the talent that God entrusted to him. He was fit, ready for action, and – due to the preparation for the South African and African Championships – he was mentally strong. However, four months without any contract or promise of a contract forced him to make the unprecedented decision to pack up, sell everything, and return to South Africa.

"He gives strength to the weary and increases the power of the weak. Even youths grow tired and weary, and young men stumble and fall; but those who hope in the Lord will renew their strength. They will soar on wings like eagles; they will run and not grow weary, they will walk and not be faint." – Isaiah 40:29-31, NIV

Reinardt and his wife, Leilani

With the words of Isaiah 40:29-31 in his heart, a strange peace came over him. With the knowledge that professional cycling was over, for then, he touched down on South African soil.

God's timing is His own. Sometimes it feels to us as if He is late, but He is always on time.

Two hours after his arrival, Reinardt received the long-awaited dream phone call from his future team manager, who confirmed his place as one of the chosen nine riders in the Lotto Dstny team. Reinardt would put pen to paper at lunchtime to make his third Tour de France a reality. Within 48 hours, he flew to Europe to move back into the same vacated apartment. *"The day I signed the contract with Lotto Dstny in April 2022, it did not mean that I would be part of the Tour de France team of eight. The entire group consists of 29 riders, and the best eight are usually selected, where each has a specific role to fulfil. A rider must first prove himself several times before he can be considered for a team. At that stage, the expectation that I would participate in the tour was zero. It was unheard of in cycling for anyone to be without a contract in April and then compete in the Tour de France in July. I count it as a miracle of God in my life."*

"It is in times of uncertainty that one must remain calm and keep trusting. God expects us to do our part, hang in there, and work hard. We cannot afford to just sit back and expect everything to work out. We must work hard and believe. Because when your reward comes from God's hand ... it is always greater than you expect."

He gives **STRENGTH** to the weary and **INCREASES THE POWER** of the weak. Even youths grow tired and weary, and young men stumble and fall; but those who **HOPE** in the Lord will **RENEW THEIR STRENGTH**. They will **SOAR** on wings like eagles; they will run and **NOT GROW WEARY**, they will walk and **NOT BE FAINT**.

What do you think is the biggest obstacle in men's lives?

Men are traditionally seen as the providers in the home. When a man does not meet the needs of his family, major psychological problems can arise. Every man wants to take care of his family, but when they suffer, men blame their own shortcomings, and this puts incredible pressure on them in society.

How would you like to be remembered?

I would like to be remembered as someone who never gave up, despite things that may have gone wrong; as a man who had the perseverance to pursue his dreams. Someone who inspired, not just by cycling, but by just being who I am.

The day before the SA championship, Reinardt shows his brother that he is ready

Your message to South Africa

Life is a journey, not a final destination. We are so focused on the end goal and do not celebrate or enjoy the present. When you reach your end goal – well done! But enjoy the growth and experience along the way because that is how memories are made. In tough times, put one foot in front of the other. Do not measure yourself by your final destination. We, as humans, are insatiable creatures, we will never be one hundred percent happy with what we have achieved, so enjoy the process!

"My new team kit for the 2022 season!"

Christmas dinner with the family

Ine-Marí Venter

Ine-Marí Venter, born in Pretoria on the 21st of April 1995, is a South African netball player. The 1.92 m tall Ine-Marí began her netball career with TuksNetball, followed by Gauteng Jaguars in the South African Brutal Fruit netball cup series (2015-2018). In 2017 she donned the green and gold and stepped onto the court for the South African senior national team after representing the u19 national team from 2014 as well as the u21 national team from 2015. At the 2018 Commonwealth Games, the talented Ine-Marí caught the eye of Simone McKinnis, head coach of the Melbourne Vixens. Ine-Marí made South Africa proud in this Australian team's 2019 season, and also in the 2020 season as a player for the Queensland Firebirds. Since 2021, she has been playing for the Saracens Mavericks and is also currently playing goal shooter for the Proteas.

My love for sport began... *next to the netball court in Pretoria. My mother was a Transvaal netball player and, as a little girl, I ran around on Tukkies' netball court during her training sessions. In primary and secondary school, I excelled in athletics, hockey, and squash, but netball chose me and stole my heart. It was the one sport that, each year, I could not wait for the season to start. All the other sports were afterthoughts, something I could do while I waited for the netball season to begin.*

If I was not a sports star, I would... *become a veterinarian. My love for animals is unprecedented. For career day in grade 2, as eight-year-olds, we had to wear an outfit portraying what we would like to be one day. Dressed in my aunt's nursing uniform with epaulettes on my shoulders, I proudly stood there as a vet! However, it was much later in my life that I realised sport and netball took up a lot of my time and had become a more important focus. Although I applied, I was never selected for veterinary medicine or veterinary nursing, but I did complete a year's course in veterinary nursing before my first professional netball contract and I obtained my BScAgric degree in animal science.*

I am incredibly grateful for... *my family. We are a small family who are very close to each other. In the midst of numerous personal challenges that my mother had to face, she always supported me. She was and is my number one supporter, with my father and stepmother close behind.*

If I could edit my life, I would... *not change anything. I believe that everything in my life happened for a specific reason. It is not always explicable, but everything that happened played a role in making me who I am today as a woman. If I could perhaps make one* small adjustment, I would have studied a little harder and not just relied on my short-term memory. I would have worked even harder in my off seasons. But I would not want to tamper with the bigger picture and choices because that would have changed the excitement that I had experienced as well as the end result. I know why I have to be here now.

One of the biggest lessons I learnt this year... *is about God's goodness in my life – something that my identity is established in. It was an interesting and difficult year in my personal life, as well as my sporting life. I got to know God in a different way and began to see His hand in all aspects of my life. I experienced how He guided, protected, and held me. I had to separate my identity from my sports career because often it is so intertwined. I had to realise that I am more than just a netball player; I am a woman in His eyes.*

My greatest achievement... *I do not yet see in my personal life, because I am not married, or a mother or a businesswoman. I am thankful for my degree in animal science. The university kindly included my honours year in my degree, and I could play for the Jaguars and Protea teams while still studying. It took careful planning, and I did not always do as well academically as I had hoped. However, I wanted to fall back on something substantial and that I really liked when I retired from netball, so I gritted my teeth and just persevered.*

The Bible verse that carries me...
Depending on the seasons in my life, there are different verses that I lean on, but the one verse I hold on to, especially on the netball court, is:

Esther 4:14,
"Yet who knows whether you have come to the kingdom for such a time as this?" For every moment in my life, there is a reason. God put me there to live out a purpose, to make a difference, or to learn something.

Ine-Marí during her adventures

MY STORY
Ine-Marí Venter

Ine-Marí, the middle child of three children and one of two daughters (on her mother's side), grew up in a close-knit and supportive family. She is one of five kids (if you take her stepsister and stepbrother into account). It is a family full of love – one that makes their choices and decisions around Christian values, who go to church, and who do the right thing. But when things like molestation, unemployment, identity crisis, financially difficult times, pornography, and lust were a reality, that it is when Ine-Marí wanted to close the door on these past topics and hide them from the world, out of fear of what people might say. It is also precisely in that hidden place where the enemy finds its foothold and exercises control over one's thoughts, dreams, and being. It becomes the place where he imprisons you in fear. But Ine-Marí knows the God of second chances, a true Saviour, Provider, Father, Friend, and the only One who offers true forgiveness!

At a very young age, she had to outgrow her childhood. Ine-Marí's mother, a deeds typist, lost her job during the South African recession and, within six months, was forced to sell not only her house, but her car and some of her possessions in order for them to survive. Ine-Marí had to move in with her father and, while she wrestled with some challenges as a high school girl herself, she had to change her thinking about work and provision and sometimes even help support her mother financially. From a young age, Ine-Marí learnt the value of taking on responsibilities; she learnt the power of transformation and gratitude. It is also these experiences that taught her the biggest life lessons about her future, as she had to work through her fears and questions.

> **"I thought that things would be easier and everything would change the day when, as a young teenage girl, I gave my heart to the Lord and was baptised."**

"I was an active member of our church and it was my big declaration to the world that I was allowing God to take control in my life. I wanted to uproot the sinful nature in me. I wanted to believe that I would never again bow the knee to the temptations that had crippled me for so long. I did not want to feel bad about my thoughts and actions anymore ... because I was tired of constantly feeling guilty. For too long the enemy had the upper hand..."

But Ine-Marí had to learn that Christianity is not a crash course with quick fixes. Overcoming addiction and the enemy takes time, patience, and working on yourself.

Ine-Marí was in her second year at university when she attended a youth camp. One morning the men and women were separated. Some of the female students gave their testimonies. Ine-Marí knew that she had to break open the darkness inside her and bring her shame to light, because she could no longer live in bondage. She was molested as a little girl, and this awakened her sexually at too early an age. She started experimenting with masturbation and later pornography, until it became a problem and developed into an addiction. *"I always thought that a pornography addiction was something men struggled with, until I was able to share my story that morning and realised that it is a dark problem that many other young women also struggle with! I felt alone until a few young women also admitted that this was a reality in their lives."* That night, during the praise and worship session, she felt the presence of the Holy Spirit with her.

It was the words of the Hillsong chorus, "Sinking deep" echoing over the loudspeakers that finally forced Ine-Marí to her knees:

Standing here in Your presence
In a grace so relentless
I am won
By perfect love
Wrapped within the arms of heaven
In a peace that lasts forever
Sinking deep
In mercy's sea
I'm wide awake
Drawing close
Stirred by grace
And all my heart is Yours
All fear removed
I breathe You in
I lean into Your love
Oh, Your love

"I find peace and tranquillity in nature"

That evening, Ine-Marí had a face-to-face encounter with the Lord. It was a watershed moment in her life; the experience she could always return to when other challenges arose.

"God became a reality in that moment. Even if I stumble and fall again in the future or if the enemy whispers again ... I refer back to that moment in 2015."

"It is my anchor. He is my anchor."

It is that experience that still carries Ine-Marí through, on and off the court. It resonates in her life, her career, and her future, when she is only selected as a reserve or does not have a contract. *"I found my identity in Him; my peace about who I am and where I am in my life. I started to listen to His voice and started to cut out the other noise because it slowed down my life's journey ... I can trust God and His way and process for my life."*

Ine-Marí no longer compares her life with the people around her. It was a process of making peace, bumping her head, and acceptance. She follows her heart. As a sportswoman, she still wants to excel, but her achievement no longer defines who she is as a person. Although there were some challenges before and during COVID, she still knows that God is the one who opens and closes doors. *"I understand mental exhaustion because I have allowed physical pressure, injuries, and depression to get the better of me. But I also understand that one can always learn something from every circumstance. Not everything is always God's doing. As His children, we can sometimes be pretty stubborn!"*

The Lord gave her a promise as a faithful Father, it is a promise that she still holds dear as a 27-year-old. *"The first year after I was baptised, in 2015, the Lord showed me an image. I was dancing with Him in a white dress. Then someone took over from Him. The Lord showed me my path of marriage. And although I have been infatuated many times, I have never yet had a real boyfriend. The Lord truly sheltered me and kept me pure."* Ine-Marí wants to experience and live out the values as described in John and Stasi Eldredge's book, Captivating. *"This includes the value of forgiveness for yourself, the past, and those around you. I want to keep my identity in Him, and I want to trust Him for a life partner who He has chosen for me, because I know: God knows my path, my heart, my fears, and my wishes..."*

And that is all that matters.

What do you think is the biggest obstacle in women's lives?

Our identity in God. As women, we have to constantly make adjustments as to how we look in order to live up to society's requirements. We have to constantly make changes in how we dress and be aware of the impression we create to be acceptable, and then we are still compared to each other! How the world thinks a woman should be, look, and act is not always according to everyone's own standard and quite possibly not according to

God's standard for us either. The natural beauty of a woman should be celebrated and not undermined.

How would you like to be remembered?

I would like to be remembered as someone who gave her all for her family, her relationships, and her friendships – on the netball court, for God, and for my husband one day. Colossians 3:23 reads, "Whatever you do, do it heartily as for the Lord and not for men..." May all my actions and motives be God-driven!

Your message to South Africa

The question is really, what does God want to say to us as South Africans? Because He must be the centre of our existence. Our true identity is in God. Live in the here and now. Do not compare the course of your life with anyone around you and do not miss the moment. You are only in this moment once.

Ine-Marí Venter
Exclusive interview
Scan the code to watch

"My support system"

Sandile Ngcobo

Sandile Caleb "Stix" Ngcobo, born on the 1st of August 1989, is a former professional rugby player and is currently the head coach of the Blitzboks, the South African sevens team. He is the pride of Alexandra in Gauteng, and a former learner of Highlands North Boys High School. He made his debut as a young rugby player for the Golden Lions at the 2007 u18 Academy Week tournament. His relationship with the Golden Lions continued and, in 2010, he represented them at the u21 provincial championships, Group A. Sandile's name is also linked to the UJ group, the team of the University of Johannesburg in the Varsity Cup series in 2012. His provincial career as a winger includes 36 games for the Falcons (2012-2014) – he ended the season as the leading try scorer for the Falcons in the 2014 Vodacom Cup series with four tries. Sandile also made an appearance in six games for the Griquas in 2015.

He made his entry into rugby sevens and, in 2016, was named the captain of the Academy team. Under his leadership they achieved success in tournaments during the Rome Sevens in Italy and the Geneva Sevens in Switzerland. Stix also made his debut as a Blitzbok under the guidance of coach Neil Powell and, from 2016-2018, he represented South Africa in 20 matches.

My love for sport began... *as a seven-year-old. I am a son from Alexandra, an informal settlement in Johannesburg. My English teacher, who was actually an Afrikaans-speaking man, had a huge influence on my life and changed my future. He encouraged me to participate in sports and said, "run!" which is what I did! I fell totally in love with sports and rugby. I lost my heart to sports and started dreaming big to play for my country.*

If I was not a sports star, I would... *probably have ended up in military service. My uncle practiced this profession, and it would be the natural choice for me. But then I fell in love with rugby and all I ever wanted to do after that was play rugby and be of service within the rugby system that changed my life so positively. The leaders who preceded us sacrificed a lot, and established something remarkable that really works, adds value to young men's lives, and invests in people. I feel honoured to be part of this group of people.*

I am incredibly grateful to... *Kobus Vermeulen, a man I still call "dad". His unprecedented, selfless love changed my life. I am grateful to my parents who made a choice to step aside so that I could get greater exposure and develop as a person and sportsman.*

I am infinitely grateful to the rugby system at SAS (Stellenbosch Academy of Sport) and the leadership there. Finally, I am grateful to my wife and our little daughter. Being a husband and father is a dream come true.

My greatest achievement is... to put my hand on the Springbok on my chest as a player, to see my family's surname on the back of my rugby jersey, and to play for my country as a Blitzbok. I wanted to make people proud of me. Today, as the head coach of the Blitzboks, I have the privilege of investing in players.

The Bible verse that carries me...

Philippians 4:13, NKJV,
"I can do all things through Christ who strengthens me."

MY STORY
Sandile Ngcobo

There is power in a name. The words that are spoken about you have the power to build and contribute to your character, being, and calling on your life.

His name is Sandile Caleb Ngcobo.

Caleb is a Hebrew name meaning "faithful", "wholehearted", or "brave". Some people also think that it might mean "devotion to God". The name is derived from two Hebrew words, *kal* and *lev*, which means "wholehearted" when joined together.

It describes Sandile's being and character. He is like his namesake that we read about in the Bible; a young spy who had the heart and courage of an entire army:

The story of Caleb, a faithful man of God, begins in the Bible book of Numbers. After being freed from slavery in Egypt, the Israelites were led by God to the very border of the land of Canaan, a land "flowing with milk and honey", the land that God promised they would inherit (Exodus 3:8, 17). Moses chose twelve men, one from each tribe, to explore the land. Among them was Caleb, who represented the tribe of Judah.

The twelve men spied out the land for forty days and then came back to Moses. They reported that it was indeed fertile, but that its inhabitants were the mighty descendants of Anak. Terrified by the size and strength of the Canaanites, ten of the spies warned Moses not to enter Canaan (Numbers 13:23-33). Caleb silenced the grumbling, frightened men by saying, "We should go up and take possession of the land, for we can certainly do it" (Numbers 13:30). Caleb took this stand because he followed the Lord wholeheartedly (Joshua 14:8-9). He knew about God's promises to the Israelites, and despite the obstacles he saw with his own eyes, he still had faith that God would give them the victory over the Canaanites.

From an early age, Sandile, the young son of Alexandra, would experience a calling on his life for something greater than he could dream of. God's grace rested on him, and he would never fully understand why God chose him, among all his other friends in the informal settlement, for something greater.

Another name in this story is Kobus Vermeulen. By profession, he is currently the headmaster of Curro Hermanus, but as a person, he was the man who, 26 years ago, gave Sandile the chance for greater exposure to life. *"I was seven years old when Kobus approached my parents with a request to take me under his wing. Kobus had no children of his own; investing in young people was his heart's desire and calling. As an English teacher at our school in Johannesburg, he was a well-known figure in the community and someone my parents could trust. They made the difficult choice to leave me in his care with the promise that the exposure he could offer would unlock a new life for me. For a family in Alexandra, any guaranteed promise was better than the uncertain future on the streets of the informal settlement."*

Sandile, or "Stix" as he was dubbed by friends and family, would come to know the paternal love of an Afrikaans-speaking man across cultural lines. For Sandile, the negative racial perception and judgement about a so-called "privileged life" decreased day by day. With the experience of unexpected love and acceptance, the high walls of his truth behind which he hid as a young boy began to crumble. This was because he was experiencing a greater truth – the truth of heartfelt care, love, exposure to opportunities, discipline, and hard work.

"For Kobus, it was important that I did well in my schoolwork and sports. There were constant lessons in common courtesy, language, and how to treat women with respect. I had to practice opening a door for a lady, but I also had to be able to fish and read well. Then I started playing rugby. My natural talent and speed opened doors, but my work ethic would see me through. There were always players more talented than I was, but I was willing to do the necessary hard work."

Sandile kept in touch with his parents and the support of the proud Ngcobo family motivated him to not settle for less than the green and gold. However, it was during his provincial career that controversy in rugby circles robbed Sandile of his passion for the game. He retired from rugby and walked away from his beloved sport because he could not live with a betrayed heart.

He hung up his rugby boots, accepted a job at the OR Tambo International Airport, and returned to his parental home after 13 years. He took care of his elderly parents, provided financially, and forgot about his dream of the green and gold, because a green overall as a truck driver was now his reality. *"My return to the township meant only one thing ... I was going the other way – which was not a good way. My forward momentum halted, and I reached the most difficult time in my life with the hardest choices to make. My brother was in prison – if I did not make better choices that would be my destiny too."*

Twelve months of monotonous normality dragged on before Sandile followed Kobus' advice – he had to return to rugby. His talent and calling were for the action on the 106 m x 144 m field. He had to process the pain of disappointment in people and former coaches, and then work hard to secure a future.

The hours of hard work at the airport prepared Sandile spiritually for what God had in mind for him. His work ethic of training hard in the gym after work every day was rewarded when the opportunity arose to play rugby again. *"God uses everything to prepare you for your next season. He had to take away my comfortable lifestyle, with a fixed rugby contract, and put me in a place of total dependence on Him to get my attention. I needed to hear His voice again and give my faith the chance to change my perception. Only after that was I able to jog out onto the rugby field again with an open mind, without blaming or wanting to take revenge on anyone from the past. I needed time to get my faith and perspective back in line with God's Word. He was gracious to give me another chance."*

It was the green and white striped jersey of the Falcons that welcomed Sandile back. This was also where Blitzbok coaches, Neil Powell and Marius Schoeman, spotted him. In 2016 he started playing sevens rugby and was named captain of the Academy team. Under his leadership, the South African sevens team achieved success in the Rome Sevens tournament in Italy and the Geneva Sevens tournament in Switzerland. He also made his debut as a Blitzbok and represented South Africa in 20 matches from 2016-2018. *"When I started at SAS, my passion for sport returned. The management style emphasises the player as a person. Results are a focal point, but it is not the main priority. Faith and family values are at the top of the list. It felt like home and, as a Blitzbok family, we were loyal to each other and worked hard to achieve our goals."*

Before Sandile's father passed away, he saw his son run onto the field with the Springbok on his chest and the Ngcobo name on his back. The day Sandile made his debut for his country in the Blitzbok team; it was his mother who sent him the photos of two life-changing events in his life:

1. A photo of him in his green overalls behind the wheel of his truck.
2. A photo of him in his green and gold in front of the cameras doing an interview.

"I now know that I have a different calling than other young men in South Africa. Why I was given a second chance to have a different lifestyle, away from the streets of what was an unbearable township life, is still a question in my heart. I have no answer except

that I have received incredible grace and mercy in my life; and I am grateful for it. Everything I undertake, I do for a greater cause; I want to honour a living God; bringing hope and courage to a dark world where sometimes only survival is a reality. But I can do nothing without God. If He does not intervene every day, again and again, all my deeds would be useless."

Today, at the age of 33, Sandile Ngcobo finds his identity in nothing other than the Lord, not even in being head coach of the Blitzboks. "This title and platform that has been entrusted to me is only by the grace of God. All my life I was surrounded by men who taught and showed me how to be a good person and leader, and now my life has to reflect that! It is a responsibility and a privilege to hold this position ... with God at the centre of my life, the enemy can come, I know God is my full back, He's got my back."

And rock-solid behind Sandile, in the background, there is Kobus – as always. At every Blitzbok game, his heart rejoices. There is no expectation. He just wanted to give, bless, and offer the young boy with the big smile, who was full of dreams, an opportunity in life. Today it is those dreams that have a ripple effect in other young men's lives.

What do you think is the biggest obstacle in men's lives?

There are three major concerns:

- *Men's absence in their households, families, and own lives is a huge problem.*
- *We eliminate the Holy Spirit from our lives and have no guide. God created us to be leaders in our country and families, but if we do not follow His voice and guidance, we will remain directionless.*
- *We have prisons that are full and women as victims of abuse by men. It is our responsibility to educate men and protect women.*

God entrusted me with the position I currently hold to have a say in young men's lives, but it should really be the responsibility of every father, uncle, grandfather, and manager to influence young men and inspire them to be better, and to raise another generation of good examples in our country.

How would you like to be remembered?

I would like to be remembered as a man who was always there for my wife, children, family, friends, and team. A man who modelled love and support. I want to be known for being there, being available, and for the fact that my word is my honour.

Your message to South Africa

This was the message in the dressing room in Sydney, Australia, that we declared to each other: "Everyone is going through so many negative experiences in South Africa. Your surname, your family's name, is on the back of your jersey and the Springbok is on your chest. It represents your people and your country. In what way can you inspire them with just your actions and no words? Which pain would you rather endure: The pain of losing for your country and people or the pain of working hard?" Everyone unanimously chose the pain of hard work.

South Africa, we will always keep persevering. There has been too much talking, we know it is time to truly strive for greatness. But we need each other. So, let's stand together.

Sandile Ngcobo
Exclusive interview
Scan the code to watch

Sandile and Raquel

Coach Stix

Ivan van Rooyen

Ivan van Rooyen, born on the 7th of May 1982, is a former professional rugby player who is currently the head coach for the Lions in the United Rugby Championship. This son from Mpumalanga and former learner of the Technical High School Middelburg played rugby in high school and as a student, but academics and tertiary education were his main focus. Although Ivan was a sevens player and also played rugby for the Falcons, he found his niche in 2009 as a strength and conditioning coach for the Golden Lions and the Lions team. He was appointed as assistant coach in 2018 and as head coach of the Lions in 2019. Under his leadership, the Lions were runners-up in the Currie Cup Premier Division in 2019. "Cash" van Rooyen, as many know him, is the son-in-law of the late Springbok centre, Darius Botha. His approach to management and his coaching style in his tenure with the Lions is based on his father-in-law's positive glass-half-full philosophy. He is a self-confessed team player and believed that the Lions could learn a lot from their 2012 relegation from Super Rugby and apply the lessons to take them to new heights. He spearheaded the Lions' fitness coaching to ensure they were the fittest franchise in the country during the Johan Ackermann-inspired renaissance. Ivan is praised by experts as one of South Africa's most gifted and experienced conditioning experts.

His spouse can be considered a member of South African rugby's royalty: Rienie is the daughter of former Springbok winger Darius Botha and the niece of Naas Botha. Ivan is the father of two daughters, Lisa and Nina.

My love for sport began... *in Mpumalanga. My father was a bank manager, and this led to us having to move repeatedly, from one town to the next. For example, I was in JJ van der Merwe Primary School in Ermelo, Witrivier Primary School, and Skukuza Primary School. During my high school years, I stayed in the hostel in Middelburg. For as long as I can remember, I have always been surrounded by rugby, cricket, and tennis balls. Rackets, bats, and rugby cones filled my world. We played all sports, always running around, there was never a time when we did not participate in one sport or another!*

If I was not a sports coach, I would... *probably be a commentator, just so that I could be involved in sports! I am definitely not a suit-and-tie type of guy; no desk job would have suited me.*

My grandfather and father-in-law were both clergymen, so I could possibly have ended up in ministry too.

I am incredibly grateful for... *my family and friends. My mother and father are amazing people and the best examples of parents and children of God. Their willingness to sacrifice their time and energy for others is inspiring and their hearts are full of love which never runs dry.*

Rienie, Lisa, and Nina are a husband and a father's dream – always supportive, always there to put a smile on my face. They mean the world to me.

We are blessed with a wonderful circle of friends with whom you can just be who you are. They are sincere and truly care.

If I could edit my life, I would... *have challenged myself more from an earlier age, I would also have challenged the people close to me even more. I am blessed to be naturally athletic and sporty, at times I feel that it has kept me from working even harder and performing better. Development is more effective the more you are willing to move out of your comfort zone. I could have started doing it from a much younger age.*

One of the biggest lessons I learnt this year... *The challenge and the reality of our work causes one to sometimes tend to want to play it safe and rather make as few mistakes as possible, instead of being bold. However, having a clear identity as an individual and team is so important. My job requires me to make the players perform under pressure and rise above their abilities. It is therefore necessary to create an energy and expectation and thereby challenge the individual as well as the team. We must inspire them to live out their passion with dedication each day, but also make them realise that they are part of a bigger picture and goal which requires them to push themselves and their teammates in order to perform beyond their expected abilities.*

Ivan, his wife, Rienie, and daughters Lisa and Nina

My greatest achievement is... *In my personal life:* To be a good husband and father in my family; supporting my wife and playing an active role in the daily life of my children. To be present when I get the opportunity to see my parents and my brother and his family.

In my career: I had the privilege (in my previous position) to work with young men and to see 16 of them become Springboks. With the other 300 who did not become Springboks, I could still experience them making spiritual and physical breakthroughs. It is a privilege to be included in such a system and to help young men to see that each one of them is an individual who contributes to the bigger picture. As a head coach, my focus today is on game plans and assistant coaches. I appreciate the relationships I have with people and that they feel free to ask for advice about their children or family matters. The support I offer now is worth its weight in gold to me.

The Bible verse that carries me...

Philippians 4:13,
"I can do all things through Christ who strengthens me."

MY STORY
Ivan van Rooyen

"Do you expect to win if you pray hard enough?" was the question hurled at Ivan van Rooyen before one of their games. It was the Lions' habit to form a circle before and after a match, to kneel and pray unashamedly in front of hundreds of thousands of spectators. *"Faith and sport are not separate in South Africa. Do not cross the line,"* was Ivan's calm reply. *"You and I are separate individuals. So, allow me to do what I want to do. We are not praying for a certain result; we process the results differently…"*

It was shortly after the 2016 Super Rugby final. The Hurricanes won their first Super Rugby title with a dominant 20—3 victory over the Lions in Wellington. Tries were difficult to come by in the wet, cold, and windy weather conditions and both tries were scored due to errors committed by the Lions. Barrett and his boot led to riotous scenes in the packed stadium of 39 000 spectators with two goals and two penalties. The Lions just could not find a way to unlock their opponent's defence and so the Hurricanes became the fifth New Zealand team to be crowned Super Champions.

It was a night that any other sportsman would want to erase from his mind forever, but it was nevertheless a moment where faith and a prayer after the game sowed a seed of inspiration and hope. *"Four men from Wellington contacted us shortly after that tournament with the news that they were so moved by the way we processed and dealt with the defeat that it inspired them to form a local rugby league team and name it after the Lions!"*

After that incident, Ivan knew: People were watching him. Every action and reaction. As an ambassador of God, a great responsibility rested on his shoulders.

Although Ivan left Mpumalanga many years ago, and the subsequent years in Gauteng left lasting and deep traces in his life, he is not ashamed of his formative years. On the contrary, it was a nice challenge to move from town to town as a youngster and get used to not only the new environment, but also the people. *"My parents still live in Delmas. When our team is in South Africa for a long enough period of time and the rugby season allows it, it is a priority for me to visit the family. We are an incredibly loving family who care about each other!"*

His university and close friends call him "Cash", a reminder of his time at the University of Johannesburg or RAU (Rand Afrikaans University). *"I was in the Dromedaris men's residence and, as was the custom, everyone was given a nickname in their first year at university. Because my father was in the banking sector, I was called 'Cash'. My roommate was 'Contract'. The nickname stuck."*

When Ivan reflects on the extremely challenging start of his tenure as the Lions' Super Rugby head coach, it is noticeable how he applies the proverbial glass half-full philosophy. *"The dream of playing rugby well and the reason 'why' we do it must never disappear. It is important to keep the dream alive. The guys who make it are the ones who keep the dream alive. Whether it is the ball boy on the side of the field, or the player who wears the rugby jersey, it is important to be enraptured by your calling and the role that you fulfil. I believe the moment anything starts to feel like 'work' and becomes an effort, you are no longer going to make a difference in other people's lives. The legends are the ones who keep the flame of inspiration burning..."*

And his flame for coaching burns bright. He likes to be part of the strategic planning because he is a loyal team player who loves the collaborative environment. *"If it was just about the title 'coach' I would have stopped a long time ago. It is a privilege to have a say in the future and dreams of the young men; to make people's lives better. But one must always confirm your 'why'. Why do you do what you do on a daily basis? When you know the answer and live according to it, other people will share in your vision more easily. And when I, in turn, believe in someone else's plan, I support it with all my heart."*

Ivan is not a very emotional person, one of his best character traits is that he is steady under pressure and tries to handle that which is within his control. The rest he leaves in God's hands and trusts that He will provide the necessary input. This outlook on life is largely due to his determination and education, but also the influence of his late father-in-law as well as that of his own father, who is a keen sportsman. The former Northern Transvaal legend, Springbok, and reverend Darius Botha's influence on his son-in-law was mostly on a leadership and spiritual level. *"It was an absolute privilege to know him. He was a fantastic father and grandfather, and a wonderful man. He lost his battle against stomach cancer in 2018, but the Botha family taught me how to process the loss of a life. It always remains important to celebrate someone's life and best qualities, even if they are no longer around..."*

It is with the same compassion and positive vision of the bigger picture that Ivan now leads his Lions team. As a coach, he feels almost powerless on the side-line when they play, but he has the privilege of investing in them five days a week. Every weekend the players have the opportunity on the field to show what the Lord has blessed them with. The camaraderie as players and friends is incalculable. The time, sacrifice, and involvement in each other's lives can be seen in the results on and off the field. And everything builds character.

"If you do not have balance in life, you tie your identity to winning (or losing). You must be rooted in Him, maintain the balance, and listen to the voice of the Lord in your life. Instant gratification is the evil of our time. Along with the tally of likes on social media."

His mission is to teach young men to use their God-given gifts and talents and be exactly who they are supposed to be; he also has to teach them to ignore others' opinions. *"Sometimes I struggle with social media. It always remains a challenge. We are all human and sometimes want to return the insult ... but then the inner voice stops me. I just wish* the public could understand that no one gets up in the morning and purposefully goes out of his way to not live up to his calling … On the other side of the television screen, those rugby players are just people who also have a hard time processing criticism…"

Ivan will always subscribe to the belief that the team is bigger than any individual – each player's identity is in God, which is within the team's identity. And when the individual is healthy, the team is healthier! With a healthy team there is faith in something bigger than just the individual himself, in a God with a protective, guiding hand.

> **"God is the steering wheel that determines the direction and is sometimes also the gearbox that makes things happen faster or slower … we just have to give Him the freedom in our lives to do what He wants to do."**

This coach and family man likes to recall many heartfelt rugby stories, as told by the Bothas around the dinner table – especially about the infamous Springbok tour of 1981 to New Zealand. It is those stories that inspire him to constantly evaluate: Who am I? And what am I doing?

With peace in his heart, he can answer today: *"I am Ivan van Rooyen, husband of Rienie, father of two daughters, son of proud parents, friend of many, and head coach of the Lions. And as long as I give my best, that is good enough for Him."*

"Family is everything!"

What do you think is the biggest obstacle in men's lives?

Men are over-zealous. At the age of 20 or 21, there is the pressure to play rugby professionally, the pressure to own a house or play in the Springbok colours. This unnecessary underlying pressure can be positive or negative, but the earlier success knocks on your door, the greater the chance of burnout. My prayer is that men aged 35 and over will have developed enough character to be able to be self-supporting at a later age – for the sake of themselves and their families. May every young man's identity be in God, and may he know who he is away from the sports field.

How would you like to be remembered?

I would like to be remembered as someone who is a sincere and loving son, husband, father, mentor, and friend. Someone who always put other people first and thereby inspired them to reach their full potential. I would like to be remembered as one who proclaimed the Kingdom through my actions.

"God trusts us to be good parents"

Your message to South Africa

In the end, you always have a choice to make a difference, and the difference you make depends on you. Sometimes we wait for the perfect opportunity to do or say something ... if you sit and wait, you will sit and wait forever ... but focus on it now and do it sincerely. Know who you are, live it. You never know who needs your message right now.

Ivan van Rooyen
Exclusive interview
Scan the code to watch

Jannie Putter

Jannie Putter, born on the 30th of November 1966, is a former rugby player. As a spiritual coach, sports psychologist, author, speaker, mentor, and counsellor he has had a lot of input in the lives of people and sports teams since 1994. Born and bred in Potchefstroom, Jannie played as a provincial and national rugby player for the former Western Transvaal (1987-1993). In 1992, he was invited to the Springbok trials and was selected to be part of the SA Barbarians team. Jannie's leadership skills were developed from early on. With him at the helm as captain, the combined Central Rugby Union Team, the Pukke (Potchefstroom University for Christian Higher Education), as well as the SA Universities team achieved great heights. His rugby career also included playing for the team of the South African National Defence Force.

From 1985-1993, he studied at the former Potchefstroom University for Christian Higher Education (now North-West University) and obtained his BA degree, an honours degree in psychology, an honours degree in sports science, as well as his master's degree in sports psychology with the subject of effective leadership of sports coaches. His involvement as a spiritual coach for well-known South African sports teams includes the Blue Bulls (2006-2010), who won the Super 14 title three times. From 2015-2019 he travelled with the Golden Lions, who won the Currie Cup in 2015 and reached the final of the Super Rugby Championship three years in a row. From 2018-2020 he also worked with the Orlando Pirates football team.

His passion and focus include working with schools, companies, and various teams (not only in sports, but also in the business world). Principles of synergy, teamwork, leadership, dealing with stress, marriage, and faith are mostly among the topics that he addresses.

Jannie is the author of a number of informative books with titles such as *Winning is for kids and parents!; Secrets of a Champion!; Game Plan for Life,* and *Mentally Tough: Proven Keys to Success.*

He is married to Tertia, and they have two children. These days he enjoys playing tennis and golf.

My love for sport began... *in my childhood. I grew up in a house where my father was my absolute hero. He was the head of the department of human movement sciences, i.e., the Potchefstroom University's sports department. He was an excellent sportsman* with provincial colours in wrestling, gymnastics, tennis, and swimming. He could truly do anything and everything! His brother, my uncle Dick, was a Springbok rugby player – so sports was a big passion of our Putter family. I followed their example and got my provincial colours in athletics and tennis, but my main sport was rugby. However, my love for sports psychology also took hold during those formative years. With my birthday falling late in the year on November 30th, most of the time I was the "smallest" in my age group. I only realised this much later in life. In retrospect, however, it was to my advantage, because I always participated in everything with great enthusiasm. I wanted to make friends, I was not always good at all the sports, and I very rarely won – probably because I was so small – but I tackled everything with excessive passion. It also became apparent, later on, that I used athletics as a hiding place. I was very young when my parents got divorced and there on the athletic field, I could express my self-pity and rage, although I would never throw in the towel. I bridged the saddest times in my life with the happiest times on the sports field. I got over the disappointment and exercised control over that which I could control. Sport was and still is a big part of my life.

If I was not a sports psychologist, I would... definitely be farming! In my heart of hearts, I am a farmer. I like working with my hands, making plans, and working in the soil. Nature grounds me and calms me down. If I want to relax, I do gardening or build something. Engineering would be a strong second choice, but then again, I enjoy people. So, I am definitely in the right profession, and who knows – one day I might own a little piece of farmland!

I am incredibly grateful for... so many things in my life. I am immeasurably thankful that I was saved from a life of self-pity, judging others, being pathetic, and doubting God. When my parents got divorced, I witnessed my mother lose herself because she felt like her life was falling apart. Today, I know how powerful Romans 8:28 is, "And we know that all things work together for good to those who love God, to those who are the called according to His purpose." I never really understood it, but today I know that everything that happened to me – the losses and hurts, the uncertainty, and my own roller coaster ride on my life's journey – was for my own benefit, to learn life lessons, and to discover that God is always there when one really seeks Him.

If I could edit my life, I would... not necessarily want to change anything. I know I certainly could have made wiser decisions, but then I would never have suffered the pain that taught me the necessary lessons I needed to learn. God's plan is perfect. You cannot wish the hurt away; it is part of becoming a wiser person. I am grateful for the past, grateful to the Lord, and I look forward to the future with anticipation. The past was to my advantage – even if it was sometimes painful.

The biggest lessons I learnt this year...

1. How important health is. I have had many injuries in the past and – because I want to sort everything out speedily and I am hasty by nature – I did not always pay the necessary attention to healing, as I should have. I am now older and wiser, and with that comes wiser decisions about what and how one approaches things. Up until the

age of 50, I could still do a backwards somersault from a standing position, but now I am a bit more careful with what I attempt. I realised that if your car needs a service; take it in for a service right away. Just because it is still running, it does not necessarily mean everything is fine. If something is broken, fix it as best you can. Maintenance goes on forever, so focus on the little things – physically, emotionally, and spiritually.

2. I learnt that we should never stop learning lessons. I truly have a fascinating job and the privilege of sharing in the lives of a wide variety of people.

3. I also learnt to go with the flow in life and not fight it.

My greatest achievement is... In my personal life, it is that I was able to keep the wonderful woman I married and restore our marriage. I was not a good husband. I was self-centred and I made a lot of mistakes. The fact that she forgave me, and that we are still together today, is a miracle because she had every right to end our marriage. Another achievement is that my children love me, and I love them – and both of them love the Lord. It is one of the most wonderful things in my life.

In my work environment, it is difficult to measure achievements. It is such a great privilege to be able to work with a team or with individuals and see the things we talked about come to fruition because it is God's principles that we apply, not man's clever ideas.

I think everything in one's life can be celebrated as an achievement. I was able to do a somersault, I passed matric, it took me six years before I published my first book – and then the following books "happened". The joy that our dogs give us can be experienced as an achievement. My work with people can be experienced as an achievement ... So, we each have our moments!

The best advice I have ever received... Start your day early, because then you will always be ahead, not trying to catch up all the time. Start your day with God and be in touch with your family. Always behave in such a manner as if your children are watching, so that they can look at you with pride and say, "That is my dad".

The best advice I have ever given... Do not listen to the news or read the newspapers – I stopped doing that in 1996. I always wanted to be informed, but eventually realised that news just pumps me full of emotional poison (worry and fear). What goes in is what comes out. Instead of wasting your energy on the reality of things (the things of this world), rather pour your energy into things like faith and hope. Read wholesome, edifying, and informative books. Listen to talks by influential people. Apply the principles. Make sure that when you do something – you do it with excellence. Make a personal choice to do everything above average. Answer your phone with "excellence"; if you are going for a run, do it in "excellence"; when you do a push up or prepare a meal, do it with "excellence"! Average is not good enough! Excellence will always make you stand out from the masses of average.

The Bible verses that carry me...

Proverbs 18:21 (NKJV),
*"Death and life are in the power of the tongue,
and those who love it will eat its fruit."*

Hebrews 11:1,
*"Now faith is the substance of things
hoped for, the evidence of things not seen."*

What I CHOOSE to say is the seed of my future (and it will render a harvest).

MY STORY
Jannie Putter

As a little boy, Jannie's mother would sit next to him on the bed, place her hand on his sore tummy, and pray quietly. Jannie never knew what she prayed, but he knew that he could always ask her to pray for him. This happened often as Jannie had developed stomach aches because of the underlying stress he experienced in his parental home. He grew up in a Christian family. They went to church on Sundays, his father was an elder in the church. *"Church was never a nice place for me. As a little boy, it was a gloomy place where people sat behind their stern masks. Faces that did not smile and a preacher who always looked grumpy or depressed."*

"I believed that God was displeased with us."

Only at the age of 30 did Jannie get to know God personally. That day changed his life forever. First, life happened to him and around him so that his character could develop, and he could become the man God had in mind. *"The road started getting rough when I was 11 years old. It was the year my parents got divorced. My father found a new love in his life and left us. My mother did not know how to deal with this humiliation and change, so alcohol became her hiding place. I had to grow up in the midst of all of this and start carving out my own picture about life, to take responsibility for my decisions and actions. I was angry and disappointed. I doubted the God my mother always prayed to."*

The reality of his life became murky, but on the sports field he could live his dream, he felt "light" – free from the darkness.

There he was in control of his life, and he could manage his frame of mind; including an inner circle of people close to his heart and keeping the harsh reality out. Jannie hid there but, without realising it, he was being shaped every day so that he could one day fulfil the role he does today – helping others to turn the pain of reality into a story of victory and not of failure!

Jannie with Daniëlle (daughter), Victor (son), and Tertia (wife)

Matthew 6:31-34 (NKJV), "Therefore do not worry, saying, 'What shall we eat?' or 'What shall we drink?' or 'What shall we wear?' For after all these things the Gentiles seek. For your heavenly Father knows that you need all these things. However, seek first the kingdom of God and His righteousness, and all these things shall be added to you. Therefore, do not worry about tomorrow, for tomorrow will worry about its own things. Sufficient for the day is its own trouble."

As the path of life unfolded, day-by-day and storm-by-storm, Jannie learnt the value and meaning of this passage of scripture. Each day brought its own challenges, and each month its own worries. Yet somewhere he had to learn what it meant to put God's Kingdom first and to start living for Him.

At that stage, Jannie was a young man of 30, with more questions than answers in his heart. With his own "clever answers" as his only guide – no mentor or someone to hold him accountable – life was whatever Jannie wanted it to be. *"I was totally off the rails. No one but Jannie and satan governed my life. I was a victim of life. I was unemployed. Broke. I was married to a stunning woman, but for the wrong reasons. We did not have children yet and were busy divorcing. I was unfaithful, lived a totally immoral life, and pornography dominated my thoughts. Nothing or no one could stop me or convince me to think differently about life. I was a victim of life."*

Proverbs 16:9 says, "A man's heart plans his way, but the Lord directs his steps." When you give God access to your heart and your soul, miracles begin to happen. Then you grasp the power of forgiveness – what it means not to be a victim, but a victor through your faith in God!

It was in response to an invitation from friends that Jannie and Tertia attended a church service of the late well-known American preacher and writer, Dr Myles Munroe. It was an honest, no-frills message and the prayer was an answer to a silent question in Jannie's heart (which, up to that point, had never been answered). *"Who of you sitting* here in front of me feels like a victim of your own life and circumstances, and you know you have shut God out and satan is sitting on the throne of your life?" Dr Munroe asked. "Who among you knows you are not going anywhere? You are totally lost ... You know about God, but you do not really know Him?" Then he said, *"If, at this moment, your heart answers just a whisper with the word 'yes' ... Get up, come forward, and surrender. Give your life to God to manage. Open your ears to hear God's voice."* At first, Jannie squeezed his eyes shut a little tighter, clenched his fists in fear, and then, after a few deep breaths, found the courage to stand up. There were hundreds of people putting one foot in front of the other, shuffling towards the area in front of the stage. Slowly and unsure of himself, but with a desperate cry in his heart, Jannie made his way to the front of the stage, and asked God to come into his life. He surrendered everything ... the pain and fears, the questions and anxiety. He placed the past, present, and his future in the hands of an unfamiliar, invisible God's hands ... because he could no longer be in control all on his own. *"It was the best decision of my life! I was not struck down by lightning and nothing strange happened to me as I walked to the front, but deep down I knew that this was my appointment with God. Every step forward was a step closer to the Lord and His purpose for my life. I had to let go and let God take control. As a reasonably realistic person, that moment was indescribably liberating."*

God uses other people to call you back to Him, but only when your heart is ready to hear His voice. God never abandoned Jannie because the plan for his life had to be fulfilled. *"God was waiting for me to choose Him. If I did not make a U-turn that morning, I would have walked further into the darkness with no escape. I had to change my thinking about God and life. Regardless of how bad I was as a person; God was and is always ready to work through us when we give Him access to our lives."*

Jannie had to meet God for himself and not see God through the eyes of his mother or the pastor. No, he had to have his own encounter with the Lord. Twenty-six years later, Jannie is still amazed at the goodness and favour of his Father.

> **"I wish I had discovered God and His divine principles earlier in my life and lived according to them, but thank goodness I made the choice at the age of 30."**

Jannie's life looks completely different now. His routines, his way of thinking, his choice of words, and his actions have changed. *"Everything in our life is determined by our habits. Establishing habits that lead to success means you have to START ... every day and never stop! Eventually, those habits become a way of life. When faith becomes a way of life, the realities of this world lose their power over you. Then fear disappears. Then worry disappears. Then one can live mastering life, and not as a victim! If your mouth is only full of the realities around you – what the news feeds you and the television shows you – worry, fear, and doubt will be your main emotions while hope and faith evaporate. The question is – which one do you choose, reality or faith?"*

The key to faith is hope. Hebrews 11:1 is a banner over his life, *"Now faith is the substance of things hoped for, the evidence of things not seen."* The more hope he shares in his daily sessions with clients, the more hope he experiences himself. And yes, the pruning process has not stopped; it remains part of daily life, exactly because he chose God as the King of his life. With that choice, there is also a certain price to pay. *"I had to choose whether I wanted to be part of this world, or whether I was willing to be sold out for God. The world has the media, platforms, and spotlights; but God's Word is clear about this. Whoever gives away his recognition here on earth receives it in heaven, and vice versa. That is my heart, it's not about prestige or how important others think you are. I answer my own phone, book my own appointments – my wife of course helps me a lot, but the onus rests on me. I take responsibility for that. I had to give something up – that human desire to be known and recognised. It is not about me – EVERYTHING is about God!"*

Romans 8:28 is so true … EVERYTHING that happens TO us happens FOR us when we love God and give Him the glory. Life is not about how important we are – life is about how important we can make God in other people's lives.

What were the words and message from God's heart for you these past couple of years? What has He shared with you about your life, character, and being, away from the sports field?

We are like ships on the sea or trees that grow. There will always be storms on the sea or branches that will bend in the wind. We will grow or break with the storms in our lives. The Lord promises that He will not send any storm that we cannot handle, and that we will never be tempted beyond what we can endure.

I work with the public and also have one-on-one consultation sessions. So, when COVID-19 hit, everything came to a standstill. When they announced the lockdown, my family chose not to use the word "lockdown" because we know the power that words have. We decided to refer to that time as "time out". In sports, they use the term when you need a break or when you want to regroup. You get time to realign yourself and recover from the struggles you faced in the game. We realised during this time out that our season had changed and that we needed to sow. It was not a harvesting season for us. We got to work and started sowing in people's and families' lives. This old-school guy who does not have much to do with modern technology, learnt all about Zoom and YouTube in one day and then hosted a mental toughness forum every day for 13 weeks from my office – half an hour sessions in Afrikaans and the same in English. At one stage, more than 100 families tuned in every day for these sessions! Even people from England and Australia! I grew and learnt the most during that time. I know that everything that happens TO me also happens FOR me.

What do you think is the biggest obstacle in men's lives?

Universally, there are three obstacles that are big snares for us:

- **Lust:** this is one of the oldest and most notorious traps that great "men" have fallen into. Today, pornography is probably the biggest disease in our world.
- **Fame:** the desire to be known and have prestige in this world. This is the so-called "rat race" where the high price you pay for climbing the corporate ladder is most often discovered too late.
- **Pride:** this is the type of pride that can turn into arrogance; a type of pride that says, "I do not need anyone. I am a self-made man."

How would you like to be remembered?

I hope when my wife arrives in heaven one day she will say, "Thank you, Lord, for the gentle, yet challenging husband you gave me!" I hope my children will say, "I had the most 'amazing' dad. He inspired me to live a full life and he showed me how to love God." I hope the people close to me (family) will say, "Jannie's word was his honour, he backed up what he said with his actions." I hope people will remember me for my child-like spirit. Matthew 18:3 (NKJV) says, "Assuredly, I say to you, unless you are converted and become as little children, you will by no means enter the kingdom of heaven." I never want to lose my child-like heart. I want to play and remain a child; I want to keep marvelling at God, I want to always stand in awe of who He is! I want the Lord to know that I do not take anything I have or experience for granted – not the house I live in, the people I work with, or the birdsongs I hear every morning. I hope that the teams and athletes I have worked with will remember me for my honesty and my willingness to do everything I taught them, myself. May no one ever turn around and think I would talk behind their back. I have fallen into the trap and said bad things, but I want to be trustworthy. I want to put my trust in God and be a true man of God. I want to live in forgiveness and be free from worldly trappings and status. I want to be one hundred percent obedient to God when He tells me to do something.

Jannie and his wife share a wonderful moment

Resistance training with his son, Victor, before his return to the USA for tennis

Your message to South Africa

South Africa, if you put your trust in people, you will always be disappointed. If you put your trust in God, you will always be amazed. We are in a daily war; a reality where satan rules, but where we do not have to live as victims of reality, rather as victors through the power of Christ working in us! Keeping your hope alive is the key to faith. When you lose your hope, you get bogged down by reality.

Every day, the reality around you is trumpeted out in newspapers and on news websites but be strong enough to ignore it and not give the enemy the upper hand in your thoughts. Give God the authority in your life because He gives you authority with your free will and the choices you make.

The reality around us means little to me – living as a realist will only make you negative. Choose to live in faith. Let us talk about what is possible – even if the world considers it unrealistic. Philippians 4:13, "I can do all things through Christ who strengthens me." Surprise yourself and live in faith!

Jannie Putter
Exclusive interview
Scan the code to watch
◀◀◀

Ruhan Nel

Adriaan Ruhan Nel, born on the 17th of May 1991, is a professional South African rugby player. In 2010 Ruhan, a former learner of Hoërskool Brandwag, attracted attention as an u19 player for the Pumas, and in the same year played in the u19 provincial championships. As a student at the University of Pretoria, he was part of UP Tuks, the university team in the Varsity Cup series. Ruhan's provincial rugby career includes matches for the Golden Lions (2012-2014) and Griquas (2015), and since 2017 he has been wearing the famous striped jersey of the Western Province and Stormers. His regular positions are full back, wing, and centre. He made his debut in the green and gold as a Blitzbok player and brought his skills to the South African sevens team at the Gold Coast leg of the IRB Sevens World Series in the 2014/2015 season.

My love for sport began... with my father. One of the first gifts he gave me was an orange rubber rugby ball. My younger brother and I played with it for hours on end in our backyard and learnt to kick and pass the ball. When my father returned home after work in the afternoon, he played rugby with us. Rugby had already stolen my heart then!

If I was not a sports star, I would... I did not want to be or become anything else! I have always only wanted to be a professional rugby player.

I am incredibly grateful for... my health. I had a big shock and bad experience early in 2023 when an incident on the field almost ended my life as I know it ... things could have been very different. I could have lost the use of my legs. I feel so blessed to have a second chance. I am also grateful to my wife and for the privilege of being a father to our little girl.

If I could edit my life, I would... To be honest, I would not want to change anything. I think one always says "if I knew then what I know now, I would..." but in reality, it is those experiences – the sorrow, disappointments, and good times – that shape you and change your way of thinking in the end. Even in the worst of times, you are never beyond the reach of God's grace, and in your best times you are never too good for His grace.

One of the biggest lessons I learnt this year... Just an overwhelming feeling of how grateful one should be. Life can change in the blink of an eye – you do not always realise what you have until you almost lose it. Even when I read this sentence back to myself, it sounds like something you hear in every second romcom or read in storybooks. I am sure a few readers will think it is something they have heard a million times, but all it takes is one wrong decision and your whole life is turned upside down. Sometimes, especially in our country, a decision is made for you – something beyond your control – that changes your life. Every day I say thank you for my health, a job, a home, and so many basic things that many other people do not have.

My greatest achievement is... to wear the Springbok jersey and to play as a Blitzbok for my country. The sevens system is a formidable one. It is a place where one experiences healthy growth. It was a privilege to develop under that kind of leadership. I also had the honour to be part of the Western Province team that won the 2017 Currie Cup. We were able to bring home the legendary trophy for the first time in years. In 2022 I was privileged to win the United Rugby Championship with the Stormers and to be part of the first Stormers team to win an international trophy. When I think back to my heroes when I was growing up, guys who also played in this jersey, I sometimes wonder how I managed to have ended up here.

The Bible verse that carries me...
I have two favourite scriptures. God says we must come just as we are; with no shame or preconceived notions about who we should be or who He will be.
He is God. He will blow your mind ... if you give Him the chance.
Everything we have and who we are is thanks to God's grace!

Matthew 11:28-30 (NKJV),
"Come to Me, all you who labour and are heavy laden, and I will give you rest. Take My yoke upon you and learn from Me, for I am gentle and lowly in heart, and you will find rest for your souls. For My yoke is easy and My burden is light."

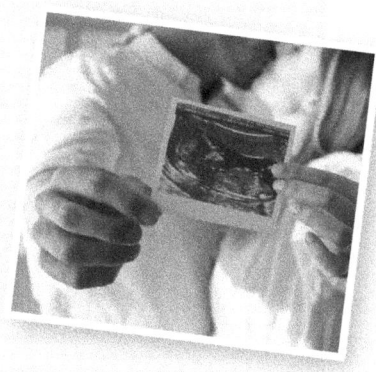

1 Corinthians 15:10 (NKJV),
"But by the grace of God I am what I am, and His grace toward me was not in vain; but I laboured more abundantly than they all, yet not I, but the grace of God which was with me."

MY STORY
Ruhan Nel

Ruhan Nel grew up in a loving home with strong principles and a focus on rugby! His father, a former rugby player in his younger days, had his career cut short after a motorcycle accident, but this did not dampen his love for the sport. On the contrary, the enthusiasm for rugby fuelled the advice and support to the two Nel brothers who both play and have played for provincial teams. It is not only Ruhan's father, but also his mother, Karen's, voice that rings out above those of the fans on the side of the field when her sons play well. Never do they miss making a phone call before or after a match, and should you ask Ruhan's parents, they consider every match as the best of his life, because that is what they believe. Do everything that you do with your whole heart – every time. Do nothing half-heartedly and finish what you start. These are tenets Ruhan lives by.

It was this mindset that enabled Ruhan to continue believing in his abilities at university, even when no rugby union came knocking to offer him a contract. He would come to the realisation that a rugby contract is not simply given to a talented player, it always a privilege (together with a lot of grace). According to statistics, only 0.004% of registered rugby players in South Africa enjoy the privilege of becoming professional players; and 670 000 candidates dream about the fifteen positions in each provincial and national team. This is where dreams are either shattered or a player starts working even harder. Ruhan would choose the latter option. From a young age, he treated every team's jersey like a Springbok jersey. *"Each new team's jersey was always the highest honour that I was entrusted with at that given time. I respected it like it was the green and gold. Under no circumstances could I just dismiss it as of lesser value. No, that jersey was what I had in my hands at that stage, and it would have been ungrateful to disregard it and compare it to a jersey of a more formidable or bigger team, because I did not own that jersey (yet) anyway. I had to prepare myself for a professional setting and could not rush the process."*

Ruhan used every opportunity to improve himself and prepare for the next season of his life because all he ever wanted to do was play rugby. *"It was rugby that led me to the Lord! I was 16 when I gave my heart to God. I was part of a group of 24 young men who got up to mischief on our u16 rugby tour in Winkelspruit. For our punishment, we were grounded. The only activity we were allowed to participate in was a church service on the same campsite where we were staying. During that church service you could place a letter at the foot of a cross as a symbolic action of your surrender and the new life you were starting. There my heart turned to Jesus, and I would never turn away again."*

However, the pruning process in his life was relentless and nowhere did he ever feel like he "had arrived" or that he wielded the upper hand. *"No, on the contrary! The pruning process never stops. Sometimes you feel very close to the Lord, and at other times you are angry and feel very far from Him. Disappointments and sports injuries at the most inopportune times can make you ask the question, 'Lord, why did You allow this?'"* Two specific incidents caused stormy seasons in Ruhan's life, times of many questions and introspection. *"In 2014 my dream came true, and I had the privilege of making my debut for the Blitzboks. In 2016, I was experiencing a breakthrough season full of highlights. However, it was during a semi-final against New Zealand in Paris that a crushing tackle brought everything to a jarring halt. X-rays confirmed that I had broken my collarbone in three places – barely four months before the Olympic Games. A sportsman's mind immediately starts calculating, drawing timelines, and asking: Am I going to be rehabilitated and will I be strong enough to play?"* If the goal is attractive enough, one will do everything to achieve it, and that is why it was such a deep disappointment for Ruhan when they announced the team, and he was not included. *"I was in tears; coach Neil Powell was in tears ... that experience is never enjoyable. I was disappointed because I worked harder in my off-season than any other player and it still was not good enough. I was angry. I stopped reading the Bible and praying. I just wanted to distance myself and figure this thing out on my own."* It was during this period in Ruhan's life that God had to reach into his life for a second time. *"I had to figure it out for myself; God is not on a rugby field as your guardian angel. It remains a sport. Our human bodies were not created to run into each other at 40 km per hour. This does not mean that God is absent on the field, no, we just have to carry the responsibility for our own choices and not blame Him when something goes wrong. Injury is a part of sports. Full stop. When something bad happens, it does not make Him a God who does not care."*

The matter was settled. It was a life lesson that would stay with him, and a moment he could refer back to when the next challenge hit.

The 2023 pre-season game in Wilderness between the Stormers and the SWD Eagles was an easy game with little to no competition. Ruhan went onto the field 15 minutes before the final whistle. It was during a last phase of the game when he tackled an opponent and another player's knee hit his neck. Unbeknownst to him, the blow did more damage than he thought. *"There was a loud crack, and everyone wanted to know if I was okay. I was lucky enough to walk off the field. In my heart, I knew something was wrong because I could turn my head to the left, but then had to hold my chin in my hand and slowly rotate my head back. The crunching sound of bone on bone was audible. Two days later, my coach's words brought everything to a grinding halt – the X-ray confirmed that my neck was broken at the C1 vertebra."* Miraculously, the vertebral fracture did not go all the way through to the spinal cord and Ruhan was able to retain the use of his limbs. *"My little daughter's face flashed before my eyes and the fact that I could still hold my wife was all that I could think about. I could still hug them. I was not paralysed."*

Tears streamed down Ruhan's cheeks; a mere 1 mm was the difference between total paralysis and indescribable grace.

Four days later, during a pre-season tour in Gqeberha, the team was due to play against the Sharks. Ruhan received a request to pay a hospital visit. In his mind and heart, he was still wrestling with the grace he was shown. What Ruhan experienced that day was a watershed moment; a moment he will never forget. *"I had to visit a young rugby player. I met Bakkies; a 19-year-old young man in a wheelchair – paralysed. When I asked about his injury, Bakkies mentioned that he broke his C1 vertebra in a tackle during a match. Another boy's knee hit his neck and his C1 vertebra broke right into the spinal cord…"*

Bakkies lay dead on the field for four minutes before medical staff could resuscitate him. However, he was paralysed from the neck down. A different life lay ahead for the 19-year-old.

"I saw a reflection of myself. I realised that it is only by the grace of God that I was not in a wheelchair myself. In the blink of an eye, I had a new outlook on life. It was as if God Himself spoke to me in an audible voice. I realised that life is not just about rugby! Rugby is not my everything, because there is so much more to live for and be grateful for."

For the first time in a long time, Ruhan would again feel the Spirit of God and hear His voice, and this time he would listen, not just hear. Ruhan set new priorities in his life, of which time with God and his family were at the very top of the list.

"Our God is merciful. He meets us where we are at our level of faith. And when you let Him, He shows you exactly who He is and why He loves you so much."

What do you think is the biggest obstacle in men's lives?

Men are proud. We have a hard time talking about how we honestly feel deep down. I am privileged to have a group of men around me who support each other spiritually. A group that you can come to once a week, have coffee together, and talk about your concerns. You often realise that you are not actually on your own. Some of the men have already been through a few things in life themselves and others are struggling with the same things as you. As a man, you take a lot on your own shoulders and are proud of the fact that you can take care of your family, protect them, and give the best you possibly can. But it all comes with challenges and that is why it is good that men have a space where they can share with friends who understand and support them.

How would you like to be remembered?

I would like to be remembered as someone who showed my little girl how a God-fearing man lives, what is right and wrong, and how a woman should be treated. I want to be remembered as a man who knew God, a man who was honest and wore his heart on his sleeve – on and off the field.

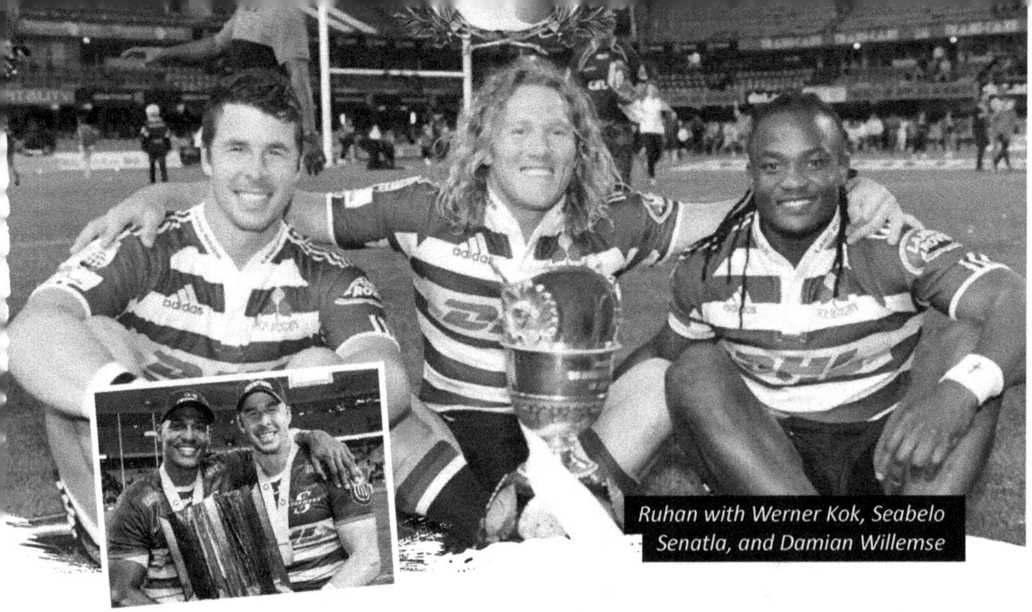

Ruhan with Werner Kok, Seabelo Senatla, and Damian Willemse

Your message to South Africa

It requires nothing but your time and giving up what is comfortable to you to understand someone else's background, culture, and way of thinking. We live in a unique country with different challenges, races, languages, cultures, and, of course, a history that has left emotional scars in many people's hearts. I was fortunate enough to attend the wedding of one of my best friends. It was in the Eastern Cape, a traditional Xhosa wedding. Although I have known this friend well for years, for the first time I really understood why he does certain things the way he does. I saw him at ease at home, among his people, one hundred percent in his culture – and he relished it. Expecting him to do things differently obviously goes against who he is and what he knows. If we do not understand and get to know each other's stories and backgrounds, there will always be friction between us. We know one way of doing things, but there are so many other views and ways that only require our time and sacrificing our comfort to explore and understand them. We have to learn to put our emotions aside and just engage. Sometimes the difficult and uncomfortable conversations are needed to move forward.

Ruhan Nel
Exclusive interview
Scan the code to watch

Ruhan with his wife, Marlé

Vernon Philander

Vernon Darryl Philander, born on the 24th of June 1985, is a former South African international cricketer. "The Surgeon", "VDP", "Vern", "Pro", or "V-Dawg", as his friends and supporters call him, is known for his medium-pace right-arm bowling on the cricket pitch. The career of the golden boy from Webner Street Primary School in Ravensmead started at a young age, and progressed to where he represented South Africa at u19 level. The resume of this former pupil of Ravensmead Secondary School includes being a player for the Western Province (2003-2004, 2015-2016, 2021-2022); the Tolchards Devon Cricket League, which is the top level of competition for recreational club cricket in Devon, England (2004); the Cape Cobras (2005-2006, 2018-2019); Somerset County Cricket Club, better known as one of 18 first-class county clubs in the domestic cricket structure of England and Wales (2012); Kent and Jamaica Tallawahs (2013); Nottinghamshire (2015); South Western Districts (2015-2016); and Sussex County Cricket Club, which is also one of the oldest of 18 first-class county clubs (2017). He also played county cricket in Middlesex, as well as for Durban Heat in the first Mzansi Superliga T20 tournament (2018), and for the Cape Town Blitz team (2019) in the same tournament.

Vernon enjoyed an extremely impressive start to his international career. He made his debut in one-day cricket (ODI) against Ireland in Belfast on the 24th of June 2007 (his 22nd birthday), where he took four wickets for 12 runs, a performance that helped seal the match for his team. He made his T20 debut against the West Indies in Johannesburg on the 11th of September 2007, and, on the 9th of November 2011 Vernon stepped out onto the cricket pitch for the senior Protea team and made his test cricket debut against Australia. He received the player of the match award after taking 5 for 15 in Australia's second innings, in which Australia was bowled out for 47 runs. It was Australia's lowest completed Test innings total since 1902. Vernon was also crowned as player of the series with 14 wickets with a run rate of 13.92. He also took five wickets during the two Tests, twice.

Some of his records and accolades include: He became the fifth player in history to take five wickets in an innings in each of his first three tests. He won the 2012 SA Sportsman of the Year award and, in 2013, he surpassed his teammate, Dale Steyn, to become the number one ICC Test series bowler.

Vernon announced his retirement from international cricket in December 2019 and, in September 2021, his name was added to the Pakistan coaching team for the T20 World Cup in the United Arab Emirates. We currently hear him as a presenter and commentator on SuperSport. He manages his non-profit organisation, the Vernon Philander Foundation, part time.

My love for sport began... *on the streets of Ravensmead. Sports on television had a great influence on us as children. We would watch Wimbledon, football, or Currie Cup matches on TV, only to go and emulate everything we saw on the screen with our friends in the street in front of our parents' houses after the sports broadcast. Every child in the community's birthday and every present that included a ball was important. This expanded our range of sports that we could play! Sometimes the competition was very serious and, at other times, we just joked around for fun. It kept us out of trouble.*

If I was not a sports star, I would be... *a family man. If I could not do sport professionally, I would have pursued my love for accounting and would probably have become an entrepreneur and businessman.*

I am incredibly grateful for... *my second, third, and even fourth chances in life. I am also grateful to my family and relatives for their support and love, even in times when we rarely saw each other, and things did not always make sense. I am very privileged to be a father and to truly know God. My life and path of faith have been a bit of a seesaw until now, but I am so grateful that God knows my heart.*

If I could edit my life, I would... *speed up the learning processes in my life. I sometimes look back and feel the bumps on my head due to painful lessons and my own stubbornness; I kept repeating the same mistakes... Now that I am older and can look back, I think with regret, as I could have learnt these lessons earlier and a lot sooner...*

One of the biggest lessons I learnt this year... *is the power of being vulnerable. I am a bit of a control freak, but after a very challenging 24 to 36 months I now know it is okay and important to show your vulnerability and talk about it. I also learnt that people around you also have a voice and, therefore, have the right to their own opinion.*

My greatest achievement is... *I think people would expect me to mention a cricketing achievement, but in my case it is admitting when I have a problem. To talk about it openly and honestly; to admit that I am not always right; that although I am a good cricketer, there are other serious and real personal life issues that need attention outside of the cricket field. There are things I have to work on every day.*

The Bible verse that carries me...

Psalm 23:4,
"Even though I walk through the valley of the shadow of death, I will fear no evil, for you are with me; your rod and your staff, they comfort me."

MY STORY
Vernon Philander

When he walked out on the cricket field with his number 24 shirt, the opposition's batsmen had to brace themselves – because when conditions were in Vernon Philander's favour, he was probably the most dangerous bowler to face. He was not a lightning-fast bowler, but with the gift of accuracy and the ability to move the ball off the seam, he was South Africa's most reliable weapon with a cricket ball. However, he was not only a brilliant medium-pace bowler, he was also handy with a bat in the lower order. *"I remember my mini-cricket days well and sometimes stand amazed at how everything turned out. Looking at my life story, I know that, as a child, I was never the best cricketer, and I never had more talent than any of the other boys. Still, I experienced a lot of God's grace in my life, and, with many hours of hard work, endurance, and perseverance, I had the opportunity to represent my country..."*

Once you set a goal for your cricket practice or any other activity in your life, you will improve. You must write down achievable goals, objectives, and big dreams, because then they can be realised – if it has the Lord's approval. It was this advice from coach James Adams that would change Vernon's outlook on life, and his approach to cricket forever. His goal was a better life for himself, his three younger brothers, his single mother, and his grandparents in the small Cape community of Ravensmead, Parow. The area is not really known for its sports stars, but for violence, gangs, crime, and alcohol and drug abuse.

"Even though I walk through the valley of the shadow of death, I will fear no evil, for you are with me; your rod and your staff, they comfort me," his grandmother Leah used to say. It was the scripture-based, strict upbringing in his grandparents' home that taught him the basics of respect, punctuality, and discipline. They were the guideposts and

God, every Sunday in church, was the true North. *"I grew up knowing how important faith, the church, Sunday school, and confirmation are. When you are young, you believe what you are told and you live according to the values that are laid down for you, but as a young man matures, and he begins to rely on his own insights, the picture starts to look somewhat different! I wanted to experience life and everything that goes with it, for myself. I wanted to find out what I believe, why I believe it, and then take my own path. Success at a young age, being a celebrity (and the fame that comes with it), a full cricket tour calendar, and the world at my feet made me headstrong and inflated my ego! I thought I was untouchable, invincible, bigger than the general public, and even bigger than the sport I loved so much…"*

"If you put your trust in something other than God, it will become a problem. Because the thing that will make you, is the same thing that will break you…" These are the words of a well-known speaker that will make anyone halt, evaluate, and re-evaluate their life. Like many other young men, Vernon would learn this expensive life lesson all too soon. After his debut for the Proteas in 2007, and an illustrious whirlwind cricket year as a professional international one-day and T20 cricketer, at the age of 22, Vernon's Protea Test cricket career was cut short in the blink of an eye. Along with that, the dream of representing his country in Test cricket at the 2011 World Cup was also scuppered. Vernon was not selected for the South African Test cricket team. *"I was devastated. Hundreds of unanswered questions washed over me as I could not understand how this could happen at the pinnacle of my career. According to me, I was ready for the big step and the responsibility of Test cricket, but in the eyes of the coaches and selectors, I was just a young man with talent … with an ego too big for the team and the Test cricket field."*

For the next few years, Vernon would do more introspection than ever before. *"Failure makes you ask hard questions. It brings you down to earth. It breaks down the self-life. Before you can find yourself again, you must find God."* He would work harder: on his game and attitude. He reached out to God, on his knees, and asked for a second chance after missed opportunities. Then he trusted that God saw his heart and heard his prayers. He had learnt to pray and trust again.

"Psalm 23:4 had to take root and become my promise. Not grandma Leah's, but my own. I had to get to know God myself and learn to love Him again. Coupled with that, I could not just focus on faith, I also had to put in the hard work in the physical world and restore damaged friendships."

Four years.

It took Vernon four years to get to a good place mentally, spiritually, and physically before the call came from Cricket South Africa and the Protea coach, Gary Kirsten. *"I do not really talk about this – my faith is a very private thing for me – but when I look back at those four years of my life, I know that I would have given up many times if it was not for my faith. I understand, better than anyone, that we all need answers about the painful things in our lives, and most of the time they elude us. I had to learn first-hand* that God allows certain challenges in your life so that you can grow as a person. It is only in retrospect that these things become clearer … when you have to apply the lessons to handle the situation better the next time and not make the same mistakes."

At the age of 29, Vernon's name was included in the South African cricket team for the 2015 Cricket World Cup in Australia and New Zealand, and he got the opportunity to make his dream come true. *"When you write an exam, you cannot expect God to pick up the pen on your behalf. You have to do the work yourself. Yes, He will give you peace, but you have to do the work. Today I know it. I still live by this principle. I apply the rules, because we live in a changing world with many variables and constant challenges."*

Looking back over the past years from the COVID pandemic to the present, those words are still a reality in his life. *"The challenges did not stop. The announcement of my retirement from professional cricket was just before COVID 19 and the lockdown period. It was an uncertain time where many questions about my life and career followed. Along with that, I lost my grandmother and my brother who both passed away, and I went through a divorce."* It was a time when he wanted to hear God's voice more than ever. *"If I did not have a relationship with God, I would have asked the nagging questions again: Why me, Lord? Why now? But this time I knew that there were more things to be grateful for than to be negative about. After every test there is something to be thankful for. I now know that I can turn to Him in the valley of the shadow of death, but also when things are going well. Regardless of what people think, I know this is a relationship that will never end."*

Vernon knows a God who gives you another chance – his idea is not to abuse God's grace. No, he just knows that as long as he tries his best, God sees his heart and intentions.

"When you live in the spotlight, you sometimes think that you have to maintain a certain image and be someone you are not. It takes years of experience and mistakes to come to the realisation that you can just be. I am now learning it through the eyes of my child and with the people of my non-profit organisation. I am serving people again and making a significant difference with a wholesome plate of food. One does not have to be 'someone special' to help the individual who is currently in his valley of the shadow of death … You will be surprised, if you sometimes just stop and help, it might help you out of your own valley of the shadow of death."

Vernon and his son, Hayden

What do you think is the biggest obstacle in men's lives?

Egos!

- As men, we like to feel good and to be right, and sometimes it comes at a price.
- The strong, tough guy character sometimes causes us to clam up and feel like we do not need to talk about it. We then rely on our own advice and get no objective input and advice in our lives. It is so important to have those behind-the-scenes conversations in a safe environment with an objective expert. We need safe platforms where we can listen to each other, hear, and give and receive advice.
- I now know that men and women play different, but important, roles. Men want to feel loved; we want to be appreciated, and it is important to know that the women in our lives needs us. It softens our hearts, but egos stand in the way of this.

How would you like to be remembered?

I would like to be remembered as someone who had a significant impact in people's lives. As a man who served his purpose. God has been good and gracious to me. And if I can do it for others, why not?

Your message to South Africa

Times are hard and we turn to our own way of doing things, but trust God who knows you and your future. Have faith and believe that He hears your prayers and, if it is His will, answers them. Believe me when I tell you: He will never leave you!

Vernon as a cricket commentator

Philip Snyman

Philippus Albertus Borman Snyman, born on the 26th of March 1987, is a former South African rugby player and captain of the South African sevens team, the Blitzboks. It is not only celebrities such as writer and intellectual Sir Laurens van der Post, actress Brümilda van Rensburg, or Springbok rugby player Adriaan Strauss who made the town of Philippolis proud. No, Philip followed their example and made a name for himself in rugby circles at an early age when he played for Gray College and, in subsequent years, donned the Cheetah jersey. From 2008-2012, Philip played as centre or wing in 59 matches for the Free State Cheetahs in both the Super Rugby and Currie Cup series. His provincial career also includes six games for the Griffons (2008-2009). Philip had the honour of donning the green and gold and made his debut for the Blitzboks in the 2008 Dubai Sevens tournament. He became part of the historic group that won their first World Series title that season and won a bronze medal at the Olympic Games in 2016. Philip was appointed as captain of the Blitzboks in 2016 and led the team in 28 tournaments between 2016 and 2019, including leading the team to World Sevens Series titles in 2017 and 2018. In the number 2 jersey, he represented South Africa at the Sevens World Cup tournaments in Dubai (2008), Moscow (2013), and San Francisco (2018), making him the only Blitzbok to have played at three such tournaments. Philip hung up his boots in 2019 as a 32-year-old player – after 63 tournaments with the Blitzboks and 276 games, during which he scored 69 tries, 14 goal kicks, and a penalty for a career total of 376 points. He ended his international career for the Blitzboks as South Africa's most successful sevens captain.

Philip is currently the assistant coach of the national sevens team. He is married to Esteé and is the proud father of two young girls.

My love for sport began... *in Philippolis, a small town in the Free State. My father was a farmer, teacher, and rugby coach. Because I was the coach's son, the older boys had no choice but to play rugby and kick the ball around with me. We were next to or on the rugby field all day, every day! With two older sisters, nephews, and a mother who were all keen sports enthusiasts, it did not take much to get everyone to throw a ball around. There was a love for sport and family, and we played sports together for hours on end.*

If I was not a sports star, I would... *most probably be a farmer in the Free State! However, since we settled here in the Cape Winelands, it would now be a difficult choice. I would probably have invested in my second love – a position in financial management. Of course, it all depends on where and in which area you find yourself.*

I am incredibly grateful for... *my wife, my two children, and my wonderful family.*

If I could edit my life, I would... *not change a thing.. I have been through many highs and lows, but because I am such a positive person who always wants to see the best in everything – including the reason behind the situation – there are few things that throw me off balance. I would not be where I am today if I had not learnt to accept many of the variables, as well as how to make the best of what is available to me. The winding roads, and even the doors that closed, lead you to where you need to be and shape you into the person you need to be.*

One of the biggest lessons I learnt this year... *is to be in the moment. As a sportsman, I tour a lot, and when you are sitting in your hotel room with two crying little girls on the phone on the other end, you soon realise that you have to make the most of every moment. Be present when you are at home, give love and play with your children, share hugs and kisses, and be there. However, when you are back on the sports field or at work, be one hundred percent present there. One cannot allow feelings of guilt to rob you of opportunities either. We must be responsible with what is entrusted to us.*

My greatest achievement is... *In my personal life, it is to have found such a wonderful wife – a beautiful woman at that! I am proud of my wedding day and the birth of our daughters. On the sports field, my greatest achievement was the privilege to wear the sevens jersey. I was 20 years old, and one does not always realise the privilege and responsibility of that opportunity. To win tournaments, represent your country at the Olympic Games, and to receive a bronze medal, is a great honour and achievement.*

The Bible verse that carries me...

Matthew 6:33,
"But seek first the kingdom of God and His righteousness, and all these things shall be added to you."

Philip and Esteé with daughters Emily and Elizabeth

MY STORY
Philip Snyman

You would think that no one can be and remain so positive all the time, but Philip Snyman knows no other way. It is more than just a survival mechanism or learnt behaviour. No, he lives what he believes, and he believes what he lives. The open-minded positivity flows from him, because he believes there is always something positive that one can take from every situation.

The best advice that young Philip would receive, remember, and always apply was very practical: *"Always be honest, sincere, and be yourself."* The toughest advice was, *"Learn from your own mistakes and not only from other people's mistakes. See what they do and how they handle it when they make mistakes, but also bump your own head and learn from it. All successful people keep their eyes open and learn quickly."*

Philip did more than just take notes. He noticed and adjusted his lifestyle and decision making.

"I decided from a young age that I was going to be the product of my own choices."

"I bumped my head a lot and ended up in dark places but refused to be a victim of my own circumstances. I chose to have a positive outlook on everything and make every bad situation the best worst situation."

This habit did not just develop overnight, it had to grow, bloom, and blossom; it is a valuable treasure in him that no one will ever be able to take away.

Philip was 17 when his parents got divorced. His father was his hero and icon.

He was the first supporter next to the rugby field and the last one to leave. The divorce ruined young Philip's life, so much so that he almost gave up playing his beloved rugby. *"I practiced rugby with him since I was five years old, but when I was 17, he pulled the rug out from underneath me. I became rebellious and started partying like never before.*

I was sad and angry, disappointed in the man who, after all these years, hurt my mother, my two sisters, and me so much with the choices he made and what he did."

Philip grew up in a Christian home with godly values and norms as its foundation. Every Sunday, the extended Snyman family sat in the Philippolis Reformed Church and, together with eight other parishioners, learnt about God and the Bible. Every Sunday just before the young Philip fell asleep on his mother's lap, he would compete with his cousins to see who could sing the loudest, then a Bible story and the lesson therein would follow. Philip never questioned God or his faith – until the day of his father's confession and the news about the divorce. Everything Philip believed in was shattered in the blink of an eye and replaced with unbelief and pessimistic realism.

"This hurt raged in me for four years. During that time, I wanted nothing to do with my father. Unforgiveness and hatred controlled me, but I refused to forgive and to forget – until one day, when God intervened and touched my heart…"

It was during his second year at the University of the Free State, on a Sunday morning, when Philip was hung over after yet another late night of partying. The cell phone beeped with a message, like every other Sunday morning before. It was another invitation to go to church. This time Philip's clever excuses could not get him off the hook, because they were all countered with an equally good answer. *"For the umpteenth time I turned down the invitation to the morning service with the excuse that I already had plans, but the answer came: 'That is okay, I am going to the evening service anyway. You are welcome to come along then.'"*

Was it the dogged, never-give-up attitude of his friend, or Philip's own conscience that wore him down? Whatever the reason, God knew Philip, and this time He would not let him get away!

That evening during the church service in Bloemfontein, the 20-year-old truly met God for the first time. *"That night changed my life. I realised what and who God really is. The comforting, calm feeling that came over me was a relief to my soul. He took away the pain and brought healing where no medicine could reach."*

It was during this phase of Philip's life that he had to find his feet in more than just his spiritual life. He also had to find stability in soul and body. With a confused heart and God's eye on him, Philip and two friends took a sabbatical from the Free State Rugby Union, accepted a three-month rugby contract in the Netherlands, and pushed searching for the meaning of life into the red. *"Those three months opened my eyes to what is valuable in my life. We would train twice a week, play one game, and the rest of the time lazed around, drinking beer, and getting up to all sorts of mischief. But it was during this time that I opened up my Bible one evening and realised that I missed my family, my country, and my faith!"*

It was the prayers of his mother and two sisters, a girlfriend, and friends that would make Philip turn back, not only to South Africa, but also to the Lord. This time everything was in line – mind, soul, and body. *"I came home, saw my father for the first time in four years, and made peace with him. Together we started farming with cattle; we went on family holidays again. Of course, everything did not always go one hundred percent well all the time, but we were able to move on and make new memories together."*

When Philip looks back now, he sees God's hand in every chapter of his life. Even in the chapters he does not want to read again.

God was there, because that is who God was, and still is, and will be forever – the One who brings restoration, the One who brings forgiveness, and the One who just wants to be given a chance to be a voice in your life.

This event brought healing and restoration to the Snyman family over the course of three years. Just in time, because in 2018 on Easter Sunday – four days before the opening ceremony of the Commonwealth Games in Australia – it was a phone call at six in the morning that made Philip sob with tears of pain, gratitude, grace, and loss. *"My father passed away that Sunday morning. All I could think of were the three years of building new memories. I was so grateful for the relationship and forgiveness. I could never have lived with the hatred and blame. I was grateful, so grateful, for a father who was my biggest hero ... the man who was my role model, despite bad choices and actions. My role model was just a human with faults. The betrayal, hatred, and pain had been real, but with the Lord's help, the decision I made to forgive my father saved my life..."*

Today, Philip still sees his father as his great role model, and even though he was not perfect, Philip learnt a lot from him; even receiving guidance on what type of father he wanted to be, and how he wanted to treat his wife and little girls.

Just as God planned it, Philip now, at the age of 35, shares these life lessons with other young men. As assistant coach of the Blitzboks, young men's eyes are fixed on him, and they take from his life's fountain of wisdom and experience. *"My first and only advice to the young men is always to make sure the Lord is and remains the centre of your life and everything you undertake ... because then you will never second guess your decisions."*

"Philip is truly a man with God as his guide." These are the words of his teammate and coach, Neil Powell, who summarises his outlook on life: *"I played rugby with him and then coached him, and in both roles he excelled. It was never about himself. Our system benefited enormously from someone of Philip's calibre as a leader and as a player, always available and willing to contribute, often at his own expense. He was the driving force behind our culture and lived it, this team and many players in it are better people because of it."*

What do you think is the biggest obstacle in men's lives?

Emotions. As men, we are naturally proud and do not like to show weakness, although it would be the best option to be able to talk about hurt, happiness, misfortune, and pain. Everyone must have an outlet. Personally, I always try to manage my emotions on the emotional scale of -5, 0, and 5. In other words: -5 is a negative reaction, 0 is a neutral assessment, and 5 is very optimistic. My emotions always remain 0, so that the bad days are not too rough, but then by nature I do not easily jump to a 5, because the road back is always too long and too difficult. Work on a scale that is functional and as stable as possible for you. Nevertheless, speak up, share your heart with others, and show emotion.

How would you like to be remembered?

I would like to be remembered as someone who had a positive outlook on life. Someone who was optimistic and tackled life with a smile and humour, without taking every situation too seriously. I would like to be remembered as someone who chose to see the light and the positive side of things, someone who loved life!

Your message to South Africa

It is so important to stay positive about our country and its people and not lose sight of who we are and can be. If everyone just focuses on himself/herself first and makes sure that he/she is the best version of themselves, we will stop focussing on other people's shortcomings. That is when we stop pointing the finger in accusation. This is when we can change our perspective with a positive result.

Philip Snyman
Exclusive interview
Scan the code to watch

Cameron Wright

Cameron Robin Wright, born on the 20th of April 1994, is a South African rugby player who plays for the Cell C Sharks in the Super Rugby, United Rugby Championship, and the Currie Cup series. The rugby career of this former student of Westville Boys High School and Hilton College is a black-and-white affair with the Sharks' emblem on his chest! Cameron wore the number 9 jersey for KwaZulu-Natal in the u16 Grant Khomo Week in 2010, he represented the Sharks at the u18 Craven Week Tournament in 2012, and in the same year also played in the u19 Provincial Championship. In 2014, he became part of the Sharks' u21 team.

As a student at the University of KwaZulu-Natal, Cameron swopped his beloved black and white jersey for a snow white UKZN Impi jersey and was part of the 2014 team in the Varsity Shield competition. He spread his wings and played for the French club, Montpellier, from 2015-2018, but returned to South Africa in 2017. The 1.81 m starting scrum half played for the Sharks again in the Currie Cup Premier Division season and in the United Rugby Championship. Cameron made his debut in the Springbok training group in 2018 under coach Rassie Erasmus and patiently waited for the day when he would wear the green and gold.

My love for sport began... *as a boy. My father always said that I could throw a ball before I could even walk! He was a great sportsman and rugby player. In the early 1990s, he played for the 'Banana Boys' as a young man. He never got the opportunity to play rugby professionally because all the contracted players still had to work to maintain a good standard of living. The Banana Boys started using the Sharks logo in the mid-1990s for sponsorship reasons. My love for sport is widespread: I was the opening batsman for my school's cricket team, played football, and much later also started playing rugby. It was the skills that cricket taught me – the timing factor of hitting the ball perfectly, the value of spatial awareness, and the finesse of the sport – that contributed to making me a better rugby player.*

If I was not a sports star, I would... *be in full time ministry. I am currently completing a theology degree with the focus on one-to-one counselling. I love God and I love God's people. My ministry seems unusual to some people, but I know that God is using me exactly where He wants to use me now.*

I am incredibly grateful for... *so many things, I feel like I have an endless list – but I am extremely grateful that I have been called and set apart by God, I am grateful for the family that He has given me, the church community that I belong to, and the talents that He has given me.*

If I could edit my life, I would... *I do not often say that I would change things in my life because I am extremely grateful for the path that God set for me. It has taught me so much and helped me to be who I am today. However, I think that if I had been less conceited and more humble at an earlier stage, it would have allowed me to remain teachable. I could have potentially caused less trauma, less grief, and would have been more of an influence in the lives of individuals around me.*

One of the biggest lessons I learnt this year... *I think the most incredible revelation that I have had this year was about God's faithfulness and goodness. If you read David's Psalms, he pleads with God in many of them and appeals to God's unchanging nature – His goodness and His faithfulness. David never points to his own good works as the reason why God should reward him. He admits that he can do nothing without God and that everything he does means nothing if God is not involved. Even thousands of years ago, he already had good insight into the grace of God.*

My biggest achievement is... *what I am most proud of in my life is my family. I am not sure if it is an achievement, a privilege, or maybe even a gift, but I am definitely extremely proud to be a husband to my wife and a father to my children.*

The Bible verse that carries me...

Galatians 2:20,
"I have been crucified with Christ; it is no longer I who live, but Christ lives in me; and the life which I now live in the flesh I live by faith in the Son of God, who loved me and gave Himself for me."

This verse helps me remember who I am, what life is really about, and how wonderful the God I serve is.

Cameron, daddy to Harper Grace and Paisley Hope

MY STORY
Cameron Wright

It is the tattoo of a roaring lion on Cameron Wright's knee that always has the commentators and the public talking.

The long black rugby socks cover the Hebrew letters and other tattoos, but the message behind the tattoos is clear: Cameron stands for what he believes in. He is not afraid to talk about his faith. No, he even writes it on his body. Consider it a starting point for a conversation or scowl in disapproval, but what you cannot say about him is that he is scared. Cameron fears no one but God. He fears no human opinion or judgement, because he has already experienced a lot in his life; he could certainly write a book. He chose prayer as healing for the wounds of the past. No scar will hold him back and no false perception will trip him up again, because his anchor is God and his foundation is firmly established in Him.

Cameron was the fiery boy with too much hate and anger for one small body to contain. Cameron's parents got divorced when he was only one year old. With his father in Vereeniging, thousands of kilometres away from Cameron and his older sister, the relationship with their father turned into a distorted Santa Claus story. Cameron saw his dad once a year for only a short time, usually with presents and during a festive celebration. After that, his father would disappear again, only to reappear after 12 months. A loving mother, but an absent father figure, led to Cameron growing up without strict discipline. The resulting consequences had a destructive ripple effect in his life. *"I was a troublemaker at school and was sometimes suspended for several days at a time. I wanted to fight to assert myself. I used rugby to hurt others and to express my anger. It was a 'legal' way for me to run around angry and frustrated for 80 minutes. Rugby was my outlet, but it was also my god."*

Cameron was performance driven. In his search for the love and acceptance of a male father figure, he would do more – do better – just to receive the approval and affirming words of mentors and leaders in the school and hostel. He saw himself as someone who was always on the back foot, never good enough. He was desperate to earn the title of 'son'. *"For a large part of my teenage years, I did not know where I belonged. My own father was absent, and my stepfather did not allow me to call him 'dad', out of respect for my own father. I experienced a huge identity crisis and never felt that I had a foothold anywhere or that I belonged."*

The unthinkable happened to young, vulnerable Cameron. A mentor, an older man who lived on the same street as the Wrights, abused their friendship – which turned into sexual abuse. Due to emotional manipulation, Cameron gave into actions that were not his choice, time and again. *"These incidents were a part of my life that I had to lay down before God the day I gave my heart to Him. It was much later in my life; I was already 20 years old then, but the raw pain of rejection, abuse, and a bitter grudge against authority figures and myself strangled and blinded me with rage. I had to give it to God to heal it. I had to get it out of my system, process it, walk a road with God, and receive healing. I had to forgive the man for the choices he made, for the deeds he committed; through God's eyes, I could also see the offender's shortcomings. I now know that each person only acts out of his own pain. I submitted to actions that were wrong and he took advantage of my vulnerability, but it was the perfect storm for the devil to thrive in."*

God, the most powerful male authority figure, would bring about a physical and spiritual confrontation with the stubborn, rugby-obsessed Cameron one morning between the pews of the Olive Tree church.

God had an appointment with him and showed up in his life in a way that Cameron never expected.

"I was an outspoken atheist who condemned Christians for their ridiculous religious beliefs. I was a young, conceited rugby player who was a god in my own eyes. I suffered from clinical depression and constantly drank too much to forget about my circumstances. Bronwen, my friend (who is now my wife), was a devout Christian and once, after another night of heavy drinking and disappointing behaviour on my part, she again invited me to church that Sunday morning. She wanted to share my life with me, but I had to agree first to heal my aching, broken heart. That morning, God and His Holy Spirit descended on me between the pews during praise and worship and I had a personal encounter."

It was a circumcision of his heart in that encounter with the only living God; a moment where a heart of stone would change into a soft heart of love with the promise and confirmation of a new life! Cameron would never turn back to his old life again. His love for God and the desire to study God's Word took hold within 24 hours, only to lead to a change of his university degree and a turnaround in his lifestyle. *"I was studying psychology at the time but changed my field of study to theology. I am passionate about God, His Word, and the church. It is a place of healing for broken hearts and restoration for hurting people. We are all imperfect people who serve a perfect living God."*

"If we, as the church, start to stand together, work together, and pray we will see how His grace, love, and goodness bring people to repentance and to rebirth."

1 Corinthians 10:31 says, *"Therefore, whether you eat or drink, or whatever you do, do all to the glory of God."*

And this is exactly what the fiery pastor Cameron Wright is still doing today! Rugby was his god, he played it to rid himself of pain and frustration, but then things turned around and rugby became the area where he could worship God. *"It may sound strange to people – the rugby field is an opportunity for me to tackle people hard, but for the glory of God! I can serve God in a unique way, with my physical body and my whole heart. The locker room and gym are my mission fields. I use my own story, life experience, the Scripture-based tattoos on my body, and my love to talk to tough men who might never go to church."*

Cameron understands trauma and what it means to be tormented by the past. He knows that pain and unforgiveness grow like mould in darkness. He does not allow potential shame or humiliation over the sin of the past to have any place in his life and shines the light on it. His life is an open book for other people to learn from. *"The biggest lesson I had to learn was to push my pride aside, to put my agenda away and not try to control people's opinions about my story. I cannot control your thinking, but if my story of pain to restoration can help someone else receive healing too, I will share my story over and over again with other people…"*

James 5:16 says, *"Confess your trespasses to one another, and pray for one another, that you may be healed. The effective, fervent prayer of a righteous man avails much."*

Cameron remains faithful to this passage of Scripture.

Today, rugby is a big part of his life, but it is not his whole life. He no longer worships it and his whole life no longer depends on whether he wins or loses. The performance-driven pressure is gone forever because he realises that he does not have to do anything more, or anything less, to experience God's love. *"In an environment where players are* idolised, I now turn the attention away from myself and give the glory to God. This is His talent in me, and I will be faithful to the territory He has entrusted to me, but the honour is and will always remain His."

The writing in Hebrew declares it clearly on his skin: *"To God I give my life."* The conceited young man has disappeared, a mature son of a living God stands strong.

What do you think is the biggest obstacle in men's lives?

Pride and lust, for sure. Men think too much of themselves and too often of women. Men love to gratify their flesh, but their flesh drags them away from the presence of God.

How would you like to be remembered?

On my memorial day, I would hope they say, "He ran his race well and he kept the faith."

Your message to South Africa

Simply: love God, love others.

Cameron Wright
Exclusive interview
Scan the code to watch
◀◀◀

Cameron and his wife Bronwen Jade

Brok Harris

Juan "Brok" Harris, born in Roodepoort on the 22nd of February 1985, is a South African rugby player. He matriculated at Hoërskool Bastion in Krugersdorp, after which he graduated from the North-West University (formerly the Potchefstroom University for Christian Higher Education). Brok started playing for the leopards as a young man in 2005, was part of the Western Province and Stormers teams in 2006-2014, the Welsh Dragons from 2014-2021, and he currently plays prop for the Stormers after returning from the Welsh Pro14 team. Brok is married to Madelein and they have three children: Divan (10), Lara (5), and Reuben (4).

My love for sport began... *in grade 1. I played rugby with my friends; we were a particularly good team that won one match after the other! We were undefeated until grade 5. In grade 7, our team was the one that everyone feared because of our excellent track record.*

My love for the game developed very naturally. It was that feeling of "winning, excelling, and celebrating" after each game, as well as practicing rugby with the group of mates every afternoon, which became the driving forces. Practically 90% of our team all chose to attend the same high school and, together, we developed even further and reached greater milestones. It was during my high school years when I realised that I had a talent, and that rugby was something I had to pursue professionally. My parents motivated me to persevere and to keep going at it. They had an enormous influence on my rugby career and their support meant everything. They sacrificed so much. There were late nights driving to and from practices; rugby tours that had to be paid for; early, frosty winter mornings next to the field – weekend in and weekend out. My father kept my fitness up to standard. I remember how every December; we would spend our holiday in Hartenbos. I first had to spend some time in the gym or put on my running shoes in the morning before we could spend the day on the beach. I was very disciplined and hard on myself.

If I was not a sports star, I would be... *a physiotherapist. I am not at all someone who can sit in an office and spend hours in front of a computer. I was an outdoors type of child from early on; on my bike or with a ball in hand playing rugby or cricket with all my mates who lived on our street. Even before I seriously considered rugby, I knew that one day I wanted an occupation that would allow me the type of freedom to be physically active; a profession that offers a new challenge every day.*

I am incredibly grateful for… *my wife. We started dating at university and this year we have been married for twelve years; we have three children. I have a lot of respect for her because she is the glue that holds our family together. She often fulfils the role of doctor, pastor, judge, policeman, and teacher in my absence. It is precisely because she can fulfil each of these roles with ease that it is possible for me to live my dream as a rugby player, whether it is on home soil or somewhere overseas. She gives me the opportunity to pursue my dream 100 % and is definitely my biggest supporter. She is the one I can talk to when things are not going well on the rugby field, and she is also the one who celebrates all the milestones with me when things are looking good.*

If I could edit my life, I would… *change nothing. I believe that everything in one's life happens for a reason. It is precisely because of the specific course of events that have taken place in my life that I have now been given an opportunity to continue my career with the Stormers. It may sound like a cliché, but there is nothing that I would want to do differently. I live with a grateful heart; grateful for the opportunity to play rugby, grateful to have had the opportunity to live and work in Wales, and grateful to have stuck with it for seven years, because it led me back to the Stormers where I intend to one day plough back into the club – and more specifically, into the youth. My time in Wales was a time of introspection where I could think about the future of my rugby career and plan accordingly – I was able to finish my coaching levels and qualifications and I knew that somewhere the opportunity to coach rugby would also come my way. I just had to trust that it would happen in the Lord's time. My choices in the past have long since determined my future and today I can say, with conviction, that I am in the best place in my personal life and career.*

One of the biggest lessons I have learnt this year… *is not to compare myself to others, because it results in you doubting your own abilities. At almost 40, I am at the end of my rugby career. Not because I no longer have what it takes to be able to play rugby at a professional level, but because I have so much younger talent around me – talent that I am busy developing and coaching in my role as a player/coach. Although I explained it like this to my coach, he told me that at this stage I still have too much to give to rugby and that I should not think about retiring just yet. It gave me a new perspective and I realised that I started to doubt myself because I was measuring myself against other (much younger) players. I had to realise that I can still make a significant contribution on the field, as a player and as a role model for the younger players. I am grateful that my coach still believes in me, even though I have had moments where I have doubted myself.*

My biggest achievement is… *the 100-game milestone I reached in my professional career for my various clubs, despite not getting any recognition for my rugby at school level. I never tasted the privilege of playing in a Craven week or being selected for the SA Schools team. The day when the call came from Nick Mallet that they needed a prop at Western Province, I grabbed the opportunity with both hands. Today I am proud to say that I have reached the 100-game milestone for the WP (120 games), Stormers (over 140 games), and Dragons in Wales (143 games).*

The Bible verse that carries me...

I have two verses that I always remind myself of, especially when I am going through a tough time:

Philippians 4:13,
"I can do all things through Christ who strengthens me"

Psalm 121:1-2 (NKJV),
"I will lift up my eyes to the hills—From whence comes my help? My help comes from the Lord, who made heaven and earth."

Lara, Madelein, Reuben, Divan, and Brok

MY STORY
Brok Harris

Brok remembers his encounter with God very clearly. It was 2008; a difficult year for him because he suffered two major injuries within the space of ten months. So much hard work went into the pre-season training and in an instant, he found himself on the sidelines. The first incident took place during a warmup match when a player fell on Brok's ankle and tore his syndesmosis ligament. After five months of convalescence and rehabilitation, as well as three matches thereafter in which he was able to play, he was back on the training field with the team every week. It was during one of the regular training sessions that he tore the ligament in his other ankle. Brok was, once again, on the sidelines and he could not participate in his beloved sport for another five months. It was during this dark season, filled with questions, that a friend invited him to church. That morning service would change Brok's whole life, because during the service he felt as if the pastor was talking directly to him. Brok cannot really recall what the sermon was about, but he remembers how he hobbled to the front on his crutches in response to the invitation for prayer... "There was a pressure and a burning within my heart; I knew that it was the Lord who came to meet me in that dark, wounded place where I found myself at that stage." After that encounter with God, Brok played 55 games in a row ... injury free.

In South Africa it is "easy" to be a Christian – many of the people you encounter are Christians. Whether it is at the church, in your neighbourhood, at work, school, or in a shop, everyone lives with similar principles.

It was precisely during a major change in their life that Brok realised how comfortable he was in his circumstances, and it was during the Harris family's season in Wales that he experienced one of the biggest times of pruning in his life.

In a foreign country, outside his comfort zone, where people do not know who God is, this was a time that tested his faith to the limit. *"I believe it was a way in which the Lord used me to share His goodness and grace with others and to sow seeds of faith where He needed them to be sown."* There was a handful of South Africans at the club who always prayed together before and after a match. The Welsh guys always found that very strange, asking questions about the reason for this custom. *"We enjoyed a beer with the team after the rugby match – as was customary back home. They wanted to know how we could call ourselves Christians, but still drink alcohol. For them this was contrary to Christianity, and they insinuated that we were 'fake'."* At times this turned into heated debates ... but Brok and the other South Africans all stood firm in their faith. Today he is grateful to be back in a community where there are shared values and principles of faith. *"I am grateful for the testing that I experienced, because I believe you grow as soon as you move out of your comfort zone."* Brok had to show in word and deed what it really means to be a Christian and today he knows that God used him to preach the Word to people who are not in the privileged position where they learn about God and interact with Him daily.

Not only was the difference in faith a challenge for Brok, but the uncertainty about a future in rugby gnawed at him. As the main breadwinner in a foreign country, he had to trust God for guidance in his career choices. Contract negotiations are always a stressful time. To Brok, one of the specific negotiations felt like a storm that just would not subside. *"The club that I played for was in financial and administrative trouble and therefore did not want to sign and finalise new contracts."* Instead of being honest about the situation, they tried to sidestep any contract negotiations with Brok. New promises were made each time – which he accepted because they sounded very promising, but the negotiations dragged on for five months. In the end they made an offer that was unfair. Financially it could not carry his family. In an instant, they had nowhere to go. Questions, uncertainty, and worries were their focus for a while, with no positive outcome. They decided to return to South Africa – without any specific plan in place. The uncertainty gnawed at Brok and Madelein, but they continued to believe and pray that the Lord had bigger plans for them. Today his wife is at the helm of her own successful business and Brok is back with the Stormers where they won the first URC title. *"We learnt that God determines our paths long in advance – we just had to realise that everything happens in His time, not ours. We simply had to trust that we were in God's hands and that He had already provided long in advance. And He did – with much more than we ever asked or hoped for!"*

When Brok looks back on the past few years, his heart is full of gratitude, because all the good gifts are only through the grace of God. *"I live in gratitude to God – grateful for a wonderful wife, three healthy children, a roof over my head, food on the table, and a talent to play rugby. I am grateful for an incredible rugby career full of milestones – highs and lows – to be able to travel and see the world, to meet influential people, and to share my love for the game with others in my role as a coach."* Since their return from Wales, and especially after the COVID lockdown, it has been so pleasant for Brok and his family to join a church again and praise the Lord in their mother tongue: "The children enjoy going to church on Sundays. They enjoy singing Sunday school songs and they are building a relationship with God, in their mother tongue..."

Quality time has taken on a new meaning for him: Time with his loved ones – parents, friends, family, wife, and children – is not a right, it is an absolute privilege. It is something that can easily be taken for granted – a hug here, a visit there, jumping on a plane to visit his parents or just to drop the kids off at school. The last greeting or first hello happened without him really realising its true value. Before the pandemic, Brok was often away from home; whether it was to play rugby or to watch a Springbok match somewhere in Europe. However, the restrictions forced him to stop; literally and figuratively. With a shoulder surgery the day before the lockdown was announced, he had no choice but to be one hundred percent present. *"I was only with my family, and it was an incredible time together."* Although the pandemic brought so much sadness to a multitude of people, for Brok it was a time with his family that he would not trade for anything. Today, he still makes time to be truly present in anyone's company; whether it is with supporters at a rugby match, the cleaners, parents, or teachers at his children's school, his family and friends, or people he runs into or helps at the shops...

> **"For the past couple of years, the word and message for me from God's heart has been to show tolerance towards my fellow man – you never know what someone else has had to go through in the last few years."**

"Something as small as a smile or a quick chat can mean a lot to someone like that, provided it comes from your heart and you are really present in that moment."

What do you think is the biggest obstacle in men's lives?

Our egos. I feel men tend to link their success to what boosts their egos – a faster, bigger, and more expensive car; a bigger house; nicer furniture; more money; more prestige in the community, and so on. Although financial success can bring you all these things, it is not going to make you a better, happier, or more "manly" man.

If men can come to the realisation that success is also determined by things that money cannot buy – such as your relationships with your wife and children, in friendships that endure the ups and downs of life, respect towards your parents (and parents-in-law), a healthy relationship with the Lord, and care for your fellow man – then, I believe men will experience fewer obstacles in their lives.

How would you like to be remembered?

I would like to be remembered as someone who did not hesitate to do what he professed. I want to be able to look back and say I led by example. I never did things to get recognition, but rather to show others that you can achieve anything, if you are willing to put in the hard work.

Your message to South Africa

Live in tolerance and give everyone a place in the sun. It is so easy to fall into the rat race for material things and to measure yourself in the process by comparing your life to other people's lives and possessions. One is so quick to become jealous of another's success that it makes you blind to what the Lord has already sent your way.

A healthy body and mind begin with inner peace and acceptance of who and what you are, what you have achieved, where your shortcomings lie, and where you are going. Only then will you be able to see the goodness in others and realise that there is a place in the sun for everyone. This will make the world a better place.

Brok Harris
Exclusive interview
Scan the code to watch

Adele Broodryk

Adele Broodryk, a marathon and ultramarathon athlete, is part of the Nedbank running team. This star from Carletonville, born on the 20th of September 1990, was the second South African woman over the finish line at the Comrades marathon in Durban on the 11th of June 2023. Her time over 87.7 km was 5:56:26 (30 minutes faster than her previous Comrades time). She is one of four women in Comrades history to break the six-hour mark. This mother of two was also the first South African woman to cross the finish line when she ran her first Comrades in 2022. She was just behind the Russian winner, Aleksandra Morozova, who had a winning time of 06:17:47, and the second placed Dominika Stelmach from Poland, who ran a time of 06:25:08.

This 2023 Comrades triumph was the highlight of a fantastic year for Adele. Among other things, she also won the Om Die Dam Ultra Marathon over 50 km. Her sixth position at the Two Oceans Marathon and a personal best of 34:48 at the Spar Women's Challenge over 10 km in Durban, were all highlights for her.

Doctor Adele has been a senior lecturer at the School of Human Movement Sciences at the Faculty of Health Sciences of the North-West University since 2013. She has a research interest in recovery, sport physiology, and psychology, as well as behavioural endocrinology. She has a PhD in human movement sciences, an MA in sports science, a BAHons in sports science, as well as a BA in human movement sciences and psychology.

My love for sport began... *in grade one. It was our primary school's sports day. I sprinted as fast as I could, but came second ... I was very disappointed. A father of one of my classmates approached my mother and asked if she would be interested in me being part of his training group, together with his son. The following year I came first at the school sport's day. That is where the running bug really bit – after that, my aim was to improve every consecutive year. However, it did not come easily; I was only able to make a provincial team in my matric year. I gave my best and trained hard for 11 years until I reached my ultimate goal – to go to the SA championship. I was finally able to achieve this in my matric year in the 400 m hurdles event. During my first year at university, I lost my love for running a little bit and merely stayed active. I wanted to focus on my academics. At the end of my honours year, I started running again and the following year I took up cross country. This is where my love for the longer distances took hold. In 2015, I completed my first half marathon at the Two Oceans race. I placed 100th and there I realised I had a talent for the longer distances. I set a goal for the following year and finished 12th. This was the beginning of my new running chapter.*

If I was not a sports star, I would... *have liked to become a physiotherapist to help athletes with their injuries. However, my mother was like a hen with her chicks and the North-West University of Potchefstroom was where I would study (only 50 km from my hometown), but the university did not offer physiotherapy as an option. I then decided to study the closest discipline to physiotherapy – biokinetics. However, as the Lord planned it, I did not make it to the final interviews for biokinetics, but succeeded to do so for sports science. This is truly where my passion lies. Where I initially wanted to help athletes recover from injuries, I can now help them reach their full potential and optimise their performance.*

I am incredibly grateful for... *my health. After a hard three years where so many of us lost our loved ones due to COVID, I can definitely say that I am grateful for good health – my own, but especially for those close to me. I am grateful for my healthy children and for the rest of my extended family. My children have the privilege of knowing their great-grandmother and great-grandfather, as well as six grandmothers and grandfathers – something I never had.*

Along with good health, I am so grateful for my mother. She was always the steadfast stabilising factor in our lives. She sacrificed herself and her time for us; every afternoon driving us to our school and extracurricular activities; in the evenings knitting away while we participated in cultural activities. She sewed, baked cookies, and started all kinds of entrepreneurial activities in order to provide everything that we needed. Somehow, she just made the finances stretch.

If I could edit my life, I would... *focus more on my sport at an earlier age. I would have liked to enjoy it more too! At school, I was way too serious. If I fell out in the heats, it was traumatic, and my mother had to pick up the pieces. A week later, I would start training again for the following year. However, at university – when athletics actually mattered – I wanted to focus on academics only.*

I would also have made better relationship choices and would have managed existing relationships better. The "normal" that I was exposed to was not healthy nor Christian at all. A broken household leads to a broken heart. The picture I had of relationships and of a father was broken, but it was my "normal". I looked for the same in my relationships. As a student I was extremely unhappy in a long relationship (and I was even engaged), but I did not know how to get out of it. In my fourth year, I met a spiritual mentor and, for the first time, realised and understood what the true extent of forgiveness was. This helped me to forgive myself, my ex-boyfriend, and my father. I was able to free myself from the unhealthy relationship and I met my husband a few months later.

One of the biggest lessons I learnt this year... *family is the most important thing. No matter what you go through, they are the ones who are always there for you through the good and the bad times.*

My greatest achievement is... *definitely my debut Comrades Marathon. I grew up in a home where we sat in front of the television, huddled under our blankets, watching the Comrades every year. It was there that the dream to one day run the Comrades began. The* plan was to finish my first Comrades, and then in the following ones to attempt to finish in the top twenty, then the top ten, top five, top three, and finally – to win it. So, being able to achieve an overall third place on my debut Comrades Marathon was a standout moment in my life and a great achievement for me. A second outstanding sporting moment was my win during the Om Die Dam Ultra Marathon – not so much because of the win, but because I was only a few seconds off the record. Why was this a standout moment for me? Because I had done my own conditioning and worked out my own training programme. It was a standout moment for me because I am a "practice what you preach" type of person. What I teach my students, I apply in my own life – and it worked!

The Bible verse that carries me...
it is probably a cliché, but for me the verse is,

Philippians 4:13,
"I can do all things through Christ who strengthens me"
This is a verse that has carried me over
the past few years. My mother always said,
"the more you do, the more you can do."

The first family photo after COVID. "The pandemic taught us that family comes first."

MY STORY
Adele Broodryk

It was the clanging of pots that greeted Adele when she walked into the house after her training sessions. Her mother was always busy with some or other entrepreneurial endeavour, as Adele often needed a new pair of sports shoes or was going on a camp. Adele's mother is her biggest fan and did everything to support her daughter's dream. However, life dealt her a few hard blows: her mother (Adele's grandmother) died when she was still young, her father was a very stern policeman. As she grew up, she experienced an unhappy marriage, was diagnosed with rheumatoid arthritis early in her life, and she also suffers from an eye defect. However, Adele's mother still got up every morning and started the day with the promise that one day her daughter would be a huge success.

Adele met the Lord at a young age. It was His role as a steadfast rock, together with her mother's guidance, that served as Adele's only sign posts, because she grew up with an absent father. *"My father was not very present in my years growing up; he was quite a stern, angry man. My image of a dad and husband was therefore completely distorted."* It was also this experience that, at a later stage in her life, caused Adele to end up in a merry-go-round of poor relationship choices. The indecision about crumbling, toxic relationships and feelings of guilt eventually drove a wedge between her and God.

> **"I resisted God a lot, because my image of a father was so distorted. I thought: If an earthly father and husband treats his family like this – his own flesh and blood – and God allows it, how will He, who is a heavenly Father, accept me? I wanted to be independent; not having to rely on a husband or father at all."**

However, God had a different plan for Adele. With the influence of role models and the soft, gentle voice of a genuine Father, God showed her a different picture; a promise of what a Christian relationship could look like and the possibility of what she could one day experience herself. *"It was only after I accepted the full picture of the cross and God's grace that I was able to free myself from the sword that I held over my own head. I have come to realise that God does not hold grudges, He does not keep a record of evil and does not have a list of all my transgressions. He is ready to wrap me in love, comfort, and acceptance every day, regardless of what I have done."*

It was in her fourth year as a student at North-West University that Adele met her future husband and father of her two children. The life she had known up to that point changed completely. *"Before you get married or have children, your time is your own. You can do whatever you want with it. When we got married, all of a sudden, I had to share my time – which was still fantastic. When our two busy little ones arrived, I had to juggle all the balls as a wife, mother, friend, daughter, lecturer, researcher, and athlete."*

During these years of adjustment, Adele's character was tested as the question of her identity constantly resurfaced. *"My identity was shaped by and trapped in my running. It determined my happiness on a daily basis. If the training or competition went well, I was a happy person."* In 2014 and 2015, Adele became obsessed with the idea of becoming a top long-distance athlete. She trained non-stop to improve herself and pushed herself to the limit ... until the end of 2015, when she started suffering from chronic pain in her foot, but she still clung to the dream.

It was during the early months of 2016 that she consulted a podiatrist. After three cortisone sessions under anaesthesia over a period of ten weeks, she still had no relief from the pain; they had to consider surgery. A huge storm raged. The initial prognosis was that she would be able to run again in eight weeks' time. Alas, she suffered excruciating pain every day for eight weeks. She had to keep her foot in blocks of ice or elevated. *"As soon as my foot dangled or was out of the ice, it turned blood red and the burning sensation would begin. My husband and I had planned an overseas trip for six weeks after the operation, but we soon realised that there was something seriously wrong with my foot – we cut our trip short and flew back home."* After it was concluded that something may have bitten Adele before the initial operation, with the result that the recovery process was delayed causing the wound to become septic, a second operation followed.

"I spent ten days in the hospital during which time the doctors tried to save my foot. The burning sensation and redness was still there every day. I wanted to give up and have my foot amputated just to find relief from the relentless pain."

Questions like "Why me?" and "Why now?" milled through her head. It was during this time that Adele rediscovered God and her dependence on Him. *"I realised that the 'independent' woman that I wanted to be would not survive this trial without God."*

It was during the recovery period in the hospital that her questions changed to: "But why not me?"

Adele found her identity in God and placed her happiness at His feet. From then on, athletics and running were no longer her sources of happiness, but a way of glorifying God. *"Every step I take is a privilege. Should I lose the joy of my running, another* winter season will follow where I will have to stop, do introspection, and allow Him to prune me."

Today she runs with a different mindset. Her favourite music that she listens to during training is Jake Hamilton, a Christian pop singer. Her jogging sessions are her time with God where she can unload her burdens on Him and wait for His voice. *"I know I can give my best in every aspect of my life because God carries me and enables me to do so. I firmly believe that God will not give me a challenge that I cannot overcome. I will always be greater than the challenge, I just have to believe and trust that I am capable of it, because God is my source of strength."*

"As for me and my house, we will serve the Lord" is written over the Broodryks' life, because this is the principle they live by and the way they raise their children.

"In good times or bad times, I am first and foremost a child of God; then I am a wife for my husband and a mother to my children. Running is a hobby and that is how it should be."

Back in the hospital after eight weeks of severe pain

A highlight moment: First South African woman and third overall during the 2022 Comrades marathon

What do you think is the biggest obstacle in the lives of women?

To juggle all the balls – to keep them in the air and set time aside for yourself. As moms, 99% of the time we put our family, as well as our work, before ourselves. We sacrifice an exercise session because our conscience bothers us: "Who will cook, pack lunch boxes, or clean?" There are many more examples of such erroneous thinking ... Yes, this is normal, and it happens to me too, but if we do not decide to set time aside for ourselves, no one else will. In the end, that "me time" makes you a better mother, wife, and colleague.

How would you like to be remembered?

I would like to be remembered as a mom who continued to live, continued to dream, and strove to be the best version of myself. As the saying goes: "A healthy body houses a healthy mind." Through my participation in sport, I know that I am a better mother for my children, wife for my husband, employee, and child of God. My dream is to sow hope for moms out there; that every one of them will also continue to live and to dream.

Both grandmothers met Ansu-May just before lockdown started

"We are privileged that our children know their great-grandmother and great-grandfather and have a total of six grandmothers and grandfathers."

Your message to South Africa

Keep dreaming and working towards your dream. Whether it is running the Comrades, riding a Cape Epic, or even just going on a dream holiday. Set goals for yourself leading up to the dream and for the outcome that you want to achieve, then set the process goals – the smaller building blocks that will enable you to make the dream come true. A heart without a dream is a heart without a beat, without hope, and without expectation.

Adele Broodryk
Exclusive interview
Scan the code to watch

Arnold Geerdts

Arnold Geerdts, born on the 31st of March 1961, is a professional media personality. With years of experience in front of the cameras, behind the microphone, and as a journalist, this son of Springs, Gauteng, is the gold of the City of Gold. He is lauded for his comprehensive knowledge of sports, but is also recognised as a storyteller, prestigious master of ceremonies, corporate trainer, voice artist, producer, speaker, and entertainer with great empathy for his fellow man. The former pupil of Hoër Seunskool Hugenote in Springs first delivered the *Springs Advertiser* as a schoolboy, before he began writing for the newspaper as a sports journalist in 1983. From there his path led to higher heights. As a bilingual sports guru Arnold was afforded the opportunity to become a well-known television anchor and radio presenter. He made his debut in broadcasting in 1984 on the airwaves for Radio 5 and Springbok Radio. In the same year, he made his television debut as a television sports news anchor during the *News at Eight* – in both English and Afrikaans. Arnold is a two-time winner of the prestigious SAB Sports Journalist of the Year Merit Award. His list of broadcasting highlights includes his Comrades Marathon broadcasts, the Barcelona Olympics, the Australian cricket tour of 1993/1994, more than 100 international rugby matches, 550 Super Rugby matches, and more than 75 golf majors. He was SuperSport's studio anchor for six Tour de France races and is a senior correspondent for the news channel, SuperSport Blitz. Arnold is a keen golfer, with a handicap of 12, and has also run more than 160 marathons and ultramarathons. The eleven-time Comrades athlete's personal best time for a marathon (42.2 km) is 2 hours and 29 minutes, which places him among the top 100 in South Africa.

His journalistic interviews include living legends such as Gary Player, Lance Armstrong, Jack Nicklaus, as well as Olympic gold medallists Kelly Holmes and Linford Christie. Prominent leaders and celebrities who have spoken into his microphone include the late President Nelson Mandela; former presidents F.W. de Klerk and Thabo Mbeki; actors Arnold Schwarzenegger and Morgan Freeman; entrepreneur Richard Branson; singer Chris Rea; as well as cricket heroes such as Richie Benaud, Sir Don Bradman, Sunil Gavaskar, and Shane Warne.

My love for sport began... *I have no idea where it came from, honestly. I was the only one in my immediate family who loved sports, played them, and eventually made it my career. From a young age I played rugby in the backyard and imitated Gerhard Viviers with his sports commentary ... When I was five years old I told my mother that one day, when I read the news on the radio, I would not make any mistakes!*

If I was not a sports star, I would... *without a doubt be a preacher. It was either a reverend or sportswriter and announcer. As it turns out, I now do both. God has hidden plans for all of us, not so?*

I am incredibly grateful for... *I recently wrote in my little black book, "I give thanks for my wife, my children, my life, and my health; thank you for my longing to learn more and be better and for my inner search for God. Without each one of these wonderful things, my life would not have meaning at all."*

If I could edit my life, I would... *That thought has crossed my mind so many times and I think I know now: I would change NOTHING, because I am the sum total of all the things that have happened in my life. I do not think that things happen to us, they happen for us and so, all these things are necessary to transform us.*

I was once on a beach in Katakolon in Greece – the whole beach was full of these golf ball-sized stones, all of them almost perfectly round. They had been tumbled, knocked, rolled, and turned by the ocean. This is what happens to us too: As life sands us down, the sharp edges become smooth, and we are (hopefully) nicely "rounded off".

One of the biggest lessons I learnt this year... *was that there is a long-lasting (this sounds like a toothpaste commercial) plan for our lives. My spiritual father, Dawie Spies, and I recently talked about exactly this – about the "legacy" that we can start. It might really only become apparent after three, four, or five generations. And it is not us; it is our obedience that must fit into Abba Father's plan, like Moses, King David, Rahab, or Ruth. They ended up being part of Jesus Christ's bloodline. Two of them were murderers, one a prostitute, and the others were supremely loyal. If we realise that it is all in God's plan, then there is finally a legacy, and we will probably never see it here on earth. That is okay with me!*

My greatest achievement is... *yet to come! It will be the day I stand before God the Father.*

The Bible verse that gets me...

Exodus 33:14,
"And He said, 'My Presence will go with you
and I will give you rest.'"

Lily, Kinah, Lileah, and Shiloh: "The apple of my eye"

MY STORY
Arnold Geerdts

In 1 Chronicles 21, King David's ego gets the better of him. The Bible says, *"Now satan stood up against Israel, and moved David to number Israel. So David said to Joab and to the leaders of the people, 'Go, number Israel from Beersheba to Dan, and bring the number of them to me that I may know it.' And Joab answered, 'May the Lord make His people a hundred times more than they are. But, my lord the king, are they not all my lord's servants? Why then does my lord require this thing? Why should he be a cause of guilt in Israel?'"* David is advised not to do this, but he still does as he pleases. More than 70 000 of his men had to die as a result.

Arnold Geerdts refers to this biblical wisdom when he talks about his life. *"If we want to do things in and out of our own flesh, it leads to trouble. We must pray for wisdom to be able to discern this, and for obedience to hear it, listen to it, and respond in the right manner."*

This is precisely where the problem comes in.

> **As children of the Lord we hear, but do not always obey and then we miss His will (and sometimes bruise ourselves in the process).**

Thanks to God's grace, these lessons build character in us, and we become those with inspiring testimonies, not just those with impressive lives.

Arnold knows all about bumping your head – his own as well as the butting of heads with those around him. He is well known in South Africa, but the prestige goes hand in hand with great responsibility and being diplomatic. Yet he never hesitates to admit that his faith is his first priority. *"It was not always easy for me, especially not in the secular media world. I am sure that my Christianity cost me a long-term position. On the other hand, I was also once asked to say grace at a corporate lunch table. This was after working for years at a top car company and facilitating their classes. They asked me to pray because they could hear that I was a Christian and they respected that. To me, that was wonderful!"*

He is recognised and celebrated as one of SuperSport's (an international sports brand and broadcaster) most established presenters. Back in the day, they did not use a script or an autocue (an electronic device that shows the words for the television presenter to read). It was simply his own fluent ad libbing skills, vast knowledge, and passion for sports that he could rely on to captivate viewers. Though, in his own life he sometimes "stumbled over his words" and landed on his knees. *"Man, I have experienced more storms in my life than a veteran ship captain around the Wild Coast has ever experienced. I have two painful divorces to my name. I disappointed two boys. There are people that I have hurt and behaviours that I am not proud of. During a home invasion almost twenty years ago, Lily and I were held up in our own house. In the middle of that ordeal, I asked the Father, 'What is really going on here?' As if He was standing next to the bed, where we lay tied up, He said to me: 'If you die here tonight, you will come to Me. So, what are you worried about?'"*

This personal encounter brought about other insights in Arnold's life and strengthened his relationship with God. The wonder of God's grace is that we can move on, repent, ask for forgiveness, receive it, and then forgive ourselves. *"It is one of the gifts that we may not always fully apply – to forgive ourselves. It frees you from feelings of guilt. As my dear friend and brother in Christ, Joe Niemand, wrote in one of his songs: 'Like a man who drowns in water up to his waist,' guilt is just the same!"*

As a wordsmith, Arnold had to step away after years in front of the camera and get used to a new season, but when a talent is also a vocation, it is much more difficult to just lay it aside. However, the doors closed and stayed closed, and Arnold had to make peace with that. *"It took me almost a year to come to terms with the fact that this was just one part of my life and that there is so much more to me than just one thing. Men are so prone to seeing themselves as their work; as a doctor, professor, television presenter, whatever! It is not you; it is just one of the parts of who you are, but we get so lost in those things that we do not always consider the other parts of our life as equally important. Our lives are like pies, there are many parts that must be divided equally; the dish that it is baked in is the grace, strength, and the miracle of God."*

Today, Arnold's voice still resonates in the ears of radio listeners daily. He takes his place on the yellow sofa in a breakfast programme on KykNET's sports insert every week, when he gives an overview of the weekend's sport. As a veteran, he now lives his grandfather's key to success and likes to pass it on to young people. The advice: Keep your mouth shut and let people think you are stupid instead of opening it and confirming it! Arnold knows that there is nothing wrong with listening instead. *"In her book, 'Time to Think', Nancy Kline writes that most people listen to others with only one thought in mind: to already have an answer ready when the other person stops talking. It is good advice to just keep quiet and really listen."*

Arnold's voice is distinctive, his sports knowledge reliable, and his character is that of a child of God who is sure of one thing in life – God's love and grace.

"The love of my life and my lifesaver, Lily"

"One of my favourite photos of my girls"

"People are going to hurt, judge, and disappoint us.
We are going to do the same to others and ourselves.
The 'COVIDs' of life are going to come, whether it is a physical
virus or a spiritual one. We are going to be tested."

For this enthusiastic sports fan, sport is as much a part of his life as breathing is, but today Arnold knows that he is not the voice, only the messenger.

What do you think is the biggest obstacle in men's lives?

To trust and follow our own heads. In 1 John 5 we are told to ask for wisdom and God will give it ... without condemnation. Making that request requires wisdom. We must realise this! We fight against it. We often do not even want to ask for directions.

Just ask Him, as simple as that.

How would you like to be remembered?

I would like to be remembered as someone who did not ask at the end, "I wonder what if?"

Your message to South Africa

Do not lose heart. Miracles happen around us daily. Be on the lookout for them. Pray that they can become a reality and be a part of it. Trust in Him and live accordingly. And just by the way, I am also talking to myself here.

Jesus said we will do greater things than He did. It can be like that. It just takes faith. Believe without ceasing!

Arnold Geerdts
Exclusive interview
Scan the code to watch
◀◀◀

Muller du Plessis

Hillegard Muller du Plessis, born on the 25th of June 1999, is a South African rugby player who represents the Sharks in the United Rugby Championship and the Currie Cup series. He is a former sevens rugby player for the Blitzboks. This former resident of Bethlehem in the Free State's love for rugby blossomed early in his life. He caught the eye of rugby experts as a primary school learner in Reitz, and represented the local provincial team, the Griffons, at u12 level. After relocating to the Western Cape, he represented the Western Province in 2012 at the u13 Craven Week tournament. The former Paarl High School learner has worn the white and blue striped jersey for several years and has played in a number of rugby tournaments including in the u16 Grant Khomo Week (2015), the South African Rugby Union's High-Performance Programme (2016), the u18 Craven Week tournament (2016), and South African Schools group for the u19 International Series. In 2017, Muller led Paarl Gymnasium's first team and was again included in the Craven Week team and South African Schools group for 2017. He signed a contract with the Sharks in Durban and joined the SAS Rugby Sevens Academy in Stellenbosch. Muller managed to maintain a good balance between fifteen-man rugby and sevens rugby. He was part of the South African team for the u20 World Rugby Championship in France (2018) and donned the green and gold of the Blitzbok academy group when he participated in two events in the 2018 Sudamérica Sevens, with victories in Uruguay and Chile. Shortly after joining rugby sevens, Muller made his debut for the senior Blitzbok team at the 2018 USA Sevens tournament. Muller has the privilege of being part of the Blitzboks team that won two World Rugby Sevens titles as well as a gold medal at the Commonwealth Games in 2022 in Birmingham.

My love for sports began... *as a little boy of five years old, playing with my friends on our family farm in Bethlehem. The love of sport is in our blood. My father was a Transvaal fullback, and the strength and conditioning coach for the Lions. My older brother, JP, also played rugby. I wanted to emulate JP and therefore joined in when my father worked out an exercise programme for my brother. During the holidays we would get up early and train, play touch rugby with the children on the farm every afternoon, and spend hours in the "gym". I loved horse riding and enjoyed the freedom and space on the farm. I also knew from a young age that there is a greater purpose behind playing rugby; that rugby would indeed be part of my vocation, but that God would use it for a greater purpose to honour His Name.*

If I was not a sports star, I would... *go into the ministry. I am still young, and I already know where my heart is outside of rugby. I love children very much and I know that I will be involved in children's ministry in the future.*

I am incredibly grateful for... *my family, as well as my grandpa and grandma. We are a normal family that has had to overcome challenges, but we are a unique, close-knit family who loves the Lord very much and puts Him first in everything. My father, Charl, not only asked us what we wanted to be one day, he also stepped in and helped us to get there. He was involved in everything in our lives – from working out exercise programmes to taking us fishing and teaching us about the outdoors. My mother, Anneline, is a phenomenal woman! I have a very close bond with her. I can ask her for advice or to pray for me, anytime. She is the spiritual support. My grandfather, Danie, was my best friend. He taught me about the Lord and the Holy Spirit, and my grandmother, Hettie, is a precious woman – my second mother. I am also grateful to the Lord who guides me daily; I thank Him for the mentors around me on the rugby field who speak into my life.*

If I could edit my life, I would... *not change anything. I would just have more joy and happiness in every season because I know God is in control.*

One of the biggest lessons I learnt this year... *we can make our own plans, but God is the One who lays out the way for us, and we must keep our spirit in tune with Him so that He can be the light to the future.*

My biggest achievement is... *to be in the u20 Springbok team, as well as being able to participate in the World Cup Sevens and Commonwealth Games.*

The Bible verse that carries me...

Philippians 4:13,
"I can do all things through Christ who strengthens me."

"My whole life in two photos; mother, grandmother, grandfather, and father"

MY STORY
Muller du Plessis

Muller du Plessis mastered Sesotho growing up on a farm in the Free State. The words over his life are:

Molimo oa rona, Ke tšōmo, monna, ntho e 'ngoe le e 'ngoe in life ba ka. In other words, "Our God, He is the legend, the Man, everything in my life!"

Muller would realise from an early age that God is real, that He does not break His promises, and that He has a definite plan for Muller's life. This included rugby, but Muller also knew that rugby would not be the main focus. On the contrary, he knew that God would only use the game and the talent He had entrusted to him for His glory. He would place Muller in places where no preacher could go and where he could shine God's light. Muller just had to be faithful, work hard, and trust in the Lord.

His preparation for a professional rugby career began at the age of five. This Blitzbok did not realise it at the time because he was just imitating his 13-year-old brother, JP, who had been training with their father, Charl, since he was nine years old. Charl was a former Transvaal team fullback and Lions fitness coach. With the help of his brother-in-law, a doctor, he developed a training programme that used elastic bands to improve the player's functional strength (strength in movement), increased speed, fitness, and developed motor skills. The boys followed a strict training regime, even during school holidays at the coast. When other children slept in, the two Du Plessis brothers woke up early, trained hard with their father, and only after that were they allowed to go to the beach. In the afternoons, they would train again.

"Sometimes we did not have anything to hook the resistance bands onto and had to use a wheel or the tow bar of our car! Then we just cracked up laughing. It sounds a lot like boot camp and there were times when we wished we could 'just be normal' too, but I could not sit still in any case, and every session was fun and stimulating in a way."

Muller saw the passion for God, life, and people in his grandfather and family. He wanted to feel and model the same passion. Even if it took hard work, or if he had to do something different to obtain it, he was willing to sacrifice everything to hear God's voice and plan for his life. Muller did not hold back and even after hours of hard physical exercise; he would spend time in the Word of God on the bed next to his grandfather. Grandpa Danie was bedridden, a man after God's own heart who studied theology and knew and understood the work of the Holy Spirit.

Hours, months, and years of conversations about the Bible and who God is led to an experience with God on one afternoon.

It was a moment that would change Muller's life so much that he would never be able to turn away from God. "I was 16 years old, just a normal young man who sometimes played the fool but had opened myself to the Spirit of God. It was one afternoon, like many others; I was sitting with my grandfather on the bed. That day in a silent prayer he asked the Holy Spirit to come over me, fill my body and life, and never leave me. In that moment, everything went pitch black in front of me. Just like with Paul in the Bible – a man we had talked about a lot, someone who wrote two thirds of the New Testament – for a moment, I was struck blind. My body shook gently in response to the weighty power of the Holy Spirit and although I did not want to do anything to stop it, I could not have done anything to stop it anyway. God was present, His Spirit was with me, in me, and over me ... I knew 'something' had happened and I knew that I would never be the same again."

It would be the best experience of his life. A spiritual pointer to which he could refer, a watershed moment in his spiritual journey. The young Muller would still be a normal 16-year-old boy, but the Holy Spirit walked with him. He could have fun and enjoy life, but the responsibility was on his shoulders to put God first in everything. "I just wanted to grow in the Spirit. I remember how my grandfather always said that in the spirit, we were the same age ... and because I never wanted to disappoint God, every choice I made, everything I had to give up, was never a problem for me ... I want to please Him much more than any human being."

Muller's group of friends and the circle of influence on his life became smaller, because opposition to such a drastic choice of faith was inevitable. For many people, God and sport cannot be mentioned in the same breath. Many people questioned Muller's convictions, but he was on one path – it was forward with God. In God, for God.

"Jesus was on earth as the perfect human being – He experienced a lot of opposition. Not everybody liked Him, but that did not stop Him from doing the right thing. In the end, it is not about us and our lives and wishes. It is about God and His calling for us."

Muller bases his life on Philippians 4:13 and knows that he must function in an imperfect world. However, he serves a perfect God who guides him regarding the big decisions in his life: from injuries and standing on the side-lines for months, to career choices, dreams, and disappointments. He consults God in everything.

God has indeed entrusted Muller with a role as a sports person in South Africa. He trusts him with the prestige, but the price he pays is obedience to God. "It is a small price to pay, because I know God sees my future! I am full of shortcomings and have tried to do many things in my own strength, but then I realised – my talent is not mine and I am only here for God to use me as He sees fit. God is everything in my life and career. If I have to sustain an injury again tomorrow, I know that I can fall back on God. If I have to retire from rugby tomorrow, I will leave everything and follow God's purpose for my life. My 'purpose' is in God, and I want to be part of His Kingdom team. For now, I am committed to play sport, because that is what He entrusted to me, but rugby is just a platform to proclaim His Name..."

What do you think is the biggest obstacle in men's lives?

Pride. Men are too proud.

Pride keeps us from God. We must accept Him and surrender to His calling in our lives. I realise that every generation has grown up with expectations that a man must be strong and show no emotion, but I also realise that this can prevent you as a man from walking with God.

It is also important that we acknowledge God in our lives. We are not always good enough, but with Him in us, we are good enough for any task.

Finally, we must leave it up to Him to guide us in our career and decisions about our family. He knows our future.

How would you like to be remembered?

I would like to be remembered as a God-fearing man with the signs of the fruit of the Spirit in my actions and behaviour. A man who not only talked about God, but lived Jesus.

Your message to South Africa

Surrender yourself to Jesus and His Kingdom. Pursue His will for your life with all your heart and know Him as God. Go out to serve people and make a difference in the world. Make an impact with the talents that God has given you and radiate His light to everyone. Trust Him with all your heart.

Muller du Plessis
Exclusive interview
Scan the code to watch
◀◀◀

Anruné Weyers

Anruné Weyers, born on the 3rd of November 1992, is a South African three-time Paralympian. With an underdeveloped left forearm due to a birth defect, she competes in the T47 disability category. As a young 9-year-old, she first stepped onto an athletic track at the Northmead Primary School in Johannesburg. The 1.67 m tall athlete was as fast as lightning in the 100 m, 200 m, and 400 m. Her natural talent, perseverance, and hard work led to a string of silver and gold medals at the IPC Athletic World Championships from 2011-2019. Anruné represented South Africa in her first Paralympic Games in 2012 in London, winning two medals: silver in the 400 m and bronze in the 200 m. Later that year, these medals were stolen at an airport. Anruné's 2016 Rio Paralympic Games produced a brilliant performance with a silver medal in the 400 m. August 2019 paved the way for the start of a remarkable athletics year for Anruné with a gold medal in the 400 m, silver in the 200 m, and bronze in the 100 m at the 2019 World Para Athletics Championships in Dubai, and a new world record of 55.60 for the 400 m at the Flanders Cup in Huizingen, Belgium. The highlight of her career was when Anruné won a gold medal in the 400 m T47 category at her third Paralympic Games in Tokyo 2021, with a season's best time of 56.05.

Anruné is an entrepreneur and foundation phase teacher. She is married to Stefan Weyers and is the mother of their son, little Janz.

My love for sport began... *in grade 3. I attended a lovely school but was bullied from childhood because of my little hand and had to brace myself for children's mean comments. A friend invited me to go to athletics training with her. I did pretty well in cross country that season, and a love for running developed overnight. It was the freedom of running that made my heart beat faster, put a smile on my face, and helped me to accept my disability. During the December holidays, while other children were eating ice cream and playing, I wanted to train with my dad and grandpa to get even better and to stay fit for the athletic season in January. It was the patience of my coaches at school, together with the knowledge that God gave me this "being different" as a gift, that only made me more determined to excel. Running became a big part of my life and I had to unwrap and explore this "gift" year after year, season after season, to discover the purpose of my life.*

If I was not a sports star, I would... *have liked to be a flight attendant! I remember it so well; I was part of an athletic training camp for eighth graders. I loved running, but* never thought that I would have the ability to compete at the highest form of our sport – the Paralympic Games. We were a group of Christian kids with strong Christian values and that evening the facilitators asked us to write down our dreams ... I wrote that I would like to become a flight attendant!

I am incredibly grateful for... *my support system throughout my professional sports career; my husband, family, and friends; as well as my Paralympic family and coaches. I am also grateful to the Lord for His grace and favour in my life and for His guidance in every season of my life. Our pregnancy was a journey of faith and I believe that I am holding our boy, my next gold, in my arms.*

If I could edit my life, I would... *probably not change anything. Life happens, as it should – everything happens for a reason. Looking back, I am grateful for the growth experiences in my life and my sports career. I am the woman I am today because I am grateful for everything I have experienced. If I had to go back, I would not be so hard on myself. In primary school, I was sensitive about my hand. I overanalysed everything and brooded too much about things. It was exhausting! I would like to say to a younger Anruné, give it to the Lord. When your lot in life and profile look different, things are a little more challenging, but see the beauty in the situation and do not fret about the small things.*

One of the biggest lessons I learnt this year... *is to control what you can and leave the rest to the Lord. We were so privileged to welcome our little son in April 2023. Our path was very different, because we had to go for IVF (in vitro fertilisation) treatments. At that point we had been married for five years and Stefan, who is an incredibly peaceful person, walked this road with me. The privilege of falling back on the prayers and support of family and friends is special. I learnt: When you can be there for someone, be there – during the good times and the bad. You do not always have to give something to someone. Prayer, an ear to listen, and a message carry so much weight. It is important to show that you care and to reach out. I also realised that it is important to enjoy every season to the fullest! I encountered one of my biggest challenges when I was 27 weeks pregnant. I could no longer run because of the discomfort. Running is such a big part of*

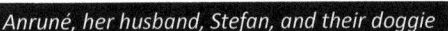
Anruné, her husband, Stefan, and their doggie

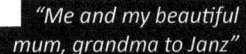
"Me and my beautiful mum, grandma to Janz"

my life, but God was teaching me that He would also meet and use me in other ways. I discovered a new appreciation for alternative ways of exercising. Going for walks with people who needed me became a priority, as well as being in nature and listening to music.

My biggest achievement is… the gold medal at the Paralympic Games in Tokyo 2021. I had an interesting road full of challenges to get there. It was the words of the song by Jeremy Camp, "Keep me in the moment", that kept me going. My desire was to run with God and when He waved His healing hand over me before the Games, that is exactly what I did. I brought glory to Him on the day of that race. He used me as a vehicle to prove His greatness – and I know it!

The Bible verse that carries me…

Jeremiah 29:11,
"For I know the thoughts that I think toward you,
says the Lord, thoughts of peace and not of evil,
to give you a future and a hope."

"My family welcoming me back home in 2021".

MY STORY
Anruné Weyers

At school, she was given the label, "the one-handed girl who runs".

Harsh words from children's mouths, but it was these harsh words that inspired the young Anruné to unwrap the "gift" God gave her, and to discover the reason behind the gift. She was different; she just had to figure out why.

The blood supply to her left hand was obstructed while she was developing in her mother's womb. Anruné must have been lying on her own little arm during the pregnancy and this resulted in her left forearm growing and developing slower. At birth, her parents and the nursing staff were dumbfounded by the deformed, shrivelled left hand, as there was no sign of it on the ultrasound scans. *"My grandfather immediately told my mother, 'This child is going to bring a lot of happiness and joy into your life.'"* From that moment on it was decided that Anruné would not be treated any different from other children. However, sometimes plans had to be improvised when she wanted to do something like skipping, where a second hand was a necessity, but otherwise she was treated just like any other little girl – with all its ups and downs.

And there was a lot of it – falling and getting up again!

It was 2009, Anruné was in her grade 11 year. Sitting on her bed in her room, she gave her heart to the Lord. She remembers it well because she wrote the date down in her Bible. *"Sometimes I wish that I had really made the Lord a part of my life earlier, because it might have made things a little easier. But He waits for your heart to be ready and then He receives you with open arms..."* Anruné lived a principled life, but the questions kept plaguing her – until one afternoon in November 2010. It was a day that she, for the umpteenth time, sat down at the Lord's feet with her Bible open on her lap. *"I asked God to explain my life's path to me ... I wanted to know why I was born without a left hand and why He made me that way. What was the purpose of it all? Why did He allow this?"* It was in the quiet of that intimate time with God where He met with her ... it was in that moment when Anruné truly made peace with her path and appearance. On that day, "Pietie" was born: Anruné's left hand would get an identity of its own! *"I finally had to embrace, accept, and celebrate the thought of being different. I realised that God made me different, precisely to change the world's perception of disability. I have the* profile of someone that people are not used to, and my goal is to, in cooperation with God, change people's mindsets and open their eyes to see the beauty and uniqueness of everything, in everyone."

Her personal experience with God would change Anruné's outlook forever. As part of the South African Paralympic team in London 2012, she also began to look at people differently and was amazed at the greatness of God! It was her fellow track brothers and sisters who would teach her the greatest life lessons. People without hands who ate with their feet; people with hearing impairments who could easily read lips and follow an entire conversation. Athletes without legs who would line up in starting blocks or swimmers who could complete a full pool length without arms or legs! *"It was one of the most special moments in my life! I was amazed at the courage in people and the honour they gave God for their talents and skills."*

It was a foregone conclusion. She would always bring glory to God – in the good races as well as the bad races, and even in times of injury, illness, and an unprecedented COVID-19 pandemic. The diagnosis on the 13th of July 2021 was disastrous. Not only was Anruné infected with the dreaded COVID-19 virus, barely seven months before the Olympic Games 2021, but the MRI scan for a torn hamstring also indicated a cyst and a problem with her spine. Anruné had no choice but to fight through the tears and despair. *"My coach, Dr Suzanne Ferreira, challenged me one day with the question: 'Where do you see God in the pain?' She sent me the song, 'Keep me in the moment'. I played the song, listening to the words for days on end in my house while sitting with a cortisone oxygen mask over my mouth … God gives breath, He gives life, and He gives strength … It is during that dark time that I got to know God in a different way."*

Anruné would come to know God as a physician, and the desire to run with Him and bring honour to the One who is so faithful in her life overwhelmed her heart. It was the words in an email to her team doctor and coach that finally silenced the noise within her.

"If it is God's will, I will run in Tokyo and then I will run with Him. Full stop. Tetelestai."

In the run up to the Tokyo Paralympic Games of 2021, she shunned all social media. Armed with God's promise of healing and the words of the song, "Keep me in the moment", she wrote the phrase, *"Me plus God running together"* on the Tokyo wall of remembrance. The world's picture of who she was supposed to be was finally erased … Anruné could just be. In the heat of the battle, she was calm. From the waiting room to the track, she quieted her mind and for the first time in her life. Anruné ran a perfect 400 m with a perfect pace … *"As if in a dream, at the 100 m mark, I said to myself, just trust Him…"*

The photo at the bottom of the page is of Anruné at the finish line ... on her knees with her hands in the air, her eyes closed, and her face to heaven. A photo that will live forever in the Paralympic archive. *"The gold medal around my neck was just a sign of what God can do when He intervenes in your life ... He ran with me. He is the gold in my life."*

What do you think is the biggest obstacle in women's lives?

We are incredibly strong, but sometimes we think that we can handle everything alone. We do not share our hurts and questions, and we compare ourselves to everyone around us. The biggest thing that we should do is appreciate one another for who each individual is and to tell each other that.

How would you like to be remembered?

I would like to be remembered as a spontaneous, caring person who always let God's light shine and saw the beauty in everything; as someone who easily forgave and forgot; the one who was a willing ear, who loved to pray together, and celebrated others' highlights with them!

Your message to South Africa

May we stand together more, sing together more, pray together more, and lift each other up in a positive attitude.

"Stronger together!"

Anruné Weyers
Exclusive interview
Scan the code to watch

James Murphy

James Murphy, born on the 30th of November 1995, is a rugby sevens player for the South African national team, better known as the Blitzboks. The former learner of Bishops Diocesan College showed his mettle in hockey, water polo, and athletics, among other things, before his love for rugby and rugby sevens blossomed at university. The 1.89 m tall James put on the green and gold and made his debut at the 2018 Hong Kong Sevens tournament where South Africa came third. However, they returned as the feared opponents and in the 2019 Singapore Sevens tournament they walked away with the laurels. With his motto for life written on his heart – "It is not about how hard you can hit; it is about how hard you can be hit and keep going on" – he formed part of the team that won the 2018/2019 HSBC Sevens World Series (The HSBC Sevens World Series is played in ten countries on five of the six continents. The United Arab Emirates, South Africa, Australia, New Zealand, the United States, Canada, Hong Kong, Singapore, France, and England each host one event). James was also part of the team that represented South Africa at the 2022 Commonwealth Games, as well as the World Cup Sevens tournament in Cape Town. Not only does a gold medal from these Commonwealth Games adorn his wall, but also a BCom degree in economics and management science with a double major in finance and logistics. His doctorate in financial planning (CFP) is on hold for now but will definitely be obtained.

My love for sport began... *at home, it is thanks to my parents and older sister. I was a terribly busy little boy and my teachers' comments on my report cards were always that I talked a lot. My father and mother knew that I needed to be kept busy and stimulated, which meant that they turned everything between my sister and I into a competition. My father would throw a ball and then encourage my sister, who is two years older than me, to run even faster to beat me to it. Just because I was the youngest did not mean everyone was going to stand back and just let me win. I had to work hard for it. These games led me to develop strong perseverance and to be extremely competitive. Looking back at my childhood, I am incredibly grateful for the way my parents raised us.*

If I was not a sports star, I would... *All my life, the corporate world has been an attractive end goal for me. However, as I matured as an individual through the various lessons of life, my passion has been developing more and more to be involved with people and to be a public speaker. Anyone who knows me will know that telling a story is one of my favourite things to do. I really love the finer details and I like to pay attention to the* smaller aspects of a story, to clearly outline the context. Acting as a public speaker is a great passion of mine and it is something I am very comfortable with. So, although a corporate family business is something I have always aspired to, the idea of being a presenter has occurred to me a few times.

I am incredibly grateful... *to my parents, for everything they sacrificed to support me in all I undertook as a schoolboy and young man. They had to overcome a lot of obstacles themselves, but it was never too much to ask. I am grateful for the sevens system and coaches who shape us as players on a daily basis to be better men in society and for our future wives and children. I am grateful to God for giving me the chance to be an instrument for Him, someone through whom He can work to show His goodness.*

If I could edit my life, I would... *I think the only change would be to discover God and His influence a little earlier in my life. Still, I would not want to change my journey because that is why my rediscovered faith is so strong.*

One of the biggest lessons I learnt this year... *is that we are only on this earth for a brief while. What you own (physically) means very little in the bigger picture. In heaven, your heart is your currency – whatever you have in this life is temporary.*

My biggest achievement is... *being part of a team that won a gold medal at the 2022 Commonwealth Games.*

The Bible verse that carries me...

Psalm 27:1,
"The Lord is my light and my salvation –
whom shall I fear? The Lord is the stronghold
of my life – of whom shall I be afraid?"

"My family, my everything!"

"It is not always about the trophy, but the character building that takes place."

MY STORY
James Murphy

James was one of the shortest and smallest boys in grade 8, the mirror image of his father – the two of them a strange exception, precisely because good rugby blood flowed in the veins of all the Murphys. All the men in James' family played as captains for provincial, national, or club rugby teams and left their mark in the rugby world of South Africa. As a small boy, James sat in the backyard of their house in Johannesburg and dreamt about his chances of being selected for the Springboks. Although the English rugby legend and fly half, Johnny Wilkinson, was his hero, it was the Springbok on the chest that called louder. However, James' stature was just too small for the contact sport. He was brilliant at water polo and swimming, as well as a sprinter of note and a superb player, but as for a rugby match, that would always remain on a friendly basis or as touch rugby on the beach.

It was a foregone conclusion and James made peace with the fact that a future in the green and gold could only be a possibility on a hockey field. It was this dream that inspired the young James Murphy enough to stay super fit and healthy. He was willing to work hard because he wanted to represent South Africa as a sportsman and go to the Olympics, until one fateful evening during a 100 m sprint with a thigh muscle tearing and the subsequent months-long healing period. James would not play in any tournament or main playoff games, which would ruin his chance of a hockey scholarship at Stellenbosch University. He would have to earn his merits with his academics and work even harder to impress Maties' hockey coaches.

However, one phone call changed the course of James' life irreversibly. Thanks to his speed, he was invited as a student of the Akademia residence to be a winger in the first year rugby tournament. James was focusing on hockey, performing with a rugby ball in hand was not at all on his radar. But as "Murphy's" Law would have it, it was his name that shone among the top fifty u19 rugby players' names!

It is when God intervenes that miracles happen, and that is exactly what James experienced. *"I was not even supposed to play a rugby match, let alone make the team. But it was the words of coach Ian Campbell-McGeachy – or as we called him, Mr Miyagi – one afternoon after a speed session, which rekindled the love for rugby in me. 'I am going to make you a Blitzbok,' he said. I was astounded, but everything inside me began to believe in the impossible."*

James with Impi Visser, Ryan Oosthuizen, and Chris Dry

Believe? Faith? A strange word and concept when one has not been exposed to it for such a long time. James grew up in a home with Christian values, but a combination of life in a hostel, an environment full of people who are outspoken unbelievers, and fellow students who mocked Christianity, made James think twice about talking about God openly. *"My friends were not bad people; they just did not know God."*

> **"I also only realised later in life that it is important to know something or someone before you give your opinion about them. So, when you want to say something about God, make sure you know Him fully before you give your opinion!"**

It was during a whirlwind of events in his first and second years as a student, and the fact that he was given the chance to play for the WP sevens team, when James experienced inner turmoil. He experienced rugby highlights and played against famous names such as Ronald Brown and Impi Visser, but tore his hamstring repeatedly at the most inopportune times – when teams had to be selected. He experienced how teammates get contracts and moved up in the rugby system to other leagues and levels. It raised so many questions for him and his future was unclear. *"It was in my second year at university that I stuck the marker in the ground and decided to take rugby seriously. That, or I would regret not doing it in ten years' time. I started exercising harder than ever before, eating better, and giving up alcohol and going out late at night with friends. My whole lifestyle started to revolve around rugby."*

It has been proven time and again that what you focus on becomes your reality. James had to choose what to focus on when he was unexpectedly confronted with his friends' opinion of him. He was faced with the choice of whether it would slow him down or spur him on. *"I will never forget. I was walking past a dorm room one night, when I overheard the conversation between three of my friends. The one guy's comment caught me off guard."*

> **"He said: 'I do not know why James is training so hard, he is never going to make it anyway.'"**

"The others agreed."

In terms of rugby, James had a responsibility to himself and no one else. No one expected anything spectacular from him, and so the words stuck. With the upcoming Assupol Sevens tournament, it was his moment to prove everyone wrong. The winning team would get the opportunity to play against the Blitzboks and thus give one the chance to be noticed.

Again, fate was against James. After the first match, with his ankle ligaments in tatters, James' dream evaporated once again. According to the X-rays and doctors' opinions, he would be out of action for another three to four months. *"'Really?' I thought. 'The world and everything in it are against me!' I gave up everything to focus on rugby and this was the end of my sad story."* James was going to simply give up that night and drown his disappointment in a bar in Stellenbosch, but God had a different plan for him. *"I was limping along in my moon boot on my way from one bar to another, when I passed the Stellenbosch town hall. I was opposite the big Mandela face when a black man in a dark suit and white tie approached me from behind. The unknown man stopped me and asked if he could pray for my ankle. There, in front of surprised passers-by, he knelt down, removed the moon boot, placed his hands on my ankle, and prayed a few words. I was not quite sure what was happening."*

> **"I did not know who the man was, what his intention was, or where he had come from. But he was kind and focused on praying for me, and I welcomed that."**

James jogged on to the rugby field six days later! His team would make it to the final and thus get the chance to play against the Blitzboks. That day Paul Delport, the Blitzbok coach, saw James Murphy's game and remembered his name.

"That recovery was a medically unexplainable miracle! To this day, I do not know who the man was and why he was there. All I know is that at that moment I felt the presence of God, Jesus, and the Holy Spirit, all in one, on me. I did not fully understand what was going on, but God planned a personal meeting with me in the streets of Stellenbosch and He showed up on the night when I least expected it!"

James' journey of faith started in a powerful and miraculous way. His grandmother had to give him some guidance and, together, they went to church to discover God's calling for James' life. That was only the beginning. *"Just because I met God, it did not mean that everything now went miraculously well. No, it took time and a lot of hard work. I was invited to join the sevens academy, but I was the only player who played without a contract. I played for the Academy team, but the green and gold was just a dream at the time. Sometimes the strangest things happened right before practice, things that were out of my control, for example squirrels gnawed through the wiring of my car overnight so that it would not start, or the gate just would not open for me to drive out. This sometimes led to me being late for practice sessions as well."* But God was in control and James was willing to be honest and sincere. He was ready to work hard and gave it his all.

Not only was his name mentioned in the corridors of SA Rugby, but James was also in negotiations with Scotland and America on the day when the call came from coach Marius Schoeman. There and then, James turned down the possible international opportunity and shifted his focus to South Africa. *"This is where I needed to be and when my head and heart aligned, the dream came true."*

James Murphy made his debut as a Blitzbok at the 2018 Hong Kong Sevens tournament and, from then on, he has been living and loving the path that God has ordained for him. *"I believe in miracles! I made peace that there is not always an answer. That is okay too. My greatest desire now is just to be a vessel for Him. If God is not with me in something, I do not want it and I do not want to be there either."*

When James Murphy jogs onto the field, he stops and kneels with his palms facing up. He surrenders. Again, and again. Every time. Not for the crowd or cameras, nor to prove anything. No, James understands the power of surrender. He is not praying for a good score or a win. He prays for authority over what God entrusts to him in that moment.

"I now know that better people make better rugby players, as coach Neil Powell has told me so many times. This platform that we are given is to make God's presence known, only for a while. There is so much power when we surrender everything to God. I will do it passionately again and again, because I now know, He sees me."

What do you think is the biggest obstacle in men's lives?

There are distinct phases in men's lives, which means there are different obstacles. For a young boy who wants to be a man, my advice is to just be yourself without any excuse. I was afraid to follow God as a young man because I was scared that I might lose my friends or be mocked or bullied.

As a grown man, we face the problem that society wants to dictate to us who we should be as men, when we should rather listen to God's voice to hear who we are supposed to become. Money, provision, and appearance are just some of the things we are bombarded with.

The church gives the answer: What is provision? Yes, it is to look after your family, but it is also to be an example of good Christian principles for your family. We cannot compromise with our Christian values and live a worldly lifestyle. Be your own vessel, every man's responsibility is different, do not follow someone else's lifestyle.

How would you like to be remembered?

I would like to be remembered as someone who carried God's glory and who was an example to the people around me of how real and alive He really is.

Your message to South Africa

Be yourself fearlessly. Find God and get to know Him as soon as possible, because life is not easy, and everything is always harder without Him. Get into the boxing ring of life and make sure you are on God's side.

James Murphy
Exclusive interview
Scan the code to watch

"My support system"

Angelo Davids

Angelo Davids, born on the 1st of June 1999, is known as the golden boy of Hoërskool Stellenberg. He made a name for himself as a sevens rugby player for the Blitzboks in his regular position as winger and fullback, but he also played for the DHL Stormers in Super Rugby as well as Western Province in the Currie Cup series. In 2017, the 18-year-old Angelo was selected for the Western Province u19 team for the Craven Week competition, and selectors also included him in the u19 provincial championships. In 2018, only a year after he completed his schooling, he was accepted into the SAS Rugby Sevens Academy. In 2018 and 2019, Angelo represented the South African Academy team in various tournaments and was selected to represent the senior team at the 2018 Hong Kong Sevens. He made his debut in their 22—7 win over Japan in the opening match and scored his first try in the green and gold at the Singapore Sevens against Scotland in 2019. In 2022 he was part of the South African team that won their second gold medal at the Commonwealth Games.

My love for sport began… *with my father. He was a good athlete in his youth and my love for athletics comes from him. To be honest, I never liked rugby. I always thought that it looked very painful when the guys tackled one another, and just over a rugby ball. It didn't seem worth it.*

If I was not sports star, I would… *probably have ended up in the wrong profession.*

I am incredibly grateful for… *the fact that my mom never stopped praying for me. She continued to believe that God had a plan for my life. Even though she was not always sure what that plan was, she continued to believe and trust that He was going to use me to inspire young people.*

If I could edit my life, I would… *have made God a part of my life far earlier.*

One of the biggest lessons I learnt this year… *is not to be ashamed to preach and talk about the goodness of the Lord. Especially as young people who love the Lord, we are sometimes cautious to publicly show that we put God first. We worry about the opinions of friends, or what the next person might say.*

My greatest achievement is… *the day I bowed my knees before the altar with the words: "Lord, here I am. I surrender my life to You. Lead my life, Lord, and I will follow."*

The Bible verse that carries me...

Jeremiah 29:11,
"'For I know the thoughts that I think toward you', says the Lord, 'thoughts of peace and not of evil, to give you a future and a hope.'"

Angelo receiving his Blitzbok jersey from Neil Powell – the coach who changed his life

MY STORY
Angelo Davids

Everyone experiences different highlights in their life, but certain incidents are life changing. You can count those events on one hand, because they are those moments when God steps in and His voice becomes so clear to you that you will never be the same again.

There have been a few such experiences for Angelo Davids.

There was the morning when everything tasted, looked, and felt like rugby! The morning when the 16-year-old Angelo put on the rugby jersey with the Western Province's colours for the first time. He could hardly sleep because the excitement of what lay ahead was just too great. Similar to the Bible story about the burning bush, Angelo became aware of God's presence. The Spirit whispered to him, *"Open your Bible to Jeremiah 29:11."* It was an inexplicable event with words that Angelo did not expect, but always needed to hear. "'For I know the thoughts that I think toward you', says the Lord, 'thoughts of peace and not of evil, to give you a future and a hope.'" Angelo experienced a peace unlike anything he had ever felt before.

He received the promise that God was holding him in His hands. The promise that God had a clear plan for his life and that in the midst of adversity, He would always cause good to come from it; so that in the years to come, Angelo would be able to constantly hold on to those promises.

In 2017, in the middle of a stormy season without any focus and with doubts about a professional rugby career, Angelo had to dust off those words again and again. The questions kept coming: Am I good enough? Will I ever succeed? Will someone notice me and give me a chance? Is rugby for me? Why do all my friends get a chance to play, and I am never selected?

Grace, a calling, and talent gave Angelo the chance to represent his country, but even after successful seasons in 2018 and 2019, he was plagued by the same nagging questions that he had to turn away from in order to quieten his heart. He had to believe with everything inside of him that God was still in control, because with a serious ankle injury that brought his season to a halt and other up-and-coming young players who could eagerly take his place, his future began to look less rosy.

> *"I could not run ahead of God's plan. He had to 'bless' me with an injury and bring me to a halt to enter His rest, so that I could listen and know that it was not yet my time."*

Angelo had to wait for God's timing and, in that time, build an unshakable relationship with Him. *"Faith is everything to me. When I went through challenging times, it was not the voices of friends I relied on or their assurances that I was 'going to be okay'. It was the voice of God and my faith that carried me."*

It was in those moments that God strengthened Angelo's relationship with Him to such an extent that he would not be able to turn away again. Even when Angelo's father – his hero – turned his back on them as a family and walked out the door without any explanation, Angelo had to believe that God is good. In Angelo's eyes, his father was the one man who was perfect. He was the man who could never make mistakes, precisely because he loved the Lord so much and preached His Word.

What made Angelo turn back and cling to a heavenly Father when his earthly father walked out on them, something that Angelo blamed himself for? His faith. He was anchored in his experience that God is still there in the tough times. He clung to God's promise of blessing and not adversity, a future, and a hope.

"I needed a father figure when I was younger and could not understand why things turned out the way they did. Over the years, I have met incredible 'dads' who have kept me on track and motivated me. Coach Neil Powell was one of them and, as a coach and as a father, helped change so many of the players' lives."

When Angelo looks back at the last two years of his life, he knows that everything only brings him closer to the Lord. *"God remains faithful to His Word. His promise that He gave me as a young boy has come to pass, even during a challenging COVID period. Therefore, I will praise and worship Him with everything in me."*

> *"God's promises remain 'yes' and 'amen'."*

"I came out stronger on the other side, thanks to God. He is a God of truth."

"My school coaches"

What do you think is the biggest obstacle in men's lives?

I think that we never want to talk about our emotions, because it might be seen as a sign of weakness.

How would you like to be remembered?

I would like to be remembered as Angelo Davids, who was never ashamed of the Word of the Lord and who always preached His Word everywhere he went.

Your message to South Africa

The Lord has a plan for you and for me. Do not delay His plan. We have a choice in life. You are given two keys: one key leads to the path that is narrow, but it is the path and the plan that God has laid out for you. The other key leads to the road where the devil wants to take you away from the good path that God has planned for you. The devil is a liar. He wants to destroy you. The Lord loves you and He will never leave you nor forsake you.

Angelo Davids Exclusive interview
Scan the code to watch

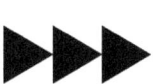

Angelo with his dad (centre) and Apostle

Angelo's two moms

Willem Alberts

Willem Schalk Alberts, born on the 11th of May 1984, is a professional South African rugby player. This farm boy from Bronkhorstspruit is a former learner of Hoërskool Monument in Krugersdorp, and his professional career includes time with the Golden Lions and Lions (2005-2009, 2020- present), 92 games for the Sharks (2010-2015), and 79 games for Stade Français (2015-2020). "The Bone Collector", as his opponents call him, is known for his strong charges (which often require more than one player to stop him) as well as his rock-solid defence. Willem's massive 120 kg build and his bone jarring tackles make him a much-feared opponent, but a great crowd favourite. In October 2010 he was selected for the Springbok squad of 39 players to prepare for the Northern Hemisphere's Grand Slam tour. He made a dream debut for the Boks on the 13th of November 2010 and scored a try against Wales in his debut tour. The "super sub" represented South Africa in more than 45 test matches and is again and again referred to as a big impact player and game changer.

At 38, he is still a formidable player for the Lions and a huge motivation for young players who are looking for guidance as well as tips for defensive skills and attacking play in the back row.

He is married to Nicolene and the father to their two little girls.

My love for sport began... *as a little boy. My father was a very good golfer, cricketer, and rugby player – so the sporting genes are in our family. I have a brother who is two years older than me, our family used to go to my uncle's box at Loftus Versveld to see the legends like Uli Schmidt, FA Meiring, and Ruben Kruger play. In later years, my sporting heroes were Victor Matfield, Joost van der Westhuizen, Ernie Els, and Hansie Cronjé. We would rush onto the pitch after every rugby match at Loftus hoping to see our icons. I think the love for sport originated there at Loftus. From as early as I can remember, I was a Blue Bulls supporter! As an adult, my loyalties naturally changed depending on the rugby jersey I wore, and with each new contract, my loyalty shifted to the new team. It is heart-warming to see all our South African teams doing well and that they are healthy. With that, I admit that probably every South African team has a special place in my heart.*

If I was not a sports star, I would... *have probably ended up in the agricultural sector. I grew up on a farm in Bronkhorstspruit and started studying agriculture. My other sporting talents were acceptable, but not brilliant – certainly not good enough to build a future as a professional sportsman. Believe me, I am very grateful for the opportunity to play rugby professionally. It is an absolute miracle and not at all what I ever expected in my life!*

I am incredibly grateful for... *the favour of the Lord in my life in terms of the people who have helped and assisted me. I am grateful for friends, teachers, sports coaches, my parents, and family, and I am grateful that my wife came into my life at the right time.*

If I could edit my life, I would... *not want to rewrite my life I could not better it. I would like to perhaps see ahead into the future to know what chapter lies ahead when my rugby career comes to an end. The unknown is sometimes scary, but with a good foundation built on God's Word, anything is possible.*

One of the biggest lessons I learnt this year... *Even though there are difficult times, we must remain anchored in God. When things are going well for you, you should try to be there for other people who are going through a difficult time.*

My greatest achievement is... *to keep going and to persevere, even if there are difficult times; to be a good husband to my wife and a good dad to my children.*

The Bible verse that carries me...

John 14:6,
"Jesus said to him, 'I am the way and the truth and the life. No one comes to the Father except through Me.'"

"Full speed! It's not that I am very fast. It is just that my facial expression changes between 3rd and 5th gear."

MY STORY
Willem Alberts

He never saw himself as a player who would one day wear the green and gold, and never did he dream of writing the name of his beloved Blue Bulls team on his CV, because Willem just did not think he was good enough to be that calibre of rugby player. As a teenager, he did not see himself as much more than a future farmer with a passion for golf, cricket, and the odd friendly rugby match. *"All boys, at one time or another in their lives, dream of pulling a provincial jersey over their heads or seeing their name listed among the famous rugby players, but then you put on your rugby boots and fall in for the second or third team and play your heart out, just because it is such fun! As a young boy, I played fly half – most of the times my name was not called out with those of the first team. That is why I always believed there were fifteen other players better than me in any position and I never allowed myself to dream beyond that."*

> **"Yes, I loved tackling guys hard and kicking a ball around, but I never thought that I would be given the chance to play professional rugby!"**

Willem still looks back with surprise and gratitude on a successful professional rugby career of 18 years. Where he finds himself today as a 38-year-old, and what he experienced in the past few years, is a miracle from the hand of God. It was more than just a childhood dream; it was God who made his purpose and calling come true; God who honed his natural talents and awakened in him the drive to work hard. *"I am still amazed at how my life has turned out. My life is clear proof for everyone that we do not control our own lives. Yes, our choices affect our daily lives, but when we let go of the reins and allow God to be at the helm, opportunities knock on our doors that only He could send!"*

For South Africa, the fans, and opponents, Willem is "The Bone Collector", dressed in the green and gold of the Springboks, or the red and white of the Golden Lions, but for his family and friends he is just a son, husband, and daddy. Willem Alberts has perfected the role of a competitive, aggressive rugby player, but as a family man he is just the opposite at home. He is the guy who loves everyone, the one who puts a smile on most people's faces, who does not start arguments, and has no interest in fuelling unnecessary conflict. No, thanks to his well-developed EQ (emotional intelligence),

Willem can sum up situations very well and uses heightened emotion to his advantage at the right time and place on the field.

However, life taught Willem this wisdom a long time ago, and sometimes in hard ways. *"I lost my father when I was only seven years old. In the blink of an eye, I lost the greatest mentor and leader in my life. Therefore, from a young age, I learnt what the advantages and disadvantages of your personal choices are."*

"Life was not easy, but I always had the choice about what I wanted out of life."

"One of the biggest lessons I had to learn was that every young man has to decide for himself whether he is going to make the right choice or not ... and then be prepared to bear the consequences of that decision. God will always be there with advice and guidance, but it will be your choice to accept it or not."

In 1992, he was only seven years old when he was chosen to appear in 7 Up in South Africa, the South African version of the Up series. This documentary television series discussed the real and serious aspects of life with children. For Willem, this included his life on the farm, the death of his father in a car accident, and his family's move to the city. *"I remember how, as a boy, I spoke earnestly in front of the cameras about God's love for His children and that He is our God, father, and friend. My earthly father figure was taken away from me in the blink of an eye; I had to make the choice to accept God as my Father. I established a quiet, personal relationship with Him. A father-son relationship that is non-negotiable; something I understood and honoured..."*

His relationship with God was important to him, and although Willem was never the guy who tried to influence other people, or who stood up and spoke loudly about his faith, he was always the man who quietly tried to make a difference. *"I did not always have all my ducks in a row. No, I wrestled with many questions throughout difficult times during my student years. Like any young man, I longed for direction, and although my mother and stepfather were wonderful parents, the final decision came down to me. I had to take responsibility for my own life and learn from every mistake, move on, and try to do better next time."*

The Lions had offered Willem a rugby contract after he completed his schooling, but he turned it down. He was given a second chance, by the grace of the Lord and a firm calling on his life, to be part of the Lions at the age 20.

"Many times in my life and rugby career I had to ask God for His advice, guidance, wisdom, and insight, because after many mistakes I came to the realisation that I could hamper my life and career because of my own decisions."

> *"I did not want to make any more unnecessary mistakes and I chose to listen to God's voice in my life and follow His guidance."*

However, Willem's rugby career was littered with injuries. These were the times that required lots of patience and faith in the promise that God's plan was still valid. *"I remember the one incident very well. It was in 2011, just weeks before the Rugby World Cup squad was due to be announced. I continued to struggle with a back injury and after an operation, I was forced to not do any running exercises for six weeks. I tried to maintain my physical fitness by cycling and swimming, but the chances were slim that I would be able to maintain the required game fitness standard. Yet I hoped, believed, and trusted God's hand in my life. I had an interesting, yet strange experience in church one Sunday morning. A woman came and stood behind my wife and me and said that she saw a spiritual cross on my back and knew that she should pray for me. No one knew about the surgery, and no one would be aware of the adjustments regarding my exercise routine. I did not know her, but I welcomed her honest, sincere prayer."*

Willem played for the Springboks in Gqeberha the weekend after that. The game against the dreaded All Blacks was the defining battle for his fitness and readiness to be included in the Rugby World Cup squad. He played well and only had to be replaced after 67 minutes. *"It was a miracle! I lose game fitness when I do not jog for a week, but I was able to play my heart out for 67 minutes straight without getting tired and without having problems with my back."*

After that match, Willem Alberts' name was among those mentioned for the Springbok team. He was truly one of the best in South Africa and represented his country in the seventh Rugby World Cup in New Zealand. South Africa did not win the World Cup that year, but for Willem it was a personal victory and an opportunity to honour God's Name.

"This was just one occasion where God's hand was visible in my life. I know He has been there many times and is here with me daily."

Willem with his biggest fans

Willem with Jannie du Plessis; Jannie's 50th test for the Boks

What do you think is the biggest obstacle in men's lives?

The obstacles in men's lives vary from man to man, but there is so much pressure in society in terms of finances and time; then there is also emotional pressure. A big problem is that men usually want to fix things or deal with it on their own; they do not want to appear vulnerable. It is therefore important to not be afraid to seek or ask for help.

How would you like to be remembered?

I would like to be remembered as someone who lived life to the fullest and always gave his best. As a man who approached life with humour, saw the bright side of life, who put a smile on people's faces, and had a lot of time for the people around him.

I would also like to be the best daddy in the eyes of my children. Someone they could look up to, who is their hero, because I loved them so much! I would also like to be remembered as a good husband to my wife.

Your message to South Africa

Know where your strength comes from in everything you do. Try to leave a heartfelt smile on people's faces. Enjoy what you do and try to make a difference every time you encounter people. We truly live in the most wonderful country! Each of us just has to do his/her part.

Willem Alberts
Exclusive interview
Scan the code to watch
◀◀◀

2023 family photo. Willem, Nicolene, and their two princesses

Grant Lottering

Grant Lottering, born on the 4th of June 1968, is a South African endurance cyclist, the founder of the Im'possible Tour, an ambassador for the Laureus Sport for Good Foundation, and an international motivational speaker. After a serious accident in 2013 – which led to five operations and almost 100 rehabilitation sessions – Grant fought back. In 2014, only 11 months after his accident, he once again took on the race in the Alps that almost claimed his life; this time successfully completing it. The feat has been described as a medical miracle. The second Im'possible Tour took place in 2015. Grant became the first South African to complete an uninterrupted solo ultra-endurance ride of 420 km through the Northern French Alps in less than 24 hours. On the 4th of August 2016, Grant accomplished something that many people thought was impossible: cycling the length of the French Alps within 48 hours. He set off on a non-stop ride of 962 km – the length of the French Alps, from Nice on the French Riviera to Les Saisies ski resort, one hour south of Geneva – which he covered in 46 hours. During the ride of two days and nights, he climbed 19 600 m over 21 peaks, which cyclists consider to be the most formidable mountains in the Alps, all while sleeping for only 20 minutes.

Grant has since crossed the entire French Pyrenees and Alps Mountain ranges in one 72-hour attempt in 2018, and in 2019 completed a non-stop 1314 km mountain bike ride from the Eastern Cape to the Western Cape in 66 hours and 12 minutes. In January 2022, South Africans witnessed Grant successfully complete his eighth Im'possible Tour in aid of charity. The ride from Plettenberg Bay to Stellenbosch, which was 750 km and took 37 hours, was by no means his longest tour, but due to the extreme heat and difficult terrain, it was without a doubt his most difficult tour ever.

On the 4th of June 2022, Grant completed his first Im'possible Tour in America, in aid of the Laureus Sport for Good Foundation USA. He triumphed in Southern California with a solo ride of 986 km in 51 hours and 40 minutes from Shaver Lake in the Sierra Nevada mountains to Big Bear Lake, north of Los Angeles, with a climb of 18 000 m.

My love for sports began... *at 12 years old. I wasn't good at school sports or team sports, but then I started cycling! On my bike I found myself and my identity. I was able to express myself through my sport.*

If I was not a sports star, I would... *be an architect.*

I am incredibly grateful... *that God chose me and considers me valuable enough to be a witness who inspires and touches the hearts of millions of people because they see God's power at work in my life.*

If I could edit my life, I would... *not change anything. All the mistakes, wrong decisions, and stupid things I have done over the years are behind me. I know our Father always has a plan with our experiences, and today I am a little wiser! I have dusted myself off, I look forward to the work that God wants me to do.*

One of the biggest lessons I learnt this year... *is the fact that I am vulnerable and weak, despite everything I have accomplished. I also learnt that it is good for a man to be vulnerable and weak. I had to admit it within myself, as well as on my knees before Jesus. I had to lift my head and reach out for help.*

My biggest achievement is... *being able to be back in the Alps only 11 months after my horrific accident and to finish the same race that almost cost me my life. All I had to do was trust God and be at the starting line. He did the rest and gave me the superhuman strength to finish.*

The Bible verse that carries me...

Isaiah 40:28-31,
"Have you not known? Have you not heard?
The everlasting God, the Lord, the Creator of the ends of the earth, neither faints nor is weary. His understanding is unsearchable. He gives power to the weak, and to those who have no might He increases strength.

"Even the youths shall faint and be weary, and the young men shall utterly fall, but those who wait on the Lord Shall renew their strength; they shall mount up with wings like eagles, they shall run and not be weary, they shall walk and not faint."

Photographer: Seb Driguez

Cycling in the Alps – for days on end without any sleep – became a spiritual journey

"I share my story with the 2015 RWB team. Grant with Jean de Villiers, Heyneke Meyer, and Schalk Burger."

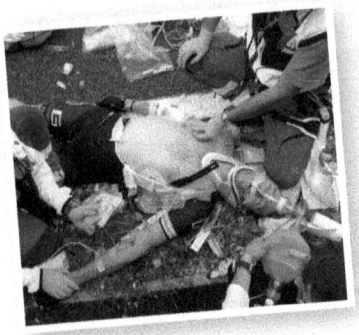

MY STORY
Grant Lottering

2013-07-21

No one ever expects the rug to be pulled out from underneath them.

Life-changing events are not usually pre-announced over a loudspeaker.

No... they just happen. They catch you off guard. It is the resulting ripple effect that can still destabilise you for months and even years afterwards – unless your foundation is built on the Rock.

Grant Lottering's life was torn apart with the death of his father in November 2009. However, it was the suicide of his ex-fiancée in December 2009 – a mere month after the death of his father – that caused him to fall and to stay down... something unfamiliar to Grant until that point. *"We mutually decided not to get married and broke up. Then she committed suicide. It was a very dark time in my life..."* Grant could not see the light, had no clever answers, and was drowning in the pain of loss – but in January 2010, at the age of 41, he found himself on his knees before God and he surrendered his life to the Lord. In this moment, Grant experienced a personal encounter with God and gave his heart to the Lord again, but this time truly and with his whole heart to never turn back again spiritually.

On the 21st of July 2013, the keen cyclist's heart stopped during a bicycle race in the Italian Alps after his body was thrown against a rock wall at a speed greater than 64 km/h. During the race, Grant did not dare hold back – as a member of an elite cycling group on the legendary Charly Gaul trail in Trento, Italy, a good race time could see him qualifying for the Union Cycliste Internationale World Championships. The accident happened on a rainy day around a blind corner. Upon hitting the ground, Grant immediately realised the severity of his condition. It was a fellow cyclist, a doctor, who stabilised Grant before help arrived. While the sounds and his vision faded away into a hazy tunnel, Grant experienced an unprecedented peace before he finally lost consciousness. He was defibrillated twice at the scene to get his heart beating again. The accident broke 22 bones in his body, and, with extensive internal injuries and bleeding, there was little chance that he would survive. After six operations and eight days in the intensive care unit, doctors just shook their heads in disbelief that Grant survived the incident at all and escaped death. However, the professional cyclist heard experts' damning words that he would never sit on a bike again. The diagnosis: paralysis.

However, Grant later realised that as a child of God, he was not afraid of death for a single moment. He had an encounter with God there in that hospital bed in Italy. He saw a vision of a clean slate and knew that he was given a second chance in life. A chance to write a new story. This served as enough incentive for him to get up and go on; to move forward! He not only was given the opportunity for a second chance, but also for a second life! *"The 21st of July 2013 was the first day of my second life."*

> *"Everything that was important to me before: my career, my properties, my money, my car, my nice clothes and watches, etc. suddenly made way for a burning passion to do God's will for my life."*

It was that vision that spurred Grant on to change his outlook on his life. From an untouchable young man who was always in control, to someone who now understands his dependence on God and cherishes the irreplaceable value of his health, family, and friends. *"I had to lose my life to do God's will for my life."*

April 2014 was the beacon for the first Im'possible Tour and the beginning of his new journey. After 11 months, six operations, and almost 100 rehabilitation sessions, Grant completed the race that once almost claimed his life. *"I believe God has given me a gift of faith. Since my accident, my whole life has been a path of faith. I have no comfort zone. My life is in God's hands with everything I do, whether it is as a professional cyclist or speaker, because I know He is preparing me for much bigger things."*

In 2016, Grant was diagnosed with cancer, but this did not stop him from living life to the fullest.

Today he addresses audiences worldwide. He talks about his death experience as well as his second chance to use his life to be relevant. He inspires others to fly high in the face of adversity and is living proof that you can fulfil your calling when you follow God's voice and persevere, even if you experience storms in your life.

With each annual solo endurance ride of his Im'possible Tour, Grant raises millions for underprivileged children around the world. *"It is important to live each day with gratitude and to focus on positively influencing others. My life is not my own. This is God's will in me. What a privilege to be able to live like this!"*

Im'possible Tour in 2016

What do you think is the biggest obstacle in men's lives?

Pride, or should I put it this way: I believe that most men have an inner fear of being wrong or admitting that they are wrong. They are afraid of failing, of being weak. Ego often stands in men's way of truly opening themselves up to God and saying, "Father, here I am. Search me, show me what is wrong in my life. Show me what Your will is."

How would you like to be remembered?

I would like to be remembered as someone whose life was relevant, who positively influenced others – especially children. I want people to see God's power in my life.

Your message to South Africa

Life is too short, too precious, and too valuable to always have to be right, better, or more important than others. Faith, hope, and love are all that matter, but the greatest is love.

Grant Lottering
Exclusive interview
Scan the code to watch ◀◀◀

Grant is helped up by Laureus chairman and rugby legend, Morné du Plessis

"I may be cycling on my own during my endurance rides, but I never ride alone! I always have a scripture for each tour."

Dr Eduard Coetzee

Dr Eduard Coetzee, born on the 8th of September 1979, is the chief executive officer of the Sharks Rugby Union. The history of this rugby prop – a son of Bapsfontein and former learner of the Afrikaanse Hoër Seunskool in Pretoria, aka Affies – only began much later in his life because cricket was his focus and main love for such a long time. However, his robust physique and strong affinity for team sports would lead Eduard's path to continually cross with rugby. He eventually played for the SA Schools rugby team. As a 21-year-old Tukkies student, he signed a sports contract with his beloved Sharks in 2000 and wore their black and white jersey for five years. In 2005, he left South Africa for an overseas offer and moved to the south-western part of France, where he lived for nine years. Eduard settled in the coastal town of Biarritz. There, he not only played for the Biarritz rugby club, but also mastered French, married his English rose, started his family, and acquired French citizenship. In 2011, he announced his retirement from professional rugby, but retained his love for the game while focusing on postgraduate studies. Eduard, who is better known in rugby leadership circles as the "champion of transformation", was appointed as the chief executive manager of the Sharks rugby union in 2019 and is praised for his views on transformation and the celebration of diversity in a team. He obtained his master's degree in inclusive innovation at the University of Cape Town and focused on inclusive business model innovation in his doctorate at the University of KwaZulu-Natal. It is clear from his dissertation on transformation (286 pages long, 90 000 words) that he indeed sees colour, "…because if we never see colour, we can never be inclusive, given the history of South Africa," he writes.

Eduard is skilled in the development and implementation of successful commercial strategies for professional sports, high performance management in sports, strategic planning, as well as financial planning. His position with the Sharks gave him in-depth knowledge of the current opportunities and challenges facing rugby organisations worldwide. This valuable experience and insight equipped him to be the driving force behind the process of developing an innovative and inclusive business model for the Sharks, ensuring the long-term financial stability of the organisation.

Eduard is married to Seren and they have three sons.

My love for sports began... *as a young South African Afrikaans boy who always loved to run around outside. I played rugby, but I really loved cricket. I had a love for people from a young age, I enjoyed team sports. I was a real team player who realised that you* can have an effect on a small circle of people who, in turn, can later have an effect on a larger circle of people and influence them positively. It was one of the best lessons I learnt early in life.

If I was not a sports star, I would... *probably have gotten involved in financial management and financial management services. I do not like studying very much, although I am still studying. This is the result of a deep root – a personal issue in my life that has pushed me to continue studying. I always wanted to prove that I am not just a rugby player and that there is more to me.*

However, I understand how sports people think. We are not high-risk people, but rather conservative, proactive people who are forced to be reactive all the time. I get bored easily and because I understand all the above aspects, it is good for me to constantly challenge myself.

I am incredibly grateful for... *my wife and family. We all love each other very much. As a family, we do not always like each other, but we make sacrifices for one another, because that is what successful families do. Sometimes one member of the family gives up his/her dreams so that others in the family can make their dream a reality. We do life together and though we do not always understand everything, we know that as long as we each consistently live with integrity, we will all reap the reward in the end.*

If I could edit my life, I would... *probably not change anything. I do not believe in regrets. I wear my heart on my sleeve. And yes, sometimes I have to curb it because my emotions run away with me, but it is also good to show honesty and sincerity. I did, however, learn that words have great power. The growth and development process has taught me that I must be quick to apologise and to correct misunderstandings. So, if my words have hurt people in the past, I would like to change that, because people, and their experiences, are important to me. For the rest of it, I am okay with living with the choices that I have made and the lessons that I have learnt.*

Dr Eduard with his family

Dr Eduard with his wife, Seren

One of the biggest lessons I learnt this year... *is that there is a lack of kindness – especially in the rugby world, a male-dominated environment. Society has forgotten how to be gentle and kind towards one another. When you arrive at your workplace, you enter that environment from a specific reality because your own environment functions in a certain way. Within the first ten minutes of arriving, you come into contact with a lot of different people whose realities look completely different to yours – perhaps full of challenges and problems that you are not even aware of. It is in times like these that kindness and caring for others can sow good seeds in someone's day, thus turning it into something positive. I would like to teach this to young men.*

My greatest achievement is... *my family and my marriage. I am very happy. I married a woman who trusts and supports me one hundred percent. My advice to my children is to always try not to plan their lives too far ahead. If, at the age of 18, I had compiled a list of what my dream bride would be like, it would not have been someone like Seren. She is English-speaking, and at that stage of my life I could barely even speak English. But our basic values are the same and when I look at my family today, I know that God's hand is in this. It is only by His grace, and I am grateful for that.*

The Bible verse that carries me...

"I have to say honestly that there is not just one particular verse that I always hold on to. I have been guided and encouraged by a variety of verses that the Holy Spirit has given me at the right times in my life. God is so faithful!"

Biarritz, France

MY STORY
Dr Eduard Coetzee

Dr Eduard Coetzee believes in and lives for transformation. He takes his truth and turns it into a reality, something that he has done daily for the past nine years. He believes that this is the only way to live in South Africa. Eduard empowers his Sharks team with the philosophy of the #ISeeColourMovement. In other words, a team that is true to themselves, their province, their community, and the collective. They are true to the celebration and respect of colour, diversity, and uniqueness. This is what makes Natal so special.

> *"Sport has the ability to evoke great emotion in South Africa. It has the power to unite like nothing else, and I have the privilege of managing a process of transformation."*

"God entrusted me with this after all these years – with all the upheavals and challenges in my own life – and I just want to be faithful to the task that He has given me..."

Eduard knows the meaning of the words: Loss and change, a new beginning, je ne sais quoi, grace and faith. And in this narrative, he wears his heart on his sleeve.

Loss and change

Eduard never had that one face-to-face experience with God. He just always knew the Lord. He was born and raised in a Christian home with strong Christian values. On weeknights they would read the Bible and have family devotions together, and on Sundays the whole Coetzee family would attend the NG Church. He was aware that his parents knew God, as they experienced the Lord's grace and love in their lives. Eduard was the youngest of three children. He was the little "medical miracle". *"Specialists confirmed that my parents would never be able to conceive their own children, thus they adopted two children: my sister Annamart and my brother Flip. Shortly after their adoptions, my mother miraculously became pregnant and I was born, the youngest of three!"* God knew exactly when Eduard had to appear in his mother's womb, he was planned by God and had a calling for a certain time and place in South Africa.

Events at a young age have a huge influence on a person's psyche. They shape a child's reality and determine his core values about himself and life. Eduard would have to deal with loss at a young age and experience one of the biggest upheavals any child could experience. *"My brother, a Springbok gymnast, was diagnosed with cancer as a teenager – it eventually took his life. I was 13 years old, and it was an incredibly difficult time in my life. Not only did I have a life-changing upheaval in my family, I also went to boarding school as I did not want to be known as 'Flip's little brother.'"* Eduard was angry at God and his family. He wanted to make sense of the loss and searched for answers in the black and white pages of his Bible. But he would have to make peace with the fact that not everything always has an explanation… on the contrary, he had to believe that God was good – in the midst of the pain.

Life would be stable for a few years after the incident. Eduard played as a prop for the prestigious rugby franchise, the Sharks. He was the pride of his parents, but he also knew that a career as a rugby player is often short-lived. Eduard therefore pushed himself to get an academic qualification, so fulfilling his purpose and calling in life.

A new beginning and *je ne sais quoi*.

> *"Every season has its rain and thunder. I had to quickly adjust my perception about challenges, because perception is everything and every challenge can make you a better person. Events make or break you, and I wanted to trust that God had the best in mind for me."*

"'Leave your country and your people,' God said, 'and go to the land I will show you.'" Armed with these words from Acts 7:3 that the Lord had given, Eduard and Seren began to dream about a life abroad. They were newly engaged and, with bright eyes and Eduard's rugby contract in hand, planned a life together in England. However, changing visa regulations would soon put a stop to their dreams. With big question marks about God's confirming scripture, they went back to the drawing board, this time without any rugby contract. *"We could not understand it. We could not have asked for a clearer answer for guidance and yet God allowed all doors to England to close. It was a mess! Prayer and words were few, but I asked for breakthrough, favour, and wisdom from God – three pillars that would keep us standing in an uncertain time."*

From what first made no sense at all, God's hand emerged with a rugby contract for Eduard at a French club! *Their* dreams included England, but God had France in mind. That day, they both learnt that God is in control of their lives and can add *je ne sais quoi* to any life story.

Grace and faith

After nine years in France, the season changed for the Coetzees who, upon their return to South Africa, were three sons richer. Eduard was the head of a family of five and had no rugby contract after his retirement from rugby, nor any other job – just the promise that they would have weekends to themselves. Eduard was offered a three-month consulting job with the Sharks. At the time he had a master's degree in inclusive innovation as well as a dream for a doctorate. The three-month contract was extended time and time again and, after a period of five years involved with the management of the Sharks, Eduard was appointed as chief executive manager in 2019.

"I was experiencing a season of breakthrough and celebration; I had many highlights in my life. Not only was my family happy, but I also had a dream position with the Sharks – I had the privilege of speaking into young men's lives and establishing a system that supports transformation. I was writing my doctoral thesis when my world came to a halt for the umpteenth time..."

Eduard never got the opportunity to say goodbye to his older sister. Annamart passed away in her sleep at the age of 47. The pain and grief were still palpable when, only six weeks after her death, Eduard received the news that his father had passed away. His parents had been married for 54 years – their marriage had a rock-solid foundation and was an example for everyone. The family was still processing the losses of Annamart and Eduard's father when the third wave hit them like a tsunami... Eduard's mother also died, only three weeks after the death of her husband.

"For the first time in my life, I experienced contrasting feelings."

> ### *"My professional career was flourishing, while my personal life was in tatters."*

"I had to focus on my studies, live up to the expectations of being the new broom at work, and also be rock solid for my family during the most painful time of our lives – all while I could barely breathe myself. It felt like I hit a wall at 100 km/h. There was no sign of light at the end of this long, lonely tunnel..."

But this is when God steps in and grace becomes tangible. People in Eduard's community, friends, and colleagues became angels without wings. When autopilot becomes the only way to survive, when the next 24 hours seem blurry and you focus on just putting one foot in front of the other, that is when one relies on faith in the God who gave us Hebrews 11:1, "Now faith is confidence in what we hope for and assurance about what we do not see."

"Looking back today, I wonder how we made it that year. Grace upon grace and faith in God who still remains good in the midst of unprecedented pain. I know now, more than ever, that things do not always make sense and that we will not always understand everything, but that is okay too."

It is the pain you feel in your heart and the lessons that cut deep that leave the biggest scars – but scars are healed wounds. They are signs of a time when the going was tough but is now in the past. If wounds still have not healed after many years, we need to ask the hard, probing questions, because it is that pain that gnaws away at us and turns into bigger problems.

"Somewhere you have to surrender control of your life and trust God, but also take up the baton and give it your best, because then you manage all the aspects of your life. God wants us to take responsibility, that is why He gave us free will. He gave us the right to words and deeds, but we must understand their power in our own lives as well as their effect on others."

When he looks back on his life today, there are not many things that Eduard would change. Everything happened for a purpose. He does, however, want to erase some of the things etched in his memory. Sometimes it takes asking for forgiveness and apologising, even if it is years later or just for his own sake... "I now know that there is no better time than the immediate, here and now, to make amends and apologise. Do it for yourself or for the sake of the other party but do it while there is still time."

Eduard knows that people have little time on their hands and that is why he works hard on the things that make a difference. With his strong leadership background on the sports field and his knowledge of the player's psyche and constant interaction with various stakeholders within professional sport, he is well equipped to accept the responsibility of creating a successful rugby culture within the union. Such a new culture will lead to long-term success – not only for the Sharks' brand, but also for every young man in the team.

"We must teach the younger generation that God is good; that He made each one unique, with our own stories; and that there will always be a breakthrough. We must teach them that we can ask for favour from God's hand and that wisdom comes from Him alone. When we understand, respect, and start living this, we will see true transformation in our lives and country."

What do you think is the biggest obstacle in men's lives?

1. Men in general, but especially in South Africa, put an incredible amount of pressure on themselves. We want to be constantly strong and in control – which is not a bad quality – but it is important to understand the value of vulnerability in the right context, with the right people.

2. It is important to teach young men that one bad decision cannot be corrected with another. Be open-minded enough to go to a mentor for guidance and make sure that the cycle of bad decisions is stopped in its tracks.

How would you like to be remembered?

I would like to be remembered as a man who always treated people well, and that when I made a mistake, I was willing to fix it immediately. I would like to be remembered as someone who had integrity and strove to try and do the right thing at all times. Not because we try to be perfect people, but to really make a difference in the way we behave towards each other.

Your message to South Africa

South Africa is in an extremely difficult place and our country is not perfect. The potential is here, but people are tired of always choosing to see the positive. Racism, poverty, and injustice are things that have been in our midst for a long time. The accusing fingers point both ways. Let us make sure the immediate circle around us is healthy. It starts with your daily actions, because if you get it right, your attitude will spill over to your organisation and then the town and, before you know it, you will be contributing towards the transformation of our country. Our #ISeeColourMovement is experiencing amazing stories in our team and among our fans. South Africa, let us celebrate each other's uniqueness and stories, regardless of who you are. And do not compare! Let us live in faith and let our light shine in this broken world that is in need of hope.

Dr Eduard Coetzee
Exclusive interview
Scan the code to watch

Hanging with the boys

Pierre Coetzer

Pierre Coetzer, born on the 6th of December 1961, is a former heavyweight boxer for South Africa and is currently a businessman in Johannesburg. He played a fundamental role in the heavyweight division of the South African Boxing Association from the late 1980s to the early 1990s. He is known as one of South Africa's best boxers of all time. His most notable fights include those against Johnny du Plooy, Riddick Bowe, Frank Bruno, and George Foreman. Pierre, a native of Pretoria, enjoyed a successful amateur career with more than 200 victories in competitions. He won the national title several times and began his professional boxing career in February 1983. Pierre took over the torch from the two legendary boxers, Gerrie Coetzee and Kallie Knoetze, when they announced the ends of their professional careers. He won his first nine professional fights, but was beaten by the American cruiserweight, Bernard Benton. In their July 1984 boxing match in Durban, lasting ten rounds, Benton won on points. Pierre made his comeback in September 1984 when he fought Bennie Knoetze to win the unclaimed South African heavyweight title and knocked him out in the third round. Pierre retained this title for seven years without having to defend it once. Over the next three years, Pierre achieved a dozen victories; including those against Larry Frazier, Eddie "Young Joe Louis" Taylor, and Alfredo Evangelista. One of his most famous boxing bouts includes the "Once and for All" bout against local heavyweight Johnny du Plooy, who won 196 of his 200 amateur bouts and scored 17 knockouts in his first 20 professional bouts. They faced one another on the 4th of August 1990 at the Sun City Superbowl, where Johnny opened a gash above Pierre's left eye with his first right and dropped him in the middle of the second round. However, the tide turned when Pierre floored Johnny twice in the second round and won the fight with a technical knockout! Due to the apartheid era, Pierre had to face difficult conditions during international boxing fights. He stayed on course, winning seven fights and earning a fight against the rising heavyweight Riddick Bowe in a World Boxing Association match. This extremely gifted American tore apart the strong South African and defeated him in seven rounds. Just three months later, Pierre travelled to London to meet Frank Bruno. The charismatic Brit beat Coetzer in eight rounds. Again, Pierre did not shy away from making his biggest dream come true and tested his skill against George Foreman in January 1993. Pierre made a brave effort and got up from the canvas twice before he was stopped in the eighth round. After losing to Foreman, Pierre decided to walk away from professional boxing with his faculties intact (after 39 wins, 27 knockouts, and only 5 losses).

Nowadays, Pierre Coetzer busies himself being a family man, father, and businessman. This 1.93 m tall former sportsman is still a South African hero.

My love for sport began... *as a little boy. I did athletics and played rugby, but in the end, boxing was my passion. When I was eight, my older brother boxed, but I took karate classes. At my first karate competition, I broke another boy's nose and, because of karate rules stipulating that you are not allowed to make an opponent bleed, I was disqualified. I decided that karate was not for me, after all. I followed my older brother to one of his boxing sessions, where I met the coach and owner of the police boxing club. Uncle Daan Bekker was a boxing legend and made a promise to me that night: If I was interested in boxing, and if I was willing to work hard, he would make me a Springbok boxer! He saw the talent, courage, desire, and my big feet and knew that he was onto something! My first amateur boxing fight was in Senekal, where only one other boy and I (from our club) won our fights that night; the Senekal club took the rest. After that, I lost three boxing matches and almost quit boxing, but with the guidance and advice of Uncle Daan, I pushed through and won more than 200 amateur boxing matches.*

If I was not a sports star, I would... *not want to do anything other than to become a Springbok! It was one of my biggest dreams. My height and size determined that I started boxing for my country and did not excel in any other sport. God gave me the talent and I just had to put in the hard work.*

I am incredibly grateful for... *my life. I have enjoyed a full, blessed life. I had a wonderful career with supportive parents and coaches. Today I look back on a blessed family life, a beautiful wife and daughter, a successful business (with challenges), and good health. I am grateful to the people of our country for all the support. I am also grateful for our heavenly Father's guidance.*

"With my coach, Alan Toweel"

He won the South African heavyweight title in 1984

If I could edit my life, I would... *not change a thing. I really had a wonderful career. Maybe I could have improved my academic background a little, because going through life with only a matric certificate to your name is hard work!*

One of the biggest lessons I learnt this year... *It is not something I necessarily learnt this year – you have to be big enough to admit when you have made a mistake, wise enough to learn from it, and strong enough to fix it.*

My biggest achievement is... *probably the fights against Bennie and Johnny, and becoming a Springbok as an amateur.*

The Bible verse that carries me...

I do not rely on just one Bible verse. I am "old school", I read my Bible, pray, believe in God, and trust that He will speak to me through His Word."

Pierre with Gerrie Coetzee (left)

MY STORY
Pierre Coetzer

Twenty-four bottles of cooldrink – this is what Pierre's father, Chris, would buy him the day he won his first South African boxing championship.

One bottle of cooldrink for each of his classmates so that everyone could celebrate the great achievement with him, and because the other children would never have the opportunity to brag about the title. *"My father was an incredibly quiet, open-minded man who would not make a big fuss about events. He made his presence known at every boxing match but would never be too loud or hand out big gifts as a reward after the fight – like all the other fathers did. He always said, for him, that was not what it was all about."*

Pierre, the mirror image of his father, had to learn from an early age that every interest or sport comes with conditions. If you are not willing to put in the hours of work and discipline, you should not even think about going onto the field, or in Pierre's case, climbing into the boxing ring. He grew up in Pretoria in a strict, loving home with Christian values and routine (devotions in the evenings were synonymous with dinner around the table). In their household, no one was bribed to do anything. This would not be tolerated, because if you decided to participate in something, you had to put in one hundred percent of your time and effort – not because there would be a carrot dangling in front of your nose as a reward, no, just because you agreed to start doing it.

> **"I was bullied terribly at school. My father said one day, 'You had better do something to protect yourself.'"**

"I then took up karate, but after a nasty disqualification incident, my older brother and his friends invited me to the local boxing club. That decision would change my whole life."

When he was eight years old, the young Pierre met the coach and owner of the police boxing club – Uncle Daan. That night, Daan Bekker would unlock a dream that Pierre was only vaguely aware of. Uncle Daan made a promise to Pierre that he would never break. "Uncle Daan struck up a conversation with me that night and asked what I wanted to be one day. 'A Springbok,' I declared out loud! There and then, the dream took hold. 'You have big feet,' said Uncle Daan. 'I can see you are going to be a boxer one day. In fact, you will become a very big man,' were his words. And Uncle Daan was right, because in the years that followed, I shot up. I was a 1.93 m tall 17-year-old boy boxing against 22- and 23-year-old opponents in my weight class."

An illustrious amateur career began for the diligent Pierre. Not only did zeal and passion drive him, but the self-discipline that the sport required was right up his alley. Everything had to be done one with hundred percent effort – every bit of preparation in and out of the boxing ring, hours of road running, and hours in the gym. Schoolwork came second – the dream of boxing was everything. The young Pierre's dedication to boxing was unprecedented and it led to sensational results: more than 200 victories in amateur boxing tournaments.

"It was unheard of. Not only did I box as a young boy against young men, I beat them and knocked them out! However, that was not my focus. I watched local and international boxing legends; I dreamt of the day when I would see my name written next to theirs as an opponent. I ate, slept, and lived boxing – even though it drove my parents crazy."

In 1983, the 22-year-old Pierre made his debut as a professional boxer and toured with the Springbok team to South America. Sanctions against South African athletes prevented the Springboks from representing their country with any emblem. This prevented Pierre from realising his dream of wearing the green and gold, due to protesting activists who disrupted boxing events and forced organisers to stage fights in underground parking areas.

"I always kept my head down. I was there to live my calling, to perform a task and, yes, to represent my country. It was not always the easiest or most pleasant circumstance, but in those times, I relied on my faith and quietly sought God's face amidst the noise of screaming protesters."

Looking back at the past, Pierre now sees beacons of hope like markers in the ground, during every international boxing match. There were the moments where he cried out to God for help, because when there is no family member around for support, you want God in your corner in the boxing ring. It was there on a little stool in the corner of a boxing ring that he had to hear God's voice and pray for peace, strength, and wisdom – not about winning or losing though.

> *"One prays for fruit from your labour of hours of hard work leading up to the match ... and for protection, because boxing is a dangerous sport..."*

"For most of my professional career, I was in the able hands of Alan Toweel, for whom I had the greatest respect for his wholesome Christian outlook on life."

During those moments in the boxing ring, Uncle Daan's voice would echo in his ears: "Hit, and don't get hit!" The best advice from one boxer to another. "And besides that, think! Ten rounds of three minutes each can exhaust you mentally, physically, and emotionally, and then you make unnecessary mistakes. Keep your head up. If there's one place you have to think, it's between those four ropes."

Today, Pierre still applies the comparable lessons of boxing to his life: "Do not react too hastily and do not lose your temper. Stay calm, think twice before you speak or do things. Words and actions hurt, and they cannot be erased. Do not be ashamed to talk about the Lord, because when everything comes to an end or falls away, God is all that remains. Pray when you need to pray – in front of people, for people, or on your own. However, keep it real because that is how it is supposed to be. As South Africans, we must be different from other countries' sports stars. We are children of a living God, and we must be able to live it and show it to other people! I am where I am today because of the grace of God in my life. The Lord has carried me, and I have experienced the most wonderful times in my life because He has allowed it."

Pierre's honest, individualistic outlook on life is set. That is the way he is. The giant man with the luxuriant moustache knows only one way, and that is to be honest and open. He is just Pierre. He does not want to imitate anyone else. "I live by my own advice: Be yourself. Do not be so impressionable that people make you abandon your own path, decisions, dreams, or calling. Decide what you want to do and stick to it. If you know what the right course of action is, do it."

The day when Pierre announced the start of his professional career in February 1983 was the day his father wanted to know when Pierre would retire from the ring. Like any protective father, he would support his son, but he did not want any regrets about advice not given. "My father said that every man must know his limitations and must plan for the day when he will cross the finish line. It does not help that you have a lot of money in the bank, but do not have the faculties to write a cheque. 'You have to look after yourself; protect yourself, and take care,' was his advice to me."

Pierre would make a promise that day that if he was not yet the world champion by 31, he would retire.

As he promised, and as if in the lead role of his own Rocky film, Pierre would hang up his boxing gloves after his last big fight against his greatest hero, George Foreman, and walk away from the boxing ring without any fuss.

Pierre "the Lion Heart" Coetzer may not have won a world title, but he has contributed more than his share of drama to the heavyweight boxing division. He was involved in two of the best boxing fights in South African history: Bennie Knoetze for the unclaimed national title and a spectacular fight against Johnny du Plooy at the Superbowl.

Pierre with his son-in-law, Diego (left), daughter, Charné, and wife, Sanett (right)

Boxing against three legends was a fitting end to an unforgettable career.

There has simply never been a fitter South African heavyweight with a bigger heart than Pierre Coetzer.

What do you think is the biggest obstacle in men's lives?

Uncle Daniël "Daan" Wepener Bekker was born on the 9th of February 1932, and died on the 22nd of October 2009. He was a South African boxer who won a bronze medal at the Melbourne Olympics and a silver medal at the Rome Olympics – both in the heavyweight division. He was also the South African heavyweight champion from 1955-1959 and again in 1961. Not only was he a part of my life since I was eight, but he also took every step of my boxing career with me and was in my corner for every fight. I listened when he spoke because he understood something about being human and being a man. Uncle Daan always said, 'Men are influenced too easily.' This is an incredibly negative aspect in society. It is important that every man finds and maintains his identity in God; that he stands up for what he believes in and does what is right.

I believe every man's worth just needs to be affirmed. And each man must have his own identity!

How would you like to be remembered?

As the man who only did and achieved what he had to because of a gift he received from God.

Your message to South Africa

I love our country very much. Therefore: Trust in the Lord, South Africa. Let us pray more. Be more result-driven with a mindset to do your part, and believe there is a beautiful future.

Pierre Coetzer
Exclusive interview
Scan the code to watch

Pierre with his father

Rocco van Rooyen

Rocco van Rooyen, born on the 23rd of December 1992, is a two-time Olympic athlete and South African javelin thrower. This Capetonian is a skilled and extremely competitive athlete who has represented South Africa for more than six years already. Born in Bellville, Rocco's professional athletics career includes the 2010 Junior World Championships in Canada (where he reached the final and placed sixth), the 2011 Junior African Championships, as well as the 2014 Commonwealth Games (where he reached the final and placed sixth). He also competed in the African Championships and World Championships in 2015. Rocco made his debut at his first Olympic Games in the 2016 Rio Olympic Games with a throwing distance of 78.48 m, finishing in 24th place. The World Championships in 2017 served as preparation for the Tokyo Olympic Games in 2021, where he threw a distance of 77.41 m. Rocco's personal best is 87.62 m, which he threw in Cape Town in 2021.

My love for sports began... *in primary school. I played all sports and was fairly good at most of them, but javelin captured my heart because it is so challenging. I kept practicing for hours just to master it. For me, there was no option to quit, I took on the difficult challenge and had to see it through.*

If I was not a sports star, I would... *pursue a career in education! With that said, I am currently involved in training and motivational speaking on a daily basis. I have the privilege of being part of a team as an ambassador for Life Path Health. We visit schools, corporate companies, and offer clinics on a weekly basis. Along with that, I am also in ministry. As one of the pastors, I am very involved in our congregation. I preach and am involved in some of the ministry projects. My life is very close to my ideal profession.*

I am incredibly grateful for... *the choices I have made in my life until now. Not all of the choices were perfect, but even the bad choices have contributed to bringing me where I am today and being who I am as a person. I am also grateful for an incredible wife and baby, my church family, family, friends, and people who have supported me in my sports career to date.*

If I could edit my life, I would... *not change anything. It is more important to look ahead with the knowledge of the lessons learnt from the past. I do not live in the past. I may regret one decision, but even that taught me something.*

One of the biggest lessons I learnt this year... *stay in line with what you are called to do and where you need to be, regardless of whether it makes sense or not. God will take you out of that season, should He want to move you along. I also realised that I still needed to be involved in athletics. After yet another injury and operation on my shoulder, I wanted to retire from athletics, but I did not have peace. It was as if something was preventing me from doing it. I waited. I was invited to give motivational talks while I was confused and unmotivated. However, I now realise how important it is to stay in tune with God's plan for your life, until He gives you the green light to move on.*

My biggest achievement is... *between the Olympics and Commonwealth Games, I have not yet come out on top, but I am pushing on, I will keep going. If it is up to me, I will keep coming back.*

The Bible verse that carries me...

Romans 8:28,
"We know that God works all things together for
the good of those who love Him, those who are
called according to His purpose."

Exercising during lockdown

MY STORY
Rocco van Rooyen

It was 2009, an evening in a well-known hangout in Pretoria; another night of big parties and lots of alcohol. Like so many nights before, Rocco would not think twice about ordering another drink and going to bed in the early hours of the morning. However, this time was notable because it was the evening before the Junior World Athletics Championships. This was the competition that Rocco had worked so hard for and had looked forward to for months. The championship could be the beginning of a dream athletics career, with a bright future.

However, it was also this weekend in 2009 that Rocco recorded in his journal. His whole life, decisions, and outlook on the future changed after this weekend.

With a personal record distance of 75 m+ that he had consistently been throwing over the past few weeks, qualifying for the world youth championships in Brixen, Italy, would be a given, because the qualifying distance was only 70 m. But that Saturday, the young, cheeky Rocco would be jolted, because with a distance of 69.82 m he would have to settle for second place, thus not qualifying to be included in the team. Hours, days, and months of hard work on the athletic field resulted in nothing – he walked off the field crestfallen and with a heavy heart.

Rocco was 17 years old when he decided to change his life and turn his heart, soul, and spirit to God.

> **"Something broke inside of me. I was a youngster who had no relationship with God, but I was not an evil person either."**

"I got up to mischief – but I was not bad. I immediately realised that I could not say a quick prayer on the field on the day of my competition and ask the Lord for His help, and then expect Him to bless me. No, I had to do something from my side, I had to do more. From that moment on I began to reach out to God with a searching heart." Rocco had to find out who God is and would only later understand the value of the scripture in 1 Chronicles 28:9, "...know the God of your father, and serve Him with a loyal heart and with a willing mind; for the Lord searches all hearts and understands all the intent of the thoughts. If you seek Him, He will be found by you; but if you forsake Him, He will cast you off forever."

Rocco regularly addresses schools as a motivational speaker

As with everything in his life, Rocco passionately searched for God and found Him. God did not disappoint him either. Rocco got to know His voice and followed that voice without question or doubt. During his sports career, he had to undergo five operations and suffered more than twenty major injuries. This meant hours of rehabilitation and months away from the sports field. *"I would have packed away my javelin and given up a hundred times over."*

"If was not for my faith, I would have stopped, but time and time again, God gave me a reason to keep going."

"The fact that God writes and directs our life story keeps me on track. He is with us in the highs and the lows, the disappointments, and the victories."

The scripture in Romans 8:28 is alive in Rocco's heart, because he knows that God still has the power to make everything work together for good. He also knows that God is the source of his perseverance and discipline, because discipline is the one great quality that was missing in his life.

Rocco grew up without a father figure and his discipline was low on the list of priorities. However, this was no excuse, and he had to acknowledge and throw away that crutch. God came to fill the void and Rocco wanted to be a better version of himself.

It took comeback after comeback. The opinions of people had to become less important. The words that tear down and discourage had to make way for the voices of loved ones that encouraged and built up.

> **"It is hard to stay standing when people do not understand what is going on behind the scenes and do not have all the information before they make a judgement."**

"People's advice was that I should retire from athletics, quit, and just move on, among other things. The word 'fading' echoes in your ears ... or the questions, 'Why can you not perform under pressure?' People say things without understanding the context, and then you have to just forgive and let go."

It is in times such as these when God's guidance and counsel become a reality. Your mouth becomes familiar with the scripture in your heart and the words on your tongue are no longer your biggest obstacle. You realise that this is a pruning process and that it will not only happen once in your life. The pruning process is also not only about the end goal and pinnacle of your career. It is about your character development and the people who you team up with along the way. Disappointment has a ripple effect, but you learn not to give up and to persevere. *"You are not always going to win. You are not always going to perform well either. God's grace in your life does not exempt you from challenges, but the test is how you handle it and your heart's reaction to it."*

Rocco van Rooyen knows how it feels to work hard and still not achieve the breakthroughs that others celebrate on podiums. A medal in the top three positions still eludes him, but does that prevent him from trying hard and persevering? Not at all! *"What matters is that one must remain faithful to what God has entrusted to you. My final destination is heaven. One day God is going to ask me what I did with my little bag of gold, and I want to be able to say that I multiplied it. I want to live out His version of success and make Him proud."*

There is still no gold, bronze, or silver medal around his neck, but in the meantime, Rocco models the slogan: "Giving up is not an option." The word HOPE is written over his life. He is not only a javelin thrower and Olympic athlete. No, he uses sporting opportunities to reach places and countries where other people would not have the opportunity to spread a message of God's love and hope.

"It is not what you do, but how you do it ... and who knows, maybe there is a gold medal in the future. Until then, I will try to make a difference wherever I go."

What do you think is the biggest obstacle in men's lives?

Men have the responsibility to be leaders in their households and communities. We must be strong, make an impact, and be pioneers, but sometimes character traits that have not yet developed are expected of men. Many men grew up without mentors or father figures – without love, guidance, or discipline – yet they are expected to master those qualities. They may still be immature in a certain area but must take on the responsibility of a man. When mistakes and poor decision-making take their toll, men become ashamed or angry and the ripple effect of this reaction can be devastating. Weak leaders make stupid mistakes, and thus a church community with strong father figures, mentors, and leaders is desperately needed.

As men, we must depend on God.

How would you like to be remembered?

I would like to be remembered as someone who never gave up. And if I were to give up, that I would stop to think for a moment and say, "Let us try again!" I want to be that man who persistently sowed joy and had no regrets about missed chances and opportunities.

Your message to South Africa

"Keep going!" One foot in front of the other, day by day, week by week, and month by month. If you want to turn away, bump your head, but come back – do not stay in that place for too long. Keep moving forward. Make an impact and do what you have to do. Sow God's seeds of love and selflessness ... focus on what matters. Only He knows what is going on inside of you. Stay authentic and do not walk away from what you are doing until God says that you must.

Rocco van Rooyen
Exclusive interview
Scan the code to watch

Zoë Kruger

Zoë Kruger, born on the 31st of July 2002, is a right-handed South African tennis player. She is currently number 427 on the Women's Tennis Association (WTA) ranking and due to an injury has a protected ranking with the International Tennis Federation (ITF). Zoë is the eldest daughter of former Springbok rugby player, Ruben Kruger. Her younger sister, Isabella, represented South Africa at the 2022 Junior Wimbledon championships.

My love for sport began... *when I was three years old! I grew up in a sports-crazy family. My father played rugby, my mother participated in sports as a student, and my uncle, Frans Cronjé, is a tennis coach. It is thanks to him that I picked up a tennis racket. My father painted a white line on the wall of my grandmother's garage and my little sister, Bella, and I took turns every afternoon (30 minutes each) to hit the ball against the wall for hours on end. We enjoyed sandwiches and Oros as refreshments and, because of all of this, my love for tennis developed.*

If I was not a sports star, I would... *I am currently studying law, but if I was not a tennis player or chose law as a profession, I might have liked to be a marine biologist.*

I am incredibly grateful for... *my family and the people around me who love me and see me for who I am and not what I do. Life, and life in abundance, is a privilege. It is our responsibility to ask God what He expects from us each day. We must use every minute of every day to magnify His Name in all that we do; we must honour Him for the privilege of seeing another day and experiencing life. We cannot afford to only notice the negative.*

If I could edit my life, I would... *want to live more intentionally. As a young girl, I had the privilege of touring a lot for tennis tournaments. Yet, I was too serious, things just came and went. Though I travelled through countries, I missed out on a lot because I did not focus on enjoying the smaller things in life. When one begins to live more intentionally, gratitude starts blooming. These days I research every place that I will be visiting. I notice things, I live, taste, and view things differently because I live in gratitude.*

One of the biggest lessons I learnt this year... *is to wait on the Lord's plan for your life, and not lean on your own wisdom. See God's provision in an open door; see God's protection in a closed door.*

My greatest achievement is... *divided into two categories. The first is on the tennis court: after a series of injuries and months of patiently waiting and preparing behind the scenes, I had the privilege to step on the court again and win a professional tournament in October 2021. The second is my personal life with God: It is an honour that He trusts us with His Name. We are His ambassadors and every time we represent Him, tell someone about Him, or live in a way that honours His Name, it is a privilege.*

The Bible verse that carries me...
There are two:

Matthew 6:33,
"But seek first the kingdom of God and His righteousness, and all these things shall be added to you."

Proverbs 19:21,
"There are many plans in a man's heart, nevertheless the Lord's counsel – that will stand."

Zoë with her mother, Lize, and sister, Isabella

MY STORY
Zoë Kruger

"What would life have been like if my father was still alive? What would he have said about Bella and me? And what kind of man would he have been?" These are the kinds of questions that sometimes go through 20-year-old Zoë Kruger's mind, because she is only human. Yes, she knows the right answers and yes, she has found peace in her life, but sometimes, just sometimes, she wonders... he is in a better place. He is no longer in pain and God had determined that his time on earth was done. Sometimes she looks at photos and smiles, because everyone says he was a good, honest, and kind man.

She was seven years old when her father, former Springbok rugby player Ruben Kruger, died of brain cancer.

With two suitcases each, Zoë, her mother Lize, and her younger sister Isabella, moved to America. A promising future in tennis, with more opportunities, beckoned. With sporting blood in their veins, they could not let the opportunity go to waste.

Zoë remembers how she many times wanted to hang up her racket and give up. She was a young girl in a foreign country with Spanish coaches. Their routine for her was rigid and carefully planned, because there they would cultivate only the very best tennis players. Her formative years were challenging. She had to find the balance between her heart and her head, as well as all that the schedules of a normal teenager would involve. A regular Friday night outing was out of the question, not to mention the celebrations and holidays she had to miss out on because she had commitments that included a tennis racket, a tennis ball, and hours of practice.

However, she had to decide from a young age what the motive of her heart was and why she played tennis, otherwise the lifestyle and expectations could destroy her spirit and eventually suffocate her. *"I always played tennis because it was such a big part of my life. I had big dreams and enjoyed the hard work. Until one day, something woke up in me and I realised that this was not just a hobby for me. Playing tennis is my calling."*

"This talent that God entrusted to me was something He trusted me with!"

"My life"

"Immediately, I understood my life's purpose! Every bit of pain and injury, sacrifice and loss made sense. I had to exalt God's Name in places where there are not many children of the Lord. I realised that it is not a right, but a privilege."

The new insight about her vocation made enjoyable days even more pleasurable, the unbearable days more bearable, and the doubts in her mind quieted down. Although she was alone, God was by her side wherever she went. *"'They say, 'God is a friend who sticks closer than a brother' – I lived it."*

Zoë's foundation is rock solid. She comes from a strong Christian family that prays together about everything, and even though she does not know all the Bible verses, she holds on to two that speak life into the season that she finds herself in. During COVID God became "real" for her once again. It was when she returned to South Africa – after seven years in America, a country far removed from the more principled, conservative lifestyle we enjoy in South Africa – that the role of a church community and close friends made a huge impact. She was able to pray again, learnt to study the Bible, and finally understood what she was reading, because she was on a journey with God. His revelation to her did not just happen suddenly or through the eyes of someone else, it happened during her continuous daily search for who He really was in her life.

The Lord entrusted Zoë with more than just talent. He entrusted her with the role as a sports person in South Africa, a role model and spokesperson for young girls. She had to first realise the responsibility, and then take it on one hundred percent, knowing that God will hold her accountable. She no longer talks about the sacrifices because the questions have been answered. The goal with her talent is clear. She walked away from those who did not understand or respect her choice with a hug, a big smile, and peace in her heart. *"Sometimes you have to walk away from people who do not understand your calling ... even if it hurts. God's plans are much bigger than your own plans for your life."*

She was born to stand out; born for a purpose, and she does not want to miss it.

> **"We can disappoint everyone, but I never want to disappoint Him. God's plan for my life comes first."**

"Even though I plan and do not easily shift my focus, I now know that God is in control. And that is okay."

His plan is powerful in her life, and He has the best in mind for her. Luke 11:13, *"If you then, being evil, know how to give good gifts to your children, how much more will your heavenly Father give the Holy Spirit to those who ask Him!"*

Zoë and Bella

What do you think is the biggest obstacle in women's lives?

I think there are three obstacles:
1. Women believe that they are not good enough.
2. Women are underestimated – most of the time and in many circumstances. Our abilities and emotional intelligence are not noticed or valued. People classify us and hang heavy labels around our necks about things that are not true. Along with this, men often think that women cannot do certain things. I am definitely not a feminist and understand the different roles of a man and a woman in a relationship, household, on the sports field, and in the workplace, but I think we are still underestimated. Neither male nor female is better than the other sex. There are roles created for each.
3. We sometimes have identity problems. We find our identity in the wrong things, instead of in God.

How would you like to be remembered?

I would like to be remembered as someone who gave one hundred percent in her life. Someone who wanted to help everyone around her, rather than herself. Someone who made a difference, even in the small gestures. Someone who noticed and appreciated the little things. Finally, as someone like my father: honest, compassionate, loving, and helpful.

Your message to South Africa

Your life journey is your own. No one's path or assignment should be compared with someone else's. You are called to something specific. Do not be jealous. Your path with the Lord is unique.

Zoë Kruger
Exclusive interview
Scan the code to watch
◀◀◀

Impi Visser

Impi Brecher Visser, born on the 30th of May 1995, is a Blitzbok warrior through and through! He is a rugby sevens player for the South African national team in the World Rugby Sevens series. With his build of 1.89 m and 94 kg, he is the epitome of rugby at its best and is an outstanding forward in sevens rugby, as well as a centre in the fifteen-man game. Impi, a former learner of Hoërskool Ermelo in Mpumalanga, spread his wings as a youth and played for the Pumas (2012-2013), Blue Bulls (2014-2016), and in the Varsity Cup series at the University of Pretoria for UP Tuks (2017). Impi is a keen student with a degree in mechanical engineering. In 2017, he was named one of the Varsity Cup dream team and had the opportunity to play against the Junior Springboks in a promotional match. In 2018, Impi made his debut for the Blitzboks. To date, he has played in more than 30 World Series tournaments and appeared in more than 170 matches in the green and gold.

My love for sport began... *in our backyard, where my older brother and I used to play. We kicked the rugby ball and often broke windows playing cricket outside. From an early age, I realised that I really loved sports – at school I played as many different sports as possible.*

If I was not a sports star, I would... *really like to become a veterinarian.*

I am incredibly grateful for... *my parents and the opportunities they afforded me. They made constant sacrifices to give our family the best and I will forever be grateful for the life they created for us.*

If I could edit my life, I would... *not want to change anything! I have never wanted to, and really do not want to change anything. The mistakes that I made taught me valuable lessons and have made me the man I am today.*

One of the biggest lessons I learnt this year... *is to be grateful for what I have. So many people struggle every day to obtain what I take for granted.*

My biggest achievement is... *being able to represent my country at the Olympic Games, it was a big moment for me.*

The Bible verse that carries me...

Romans 8:28, "And we know that all things work together for good to those who love God, to those who are the called according to His purpose."

Impi and his wife, Sarrah, love nature – especially the bushveld. Here they are pictured in the Kruger National Park

MY STORY
Impi Visser

"Is Impi your nickname?" Impi answered this question almost daily, but smiled and remained patient, because he understood his responsibility and prestige in our country. "Impi" – a Zulu word meaning "group of warriors" – is not a nickname, but his first name. His grandfather, uncle, and cousins also have this name. It serves as a reminder of a part of history that had a huge impact in Afrikaans culture. He is proud of his name and the name's rich history. When he talks about the future of our country, Impi Visser smiles, because this is his country with the most unique population in the world!

His positive attitude developed over time, thanks to many bumps in the road – and certainly not overnight. During his student years, Impi had to fight and defeat a multitude of invisible giants.

The fear that he would fail as a man knocked on his door non-stop for five years.

For those years, it felt as if he had not found direction in even one of the five focus areas in his life yet. He doubted his choices in the academic field of study, and his sports career had stagnated. He experienced no growth nor achieved success, and he wanted to just give up – more than a hundred times.

In those five years, Impi had to get clarity on the answer to the big question:

Exactly who was Impi Visser, and what defined his identity?

It was in his daily quiet time – the search for God's voice, time spent in prayer, and reading God's Word – where Impi finally found peace about his identity and calling. *"Many sports people find their identity in what they do and achieve, but I know now that I find my identity in God and what Jesus did for us all on the cross ... and it was not in vain."*

"Two friends also from Pongola (Jacques Rouillard and Philip Smit) and me on the summit of Kilimanjaro."

It was God's grace, Impi's parents, and the friends he made at university that became the driving force that spurred him on to achieve success in every facet of his life. *"I am eternally grateful for that. God truly blessed me, even in the times when it looked and felt like everything was a setback."*

God could entrust Impi with a definitive role as sports icon in South Africa. He could trust him with the prestige, as Impi had chosen God and put Him first in his life. *"Now I want to honour God in everything I do. In my career, there are many temptations that come in all sorts of guises, and it can rob you of joy in God – and it has happened in the past. But then I make a deliberate choice whether I want to follow the world's way of doing things or God's truth. And every time I chose God's truth."*

Whether it is fear, a question or doubt, human relationships, another pandemic, or a crisis, Impi knows that God is always in control and that he can fully trust Him. There will be bumps along the way, but God will constantly ensure growth while He protects him. Impi is truly free, because Jesus died on the cross for our sins, including his.

Quality time with his family in Ballito

Impi is very fond of sports, especially golf

What do you think is the biggest obstacle in men's lives?

To fail or to feel like a failure.

How would you like to be remembered?

I would like to be remembered as someone who lived to the fullest! Someone who made time for his friends and family. Someone who assisted and helped other people. A man of integrity and a follower of Jesus.

Your message to South Africa

I think that we, South Africans, are some of the most unique people in the world and I will always have hope for our country and our people. Each day we must try to make the country a better place and treat each other with love and respect.

Impi Visser Exclusive interview
Scan the code to watch

Family time in Pongola

"Time together with my pals will always be a priority in my life." Proverbs 27:17 (NIV), "As iron sharpens iron, so one person sharpens another."

Hennie Koortzen

Hennie Koortzen, born on the 27th of January 1961, has been involved with SuperSport as an Afrikaans rugby, boxing, cricket, football, and athletics commentator since 2001. This well-known voice and former Northern Capetonian from Kakamas developed a love for broadcasting in 1979 during his first year as a student at the University of the Free State, where he was involved with campus radio. Hennie also worked at the SABC and many community radio stations. His radio career spans a period of more than 30 years and he has received, among others, the SAB Award for the Best Sports Presenter and two Namibian 'ATKV-veertjies' for his contribution. In 2022, Hennie was inducted into the South African Radio Awards Hall of Fame as a seasoned radio personality and commentator, along with a handful of iconic personalities in the radio industry. Under his leadership as station manager and, later, chief executive officer of Pretoria FM, this radio station also received many South African Radio Awards. This former learner of Hoërskool Martin Oosthuizen still does the sports reports on Pretoria FM.

My love for sport began... *as a little boy. I really loved sports and played a bit of rugby, but I soon realised that my talents lay in other things, including talking! I was fortunate that my father loved rugby very much and when the Springboks played a test abroad, we would get up early on Saturday mornings and huddle around the radio under our warm blankets, coffee in hand, to listen to the broadcast and commentary of Gerhard Viviers. These are some of my fondest memories of my childhood.*

If I was not a sports commentator, I would... *practice as a psychologist. I took psychology as a university subject until my third year; my natural aptitude and intuition around people has always stood me in good stead. I sense it when people are upset, and I know how to encourage others. I love people and want to offer a safe haven and guidance. I always see the light at the end of the tunnel and choose to see the end of a road as the beginning of a new path. Positivity comes easily to me in the midst of life's circumstances, which throw us all a curve ball at some point or another.*

I am incredibly grateful for... *the opportunities that I have been afforded in my life. The Lord opened doors for me in areas where I least expected it, and in such a natural way. There were times when, in despondence, I wanted to turn my back on my dreams, but God always opened the way back to broadcasting.*

I am also grateful for my supportive family, friends, and colleagues. Without them, I would never have been able to maintain a successful personal life and career at the same time.

If I could edit my life, I would... spend a lot more time with my family! The misrepresentation of what is really important in life sometimes makes us slaves and victims of our own decisions. However, nothing can be more important than spending time with those you love and whom God is lending to you on your journey through life. I regret the mistakes I have made, but I consider it all a learning school for a better future!

One of the biggest lessons I learnt this year... It is important to not lose yourself in the hustle and bustle of life! The COVID restrictions made me realise that everything can still be achieved without needing those extra hours in your day. Be aware of your God-given task and calling and be obedient to His call. You will be surprised at how much time you have to succeed in much more than just your career.

My greatest achievement is... just being the best version of myself that I can be every day! God does not expect miracles from me! He performs the miracles in our lives every day – often without us even being aware of them. He does not give us a life with guarantees, but a life with opportunities and the talents to use and take advantage of these opportunities. I want to be remembered as His light bearer, despite my faults. My achievements are His achievements through me!

The Bible verse that carries me...

Philippians 4:13,
"I can do all things through Christ who strengthens me."

Hennie and Maritha on their wedding day

MY STORY
Hennie Koortzen

Hennie grew up on an island in the Orange River, about 20 km above the Augrabies waterfalls – a place where his family still farms with grapes. Hennie is familiar with the "organic" way of growing up. He knows about growing vegetables and fruits, farming with chickens, and milking cows. He understands hard work and persevering, but he also understands dreaming big. Because there, next to the canals on the island, young Hennie's dreams took flight – with a cassette recorder in hand, he walked around for hours and made recordings, narrating what he observed. Every weeknight everyone around the dinner table had to listen to his adventures of the day, but weekends were different. On Saturdays, the famous voice of radio legend and experienced rugby commentator Gerhard "Spiekeries" Viviers echoed through the Koortzen house. Saturday was synonymous with rugby, and then Hennie and his family were glued to the "wireless". Uncle Gerhard was Hennie's hero. He would carefully listen to every aspect of the commentating, only to later repeat the broadcast with the pronunciation and style copied to perfection!

Viviers' nickname was Spiekeries because that was always his answer when someone asked him how he was doing. Hennie was only ten years old, but he remembers the first test between the Springboks and the All Blacks on the 25th of July 1970 at Loftus Versfeld. It was five years after the Springboks' disastrous tour of New Zealand, and also the first series after the tour of Britain, which was marred by protesters and was equally dreadful. Hennie remembers how determined the Springboks were to kick off the series with a win. A hero was needed to secure that victory. At the time, television was only a myth, South Africans had to wait another six years for it to make its appearance, but the legendary Gerhard Viviers vividly described the match to the listeners of the SABC Afrikaans radio service. That would always stay with Hennie. The All Blacks received a penalty kick in their own half and, in the end, All Blacks captain Brian Lochore got hold of the ball. Then the Springboks' right winger, Syd Nomis, intercepted the ball and sprinted full tilt to the goal line (He had been part of the team since 1965). Gerhard was in full cry and the most memorable piece of sports commentary in our country's history followed. *"Siddie! Siddie! Siddie!"* he yelled! The final score of 17—6 in the Springboks' favour was just as sensational as the commentating – that moment would forever live in Hennie's heart ... because he too would one day yell out famous names in the same fashion. Hennie made up his mind there and then: Though he would never be able to play for the Springboks himself, he would become a Springbok announcer!

Research shows that up to 95% of people never achieve and live out their dreams, but this native of Kakamas would refuse to be part of that statistic. Hennie's first opportunity

Hennie with Toks van der Linde

Commentators ahead of the 2019 World Cup final

to serve as a sports commentator was as a first-year student at the University of the Free State with the campus radio team. A soaking wet, over-eager Hennie braved the torrential rain as he climbed up the scoreboard of the university sports fields, two-way radio in hand. From there he connected to another two-way radio in the studio to provide live commentary on the hostel rugby final. Like a mini Spiekeries, Hennie described the tries and goal kicks and kept the campus radio listeners glued to their seats.

> He would practice his technique, polish his pronunciation, and use every opportunity to try to perfect his skill.

"I was very young when, one day, I got into my car and drove to the SABC. The odds of ever getting any airtime were very slim, but I was determined, and because I was willing to learn, I was also willing to do anything. Coming from the Northern Cape, the city centre of Johannesburg was terrifying. However, the office of Christo Olivier in the giant SABC office block was a place where I would find my feet, because with his guidance and advice I got involved in the news department, and then much later in broadcasting itself."

Many people contributed to help Hennie realise his dream. God opened doors and put the right people on Hennie's path so that he could finally sit behind the microphone. However, he had to learn to trust God and leave the dreams about his future up to Him. *"When there was opposition in my broadcasting career, I always stuck to the advice of my high school teacher, Mr Erasmus:*

'If you fall, do not forget to get up.'

'Too many people stay down or do not have the courage to get up again. Everyone is going to stumble and fall at one time or another, but the question always remains – what are you going to do then?'"

Hennie would follow this advice many times because anger, sadness, disappointment, and rage were simply emotions and should not be allowed to take hold. He would choose to see things differently and then stand up again. When he looks back over his life, he can clearly see the hand of God, who always helped and guided him.

It took six years before Hennie became a well-known voice on SuperSport. This was after the much older Hennie had to take another huge chance and a leap of faith. He followed Naas Botha's advice, made a recording of himself, and simply drove to the studios of the broadcasting giant. There he handed over his recording to someone in hope that it would end up in the hands of the person who made decisions about voice artists and commentating work for SuperSport. A week later, Hennie received correspondence and was asked to refine his broadcasting style. Only seven days later, Hennie sat behind the microphone of a SuperSport broadcast for the first time. *"My life changed the day. I realised that God is the one who fulfils our dreams! I was older and wiser, but God could now trust me with the big dreams that had He planted in my heart from childhood. When we realise our dreams are not our own, but only the dreams God has for us ... He becomes a reality in our lives! And then we have the guts to tackle even higher heights!"*

His first broadcast of a Springbok rugby test was on the green fields of the Bloemfontein rugby stadium. Hennie came full circle; he was back where he started. From SABC Bloemfontein's broadcasting rookie to experienced Springbok rugby test commentator with 26 years of broadcasting experience. However, the dream coming true would not be without a hurdle or two. Once again, Hennie had to choose how and when he was going to get up... *"We all had to fly to Bloemfontein to broadcast the test, only to get to the airport and find out that there were double bookings and I had to stay behind. Immediately, I called the SuperSport management and offered to drive from Johannesburg to Bloemfontein because I did not want to miss the opportunity. Management devised a plan B. I was on my way to plane number two, just in time to hear that there were no more pilots on duty to fly the plane! I got up three hours later and decided to carry out my plan and drive to Bloemfontein by car. Fortunately, there was a bright light at the end of the tunnel, and I got a seat on another flight!"*

Hennie with his family, parents, and in-laws

Hennie's first test would forever be etched in his mind, because the late Joost van der Westhuizen took seat next to him to broadcast as a co-commentator. *"I remember the feeling of broadcasting with a Springbok hero.*

> *"It was one of the most special moments – not only to know that I was good enough to sit there, but also to watch Joost in action."*

"He still teared up during the national anthem, and with every try, he jumped up passionately. Right there, I once again realised the unifying power of sport."

The 2011 Rugby World Cup in New Zealand is another highlight in Hennie's diary. As anchor presenter, together with the famous rugby player, commentator, and television presenter, Kobus Wiese, they shared the highs and lows with the South African public. The Springboks did not walk away with the laurels, but they played every game with passion and zeal. Hennie equalled their zeal and never had to regret a single lost opportunity. *"My passion for every game is great: Whether I am broadcasting for school rugby or whether I am preparing for an international test, my preparation and energy always remain the same. I realise that this is just as important for the school sports player as it is for the Springbok player on the field. Each player's parents, fans, and friends see that match as a personal test and, thus, it is important for me to bring the* same amount of energy to the table. It remains a privilege and an opportunity – every single time."

Another big highlight for Hennie was being able to be involved as a presenter in the KykNet series, *Op die Skouers van Reuse*, where he was able to interview various sports personalities about their passion for sport, but also talk about the differences they make in the community. He says it was clear what a vital role God plays or has played in practically everyone's life and success.

He looks back on more than 30 years in broadcasting and still sees opportunities. *"My advice to anyone interested in this industry: Be on the look out for opportunities. If you know that this is the calling that God has for you, never let anyone tell you that you are not good enough. Listen to advice. Polish your technique, and then give it all you have! Because when you look back one day, you are going to wonder: How did this happen?"*

Hennie is a Springbok broadcaster and a legend in his own right. He lives in gratitude every day and still realises the grace in his life.

Hennie and Maritha during the SA Radio Awards

Having an enjoyable time at De Vette Mossel

What do you think is the biggest obstacle in men's lives?

A man never wants to be labelled as someone who "could not make it", so he will work harder and put even more pressure on himself. But somewhere in the course of his life, every man must stop in his tracks and realise that he is a child of a living God and Father who wants to take care of him. Then he must rest in the knowledge that he is only human, admit his shortcomings, be at peace, and leave his dreams to God to manage, because He is God.

How would you like to be remembered?

I would like to be remembered as someone who could make a difference where it really mattered. May our heavenly Father open my eyes to see opportunities to be a helping hand to someone on a difficult path! I would like to be remembered in the broadcasting industry as someone who was able to help others with similar dreams with practical advice and training.

Your message to South Africa

Lift your head and make sure that you give your best every day. We can all sit in a corner and complain about what is negative, but it will not make any difference. Get up every day and give your best; help where you get the opportunity to do so, even if it is just to give a smile. Focus on the little things around you that you can do. Leave the miracles in God's hands. You will have a better life and you will sow seeds so that the people around you will also have a better life.

Hennie Koortzen
Exclusive interview
Scan the code to watch
◀◀◀

Ronald Brown

Ronald Brown, born on the 2nd of September 1995, is a South African rugby sevens player and Olympic athlete. Commentators refer to him as "the speedster who is faster than takeaway food", but the former Montagu High School student is a star and the idol of every boy in that town. With the help and attention of competent coaches, 15-year-old Ronald played as fly half for the u19 team, making his mark in school rugby. He wore the Boland colours for a while before, as a keen student at the University of Johannesburg, he played in the Varsity Cup series (2014-2017). It was after an invitation to be part of the SAS Rugby Sevens Academy in Stellenbosch (2018) that Ronald made his debut as part of the 2020 Blitzbok team in the number 13 jersey and wore the green and gold for the Olympic Games in Tokyo. Ronald was also part of the South African sevens team that won their second gold medal at the 2022 Commonwealth Games in Birmingham.

My love for sport began... *next to the rugby field and in the streets of Montagu. When I was growing up, my cousins played rugby for a club in Montagu and that inspired me to try the sport as well. I fell in love with it. Touch rugby with friends in the streets of Montagu – after school, in the evenings, and over weekends – made my passion for the sport grow.*

If I was not a sports star, I would... *definitely have become an architect. I have a passion for drawing buildings and structures.*

I am incredibly grateful for... *my family. They show their support through thick and thin.*

If I could edit my life, I would... *change absolutely nothing.*

One of the biggest lessons I learnt this year... *always live life to the fullest and strive to give your utmost in everything you do.*

My biggest achievement is... *representing South Africa at the Olympic Games in Tokyo 2020.*

The Bible verse that carries me...

*Matthew 21:22,
"If you believe, you will receive whatever you ask for in prayer."*

HSBC's player of the match in the 2021 Dubai final

MY STORY
Ronald Brown

"It is cancer. Hodgkin's lymphoma…"

In that moment, Ronald Brown's world came crashing down. He was a young, strong, up-and-coming player for the South African rugby sevens team, on his way to making his debut in 2019 in the green and gold at a tournament in Los Angeles.

Everything Ronald had worked for and everything the 24-year-old had dreamt about for the previous eighteen years shattered in a matter of moments.

In November 2018, Ronald moved to Stellenbosch to take up his position in the SAS Rugby Sevens Academy, with the hope of becoming a Blitzbok. He had the support of his parents, family, and all of Montagu behind him. *"I was really glad to join the team, but God had other plans."*

In January 2019, Ronald injured his knee in a punishing training session with the team while preparing for a tournament. With the damning news that the meniscus of his knee was torn, an operation and three months away from the playing field was in the offing. He would not be selected for the team. A further hamstring injury setback extended the original recovery period from 12 to 18 weeks, and again he was not included in the team.

"After more than four months, I was finally able to return to training sessions and was chomping at the bit to train with the team in preparation for the Los Angeles tournament. I knew I could possibly make the team this time, but during practice, I experienced pain in my chest. I did not think it was anything serious and continued exercising. However, the pain worsened, and I had to go for scans."

It was the night before Ronald was to go for his visa appointment that he received the call from the team doctor, Dr Leigh Gordon. The visit to the hospital in Stellenbosch would hopefully just be a routine examination, but Ronald's life was turned upside down that day. *"I had so many questions. Would I ever be able to play rugby again?*

Always a grateful heart towards God after a game

Would I survive? What would happen to me? It felt like everything was going wrong, and I asked God if I was in the right place in my life."

This is where his path with the Lord really began.

"I grew up in a Christian home. We went to church. My father was very strict, he kept us on the straight and narrow path. My mother had a stroke 13 years ago, which affected her speech. Everything in our house changed. Everyone had to take on extra responsibilities. It was hard on my father, hard on all of us, but family was important, and we stood together and pushed through."

This time they would all rally around Ronald, the only son in the house – once again the family stood together. In this scrum, Ronald embraced God and never let go of Him. *"I began to spend more time in the presence of the Lord because I needed Him more than ever before ... my relationship with God changed, it became stronger, and I grew to love Him even more."*

"My desire to become more like Him deepened."

Ronald's weeks of chemotherapy turned into a journey of faith with his heavenly Father and his earthly father by his side. His parents' home was his safe fortress. His parents – especially his mother, with few to no words – were his life coaches on the road to recovery. Ronald lost 11 kgs – muscle mass, the one thing a rugby player desperately needs. However, this did not stop him. COVID and the overall confinement period gave Ronald a little more time. He used this time to get stronger, faster, and even more focused, while training for hours on end.

His fairy tale return to rugby stunned everyone. Ronald was stronger and faster, and his second chance at life and rugby made him even more passionate about every training opportunity. His relationship with God had deepened and this inspired his coaches and teammates.

"After this pruning process, I finally got my chance to be selected as Blitzbok and was even selected as Springbok sevens player of the year in 2021. No words can describe what the Lord has done for me. I am so grateful for His goodness. Being in His presence still makes me feel overwhelmed because I see His goodness and who He really is. It feels like He makes sure that I know I am His son and that He has chosen me, every day."

Life will always have some setbacks, be it an injury, disappointment in people, not being selected for the team, or a bad experience due to the world's ways, but one thing is certain; Ronald Brown knows the voice of his Father and he will never undertake anything without God's hand guiding him.

Cancer conqueror

Ronald played for Montagu High School

What do you think is the biggest obstacle in men's lives?

Mental health issues. Traditional gender roles and society's expectations have a significant effect on why men are less likely to seek help or discuss mental health issues. Men are often expected to be strong, the breadwinners – and with other pressures that come with these expectations, it can be difficult to open up and talk about our emotions.

How would you like to be remembered?

I would like to be remembered as a God-fearing individual who inspired other people and never gave up on his dreams.

Your message to South Africa

It does not matter where you come from – if you have the desire, willingness, and belief to achieve your dreams, nothing is impossible.

Ronald Brown
Exclusive interview
Scan the code to watch

UJ's sportsman of the year in 2021

Henco Venter

Hendrik Petrus Venter (Henco), born on the 27th of March 1992, is a South African rugby player. This former Bloemfonteiner is a nephew of the late South African rugby players Ruben Kruger and Drikus Hattingh (former Springbok lock). As a former Gray College learner, he follows in the footsteps of great rugby legends. The young Henco's rugby career kicked off in 2005 with his inclusion in the u13 Craven Week tournament. In 2008 he played in the u16 Grant Khomo week and was honoured as a member of the u16 elite group. After Henco played in the 2009 Academy Week, his future seemed set. As a player for the Free State u19 team, he represented the young Cheetahs in the 2011 u19 provincial championship and represented the Free State u21 team in 2012 and 2013 for the provincial championship. He made his debut for the UV Shimlas in the Varsity Cup series and was included in the Varsity Cup dream team at the end of the 2015 Varsity Cup tournament. In 2012 he played in his first Currie Cup match with the Cheetah on his chest during a promotion-relegation match against the Eastern Province Kings. Henco's provincial career includes the Cheetahs (2012-2018) and the Japanese team, Toshiba Brave Lupus (2018-2019). He has been playing as a loose forward for the Sharks since 2020.

My love for sport began... *as a little boy. I grew up next to the rugby field. Sport has always been in my family: Two of my uncles played for the Blue Bulls and Springboks (Ruben Kruger and Drikus Hattingh). I remember how we went to see them play and how proud I was of them. My father was a school principal and I went with him to all the first team's practices, tours, and matches, and even trained with the older children.*

If I was not a sports star, I would... *have studied theology at the University of the Free State. I have always had a love for theology – the history as well as a calling in that direction, but I also really like the business world. Owning your own business gives you more flexibility and therefore more family time, which is a big priority for me. It would thus be a marriage of theology and entrepreneurship.*

I am incredibly grateful for... *my family. Michael J. Fox says: "Family is not an important thing. It is everything." This is how I feel. I am truly grateful for my wife and my family. If everything (manufactured) is taken away from you in the end, all that you would have left is each other and your memories. I am especially so grateful for the life (and lessons) I had as a child, it has been invaluable to me, to this day. We are a very close-knit family and visit each other often.*

If I could edit my life, I would... *say to myself, "Henco, study for those Greek and Hebrew tests – you do not want to do a rewrite!" There is nothing that I would want to change. There have been many lessons that I have learnt so far in my life, and to change anything would cause me not to have learnt them.*

One of the biggest lessons I have learnt this year... *Things do not always work out the way you imagined them, and that is okay. We do not run the show, there is Someone behind the scenes who makes things work out perfectly for us (Romans 8:28).*

We are the clay; He is the Potter who is busy shaping us into something wonderful – how nice to surrender!

My biggest achievement is... *If I have to single out one achievement, it is being able to study and be a professional sportsman at the same time. It is something that required a lot of discipline and I am glad I persevered.*

There are several highlights in my life: I think of my wedding day, my graduation, the Varsity Cup we won, Currie Cups we won, and different games that demanded all we had until the end.

The Bible verse that carries me...

Isaiah 40:30-31,
"Even youths grow tired and weary, and young men stumble and fall; but those who hope in the Lord will renew their strength. They will soar on wings like eagles; they will run and not grow weary, they will walk and not be faint."

Henco with his loved ones after a tough game

Henco and his wife, Lurinda, on their wedding day

MY STORY
Henco Venter

The Lord is real for him. He makes a point of being aware of God as he lives each day, because He is his Father, his best friend, and the One he to talks about everything. *"I experience God every day. When I am one hundred percent aware of Him, I am full of energy, I am proactive and not merely reacting to things. I can then take in everything that God has given me, to make the right decisions – whether on the rugby field, in business, or in my spiritual life."*

Henco grew up in a home with Christian values and standards, and follows his parents' example. It was while growing up that he realised that God was not far off, but near. This awareness completely removed the complicated questions about God's goodness. From a young age it was a foregone conclusion: Bad things will happen because we live in a world where this is a reality, but God is always good!

> **"The world is going to ask you who you are, and if you cannot tell the world who you are, the world is going to tell you exactly who you are."**

"For me, being a Christian is to declare to the world every day: 'I am Henco Venter, and I want to be exactly like Jesus Christ.'"

However, that decision did not exempt Henco from the bumps and bruises of life. He experienced them too. There were the four shoulder operations in matric (between May and the end of January 2011). The wounds became inflamed and septic, preventing Henco from being a part of teams and competitions, which could have meant a possible positive direction in his young sports career. There were numerous times when he doubted whether he would ever play rugby again. *"Storms shape us. Nothing that comes easy is worth it. We soon forget a healing that came easily."*

Henco had to make the decision early in his life to do things differently and to think differently. The world wanted to put him in a box, but the 1.92 m tall giant soon realised that he did not have to live up to people's expectations. *"Be comfortable with not having to live up to expectations and demands. The world makes demands and wants you to*

Henco's whole family together on the farm: The Venters (Lurinda, Henco, Behan, Dawie, and Marietjie) and the De Wets (Ane, Alison, and Michal)

do things in a certain way, but then it is freeing to do it completely differently; not like the world."

With this outlook, Henco looked the world squarely in the eye, because easy choices in the moment would mean a difficult life later, while difficult choices in the moment would mean an easy life later. This point of view was a practical guideline in the uncertain times to distinguish between good and bad, mistakes and no mistakes. *"It is difficult for any young person to have discernment if you do not have a lot of knowledge yet. I have already burnt my fingers with wrong choices and relationships; those red lights that one ignores. Sometimes one has to walk the path of failure to learn and to gain wisdom."*

God could trust Henco with a role as a sports person in South Africa, with the prestige, because Henco knows who he is. *"You take wrong path, but the Holy Spirit brings you back to the right path. It is through these personal experiences that you learn who you are and why you are the way you are."*

Henco holds on to Romans 8:28, "And we know that in all things God works for the good of those who love Him, who have been called according to His purpose." He firmly believes that when we, as children of God, do our part, the Lord will make everything work together for good. He prays daily for the "guts" to make the hard choices and to push through.

His character was formed step by step, away from the sports field. Henco put the ball aside while the preacher inside him stepped forward, because at heart that has always been who he is. "The triangle of shalom, to experience peace, is spiritual wealth, emotional wealth (stability), and sufficient financial wealth (provision). I cannot have one and not the other, then there will be an unfulfilled need and I will try to fill it with earthly things. The tools in the Bible to use are the seven expressions of the Holy Spirit in Isaiah 11:

1. The Spirit of the Lord
2. The spirit of wisdom
3. The spirit of understanding
4. The spirit of counsel
5. The spirit of might
6. The spirit of knowledge
7. The spirit of the fear of the Lord

If the fruit of the Lord's sevenfold Spirit can be seen in my life, I will truly experience "shalom".

> "Everyone does and thinks differently, but the most important thing is to remember that we are on earth for Him; to bring glory to Him in everything we undertake, and to move away from our own desires and opinions."

"Life is short, tomorrow is not guaranteed … do not let your lamp be empty of oil when the Bridegroom arrives."

Henco on the farm with mother Marietjie and father Dawie

What do you think is the biggest obstacle in men's lives?

Different seasons have different obstacles. I suspect pride is the biggest obstacle: being too proud to say sorry, too proud to say "yes" to the right thing, too proud to say "no" to the wrong thing, too proud ask for help, and too proud to surrender when the time is right to do so.

How would you like to be remembered?

I would like to be remembered as an ordinary man who lived in the moment every day and gave his best for everyone and everything; that I did not just talk about my faith, but that I lived it daily.

Your message to South Africa

We must open our eyes and stand up. We are in Africa and it is not always easy in our country, but we are tough people. The Lord has given us all the tools we need to have shalom (peace) in South Africa. If you cannot change the country as a whole, start small – with your attitude, with your family, in your neighbourhood, or where you are. Positivity has the ability to spread like wildfire. It is our choice whether we want to use it or not. Talking negatively around the braai is not going to help anything, except to make you more negative.

As Carike Keuzenkamp sings in her song ,"Dis 'n land", South Africa is rich in colour and sound, it is a land of abundance to be grateful for ... but only if you decide to see it and to lend a hand.

Henco Venter
Exclusive interview
Scan the code to watch
◀◀◀

Henco, James Venter, and Werner Kok after a successful day of fishing

Henco and Lurinda enjoy coffee with his sister, Ane, her husband, Michal, and their little daughter, Alison

Warren Whiteley

Warren Roger Whiteley, born on the 18th of September 1987, is a former South African professional rugby player and currently the defence coach for the Sharks. This Durbanite's colourful rugby career includes time as a player for the Sharks (2008-2009), the Mighty Elephants (2009), more than 160 games for the Golden Lions and Lions in the Super Rugby and Currie Cup series (2010-2018), and ten games for the Red Hurricanes (2016-2018). The former Glenwood High School pupil made his mark as captain for the Lions, winning the Currie Cup in 2011 and 2015, and reaching three finals in the 2016, 2017, and 2018 Super Rugby series. Warren donned the green and gold for the first time when he played for the Blitzboks as a young 25-year-old in 2012. He became part of the South African sevens team that won the gold medal at the 2016 Commonwealth Games in Glasgow. After two years with the Springbok already on his chest, Warren also got the opportunity to make his debut for the Springboks in 2014. He made his debut against Australia in Perth and, after the regular number eight player, Duane Vermeulen, suffered an injury in the second test against Ireland, Warren was a regular in the Springboks' starting team as number eight. In 2017 coach Allister Coetzee appointed Warren as the 58th captain of the Springboks, but due to an injury, Warren missed the final mid-year test against France. The Stormers lock, Eben Etzebeth, took over as captain, and then Siya Kolisi took over the captaincy in the absence of both Warren and Eben. He retains the captaincy after the return of both players.

In 2019, after 23 tests for the Springboks, a series of knee injuries forced this proud son of KwaZulu-Natal to retire from professional rugby. He is currently investing in the talent of young players and uses his wealth of knowledge and experience as positive guidelines in his coaching.

Warren is married to Felicity and is the father of their two daughters and a son: Ava, Lily, and Samuel.

My love for sport began... *as a young boy. I really loved nature and the outdoors, I was always running around outside or climbing trees. I had a great love for individual sports in primary school and excelled in long distance running, high jump, and shot put, but though enjoying athletics, I developed a love for team sports playing cricket. It was the camaraderie and friendship that attracted me, and the fact that you worked together towards a mutual goal.*

If I was not a sports star, I would... *have gone into a creative direction for sure, or I would have become a teacher or coach that could still have an influence and make a difference in children's lives.*

I am incredibly grateful for... *my wife and family, my parents and coaches, and every mentor in my life. They have all made a huge and unique contribution to who I am today as a man. The South African public supported us in full stadiums during my rugby career and for that I am also grateful. Then of course I am grateful to God. He is my everything. He is always present, and He is my Father – the One who understands me better than anyone else.*

If I could edit my life, I would... *not change anything. I regret few things in my life. The path I walked made me the man I am today. It is here where I find myself right now, where God wanted me. Every season in my life has been a growth process. Yes, I would have liked to finish my career on my terms and finally wrapped it up, but things do not always go the way we want or expect them to. What I do have in my hands are the choices I make to learn and grow in each situation.*

One of the biggest lessons I learnt this year... *It is not necessarily just this past year, but during my rugby career. I did not make the Springbok squad in 2015. We lost the Currie Cup final against WP the previous year under my captaincy, but I also had the privilege of leading the team in the Super Rugby series. So, I expected that the new season would come, and I would just resume the captaincy again with the objective to win the Currie Cup series. However, Coach Ackies shared the news with me that Jaco Kriel would be the caption for the season, and I therefore had to take a back seat. I remember how shattered I was. I could not understand it, but after a few hours of introspection I realised that my ego had become the better of me and the captaincy and title had become my focus. It was about me and not the team. I had to learn that a leader does not necessarily need a title to lead. We all have the opportunity to lead every day. Jaco and I are still good friends and yes, we won the Currie Cup. I had to learn the hard lesson, and today I still am aware of every choice and reaction I make, and I ask the question: Is it ego or heart that is speaking the loudest?*

My greatest achievement is... *my family – my children, my wife, and who we are as a unit. We are so proud of each other and love each other very much.*

The Bible verse that carries me...

Philippians 4:13,
"I can do all things through Christ who strengthens me."
This is a verse that my mother always gave me as a young boy before the matches. I was a rather shy and anxious young man, and it always helped me to hold on to that.

MY STORY
Warren Whiteley

Warren Whiteley would never describe himself as fierce or forceful, but as a determined young man who always wanted to be the best version of himself in everything he undertook! As a child, life had already begun to teach Warren that victory is not always the order of the day and that there are more lessons to be learnt from defeat than from victory. However, he found this thought hard to stomach and only began to accept it as a high school student. *"I worked extremely hard all my life because I loathed losing. My parents never pushed me to win, instead they encouraged me to just participate, but as a little boy I had suffered from anxiety when I lost and had to come to terms with the idea that it was a part of life ... However, well-known American basketball coach John Wooden's approach to sports made an impression on me and taught me: All of life is just peaks and valleys. Do not let the peaks get too high and the valleys too deep. I had to learn this for myself, especially in our industry. Losing is inevitable and when you can let go of the fear of losing, growth will take place within you..."*

The growth was accompanied by heavy life lessons and very deep valleys where he had to choose to grow, because injury after injury hampered Warren's sports career at the most crucial times. During those emotionally challenging times Warren would often cry out, *"Why Lord? Why now! Why me?"* again and again! He did everything right, focused on physical fitness, mental strength, and kept his thoughts focused, but time and again another unexpected major injury would stop him in his tracks. *"My career has been riddled with injuries and setbacks. I was not selected for the 2015 Rugby World Cup team ... After that, my goal was to work hard for four years and then achieve my big dream – to be part of the 2019 Rugby World Cup ... only to tear my pectoral muscle in 2019 and re-injure my knee. I followed the advice, but still returned to the game too early, which was the final nail in the coffin. My knee would not recover and, in 2019, I had to announce my retirement from rugby, instead of my inclusion in the Rugby World Cup team..."*

Warren still swallows hard when he talks about his big dream which remained exactly that – just a dream. Sometimes he can manage the loss, but other times he just pushes it aside for the time being, believing that everything will work together for the good of those who love God. Even if things do not make one hundred percent sense today, he will believe that God is still in control of his life. The words of sports psychologist Jannie Putter carry weight, *"Whatever happens to me, happens for me."* Warren chooses to see the hopeful picture, even if it is sometimes blurry, because God's Word has power.

Warren with his wife, Felicity, and children, Ava and Samuel

"It is challenging at times; I will not lie. Sometimes I still want to make choices in my own wisdom and come to my own conclusions. Sometimes when I watch a Springbok test, I wonder: What if I still played? But at the same time that thought comes to me, I remind myself of where I am now, of the peace and contentment I experience, the value I now add to other young men's lives, and the fulfilling role I play."

In those moments, Warren's heart becomes quiet again, he experiences peace and then he focuses on what God wants to say. *"God is my Father. I have a close relationship with the Lord … there are difficult times where I question myself or Him, but the incredible part of our relationship is that I can talk to Him. He allows me to feel emotions: Whether I am angry, disappointed, down, or feeling totally lost, I know He is with me all the time."*

But for that awareness of God and such a personal relationship with Him, Warren had to have an encounter with the Lord. That meeting took place in the most unexpected place … between the walls of a stadium in a rugby changing room. *"As a child, I grew up in a strict Reformed Church. I rarely went to church, but as a sports-crazy high school boy, my mother handed me a small note with a Bible verse on it before every game or race. It kept the fire in my heart aflame. I kept wondering about God and sometimes asking myself: Who exactly is this God?"*

Warren was 20 years old on the day that he walked into a cell group for the first time. Johan Ackerman, the head coach of the Lions, invited the players to join, and Warren had chosen to attend. There, at the stadium, Warren would learn the difference between a personal relationship with God and simply knowing about God. *"I always felt that I had to do something to be good enough for God, but when I heard that I had already been forgiven and that God loved me despite my actions, the revelation of God's grace became a reality for me. My whole outlook changed and a new relationship with God began."* The Lions team would always pray before a game and open and close team meetings with prayer. They had the opportunity to pray for each other and a close bond developed. They were strong in spirit and in the flesh, changed people who, in turn, touched and influenced the game and other people's lives.

Today, the purposeful Warren is the defensive coach of the Sharks alongside mentors such as Neil Powell and Dr Eduard Coetzee. Together, they aim and strive for something bigger than themselves. Warren does not know if they will meet all their goals, but that is not what it is about. It is about having a common goal to strive for, something they can set their hearts on. It always remains a surprise to Warren where the Lord leads him, but he has learnt – growth does not happen on his own terms. *"Other players have reached highs, won titles, and retired at the pinnacle of their careers, but not everyone's stories are the same. My dream of a World Cup title or playing 100 Super Rugby matches did not happen. Do I blame God and hold Him responsible for my injuries? No, not at all. God remains good. It is in the low points that we grow, and the miracle of it that launches us into the rest of our lives."*

Warren, the former Springbok captain, is ready for action in his new position as coach. He inspires, leads by example, and passes on the Godly values he has learnt to the young men. *"I must remind myself every day that these are just young men – they are going to make bad choices too. My role now lies in mentoring ... it is my turn to unashamedly and courageously sow hope, because God is in our midst."*

"My pride and joy"

What do you think is the biggest obstacle in men's lives?

1. Men's egos are a significant factor.
2. Awareness of who you are is important, but you must put God's voice first in your life.
3. It is good to have your own dreams and thoughts, but it is more important to talk to the Lord about this.
4. We are imperfect beings who will make mistakes, allow God to shape you to be the man He sees you to be.

How would you like to be remembered?

I would like to be remembered as a serving person. A man who is willing to give of himself to others. Someone who is willing to put his heart on the line, make mistakes, and be the best version he can be.

Your message to South Africa

South Africa, our Father has a wonderful plan for our country and our people. We must continue to believe and trust in His calling for our country. We have a diverse culture that gives us perseverance to bounce back from any challenge. When we believe in one vision, we are stronger together as a nation. Every person can make a difference in their home, community, province, and country.

Warren Whiteley
Exclusive interview
Scan the code to watch
◀◀◀

Ava, Lily, and Samuel

Theo Bierman

Theo Bierman is an ultra-endurance athlete with All World athlete status. He is a life coach, certified Ironman coach, TRC triathlon coach, and author of the ebook, *10 Critical Steps Before Any Personal Development*. His high-performance coaching practice is built on principles of life coaching and a walk with God.

The former De La Salle Holy Cross College learner completed two full Ironman challenges back-to-back in November 2022 as part of a charity fundraiser – The Paige Project Back-to-back. It is one full Ironman (226.31 km) immediately followed by another full Ironman (226.31 km). That means 452.62 km in 48 hours! An Ironman triathlon is a great test of one's mental and physical endurance and requires a lot of preparation and dedication.

The Ironman triathlon distances include 3.86 km of swimming, 180.25 km of cycling, and 42.2 km of running.

My love for sport began... *in 2016. I was alone in the UK after a failed attempt to emigrate. My wife and children had already returned to South Africa. During that time, I started training, taking part in races and developing a real love for endurance sports, especially Ironman. However, there is another part of my story that is much more important. I am an addict who has been on the road to recovery for the past nine years. It is my inspiration to get up every morning and to exercise every day. I am a better husband, a better father to my children, and a better coach and athlete because I started on this road of recovery. When I wake up in the morning, the first words I say are, "Thank you, Lord, that I can wake up every morning." When I go to bed at night, these are also the last words on my lips. Endurance sports have become a very big part of the transformation in my life. Actually, they saved my life. I use endurance sports to serve in humility, with vulnerability, and proudly. This is the goal that motivates me every day.*

If I was not a sports star, I would... *It is a tricky question to answer because I would certainly not refer to myself as a sports star! Doing two full Ironmen back-to-back definitely drew attention – something I am eternally grateful for. But this challenge that I had set for myself was to raise money for the Paige Project, a charity I founded with three dear friends. We help raise funds and create awareness for underprivileged children living with cerebral palsy. Because I have family members living with cerebral palsy, I know first-hand what it takes to provide the necessary care. The Paige Project is thus something that I am very passionate about. Under different circumstances, I would* have liked to spend a lot more time on it, but we all have bills to pay and mouths to feed. I do what I can in cooperation with my co-directors. My career is therefore to accept the mantle that God has placed on me, humbly, and to inspire those who cannot inspire themselves, help those who cannot help themselves, and show others that there is a way out – always. I will do this with my God-given talents and use my body and mind to honour Him who gives me strength.

I am incredibly grateful for... my recovery process and surrendering to the fact that only a power greater than myself could restore me to sanity. I am 44 years old. I am now wiser and closer to God than ever before. I am grateful for second chances. He is the centre of my life. During the recovery process, He taught me that I am not the focal point. One can easily have a victim mentality. It is something I still find hard to shake, but with Jesus Christ by my side, I can live each day with the confidence I need. With this assurance and restored sense of self-worth, as a child of God, I am able to be a better husband, father, son, brother, coach, and athlete.

If I could edit my life, I would... have sought help sooner. When I look at my life holistically, I realise that much of the damage I caused could have been avoided if I had decided, as a young adult, to follow a mentor. As a teenager, I lost a parent to addiction, and I grew up without any guidance. As a coach, I now see how crucial it is to have the right kind of mentorship and guidance, both in the sports world and in one's personal development. I was young and ignorant and made important life decisions on my own. I was not equipped to take on the responsibility that was thrust upon me

Friends become family when you go through hardships together

at such an early age. However, many of the mistakes I made have contributed to the steadfast, successful, driven person I am today. I wish that my children's entry into this world was met with a sober father. I wish that I drew upon the Christian faith earlier in my life; it would have given me the foundation to get through many dark times. I understand that the only way to overcome pain is to go through it, but it did not have to be that complicated or difficult. All I had to do was give it up to Jesus, right from the very beginning, and everything would have worked out better. I am sure I would not have left such a scorched road behind me. Nevertheless, the past is the past, and I can now move forward in the right direction.

One of the biggest lessons I learnt this year... *is to understand that my own limits are firmly cemented in mental resilience, which seems to be more apparent at middle age. Mental perseverance is just like physical fitness, it is a skill that develops over time. During training or in competitions, every amateur athlete eventually comes to a decisive moment when their thinking has a greater impact on performance than their bodies. These moments can make or break an important training session or an important race and can even have a ripple effect in their lives. During COVID, I decided to go all in on understanding what my limits were. I thought I could do more than I could, but when I established what my limits really were, I was able to set achievable goals and execute them realistically. I swam, cycled, and ran 452 km in 48 hours and had to follow a "less is more" approach. The plan that allowed me to achieve this goal had to be simple, because complicated solutions do not solve complicated problems. Simple solutions solve complicated problems. We often tend to complicate our problems because we devote most of our lives to telling ourselves stories about who we are – to the point where these stories become a reality.*

Once you set realistic goals as part of a simple plan, and consistently achieve these goals one after the other, you begin to systematically destroy your limiting beliefs.

My biggest achievement is... *Apart from staying married to the woman who helped save my life, and having two beautiful children, my biggest achievement is completing a 452 km swim/cycle/run challenge in 48 hours during The Paige Project Back-to-Back. It was a life-changing event that was made one hundred percent possible with the strength, perseverance, and determination that God gave me. The result of this experience confirmed that my next challenge, whatever it may be, is completely achievable.*

The Bible verse that carries me...

Psalm 19:14,
"Let the words of my mouth and the meditation of my heart be acceptable in Your sight, O Lord, my strength and my Redeemer."

MY STORY
Theo Bierman

On the 29th of January 2014, Theo Bierman's life came to a halt. He was 35 years old. He remembers her eyes so well – the sadness with which his wife looked at him as he looked back at them through the rear window of the moving vehicle. She was eight months pregnant and as she held their firstborn, a one-year-old boy, tears streamed down her cheeks. *"I was on my way to the rehabilitation centre. It was the lowest moment of my entire life, but I made a choice to recover after all these years."*

"Everything is only made possible with the power of one. The starting point is one. That is how the kilometres stack up. Two follow one, then three follow – until one step has become thousands, but one action – the first – is the beginning. This was my first step towards recovery. The power of one is synonymous with my faith and my relationship with God, but I had to learn it step by step."

Theo was born into drug addiction – he grew up with drug addiction and alcoholism in his childhood home. Some friends and family members overcame the problem with the necessary help, but others... never did. Despite the chaos that surrounded him, it was a choice that Theo made for himself, and the course he took was the path of drug abuse. As a 13-year-old, he began the self-destructive path of self-medication. Fundamental principles for life did not exist in the framework of his life. He had to rely on himself because that was where he felt safe, it was all he knew.

God was not a reality in his life. However, when he looks back now, Theo can see the protective hand of an invisible God throughout his life. He never asked Him for guidance, but God was always there, in one way or another.

It was 2016, the third year of the 12-step Narcotics Anonymous rehab programme. Theo and his family decided to emigrate and start afresh. They packed everything and left behind all things familiar with the high hopes of a new start in the United Kingdom. However, after a few months, the dream to start anew in a foreign country evaporated with the reality of a failed emigration attempt. Theo had to stay behind, and again he would have to say goodbye to his wife and children. This time at an airport, and this time for a year. *"I could not return home with my family because I had to stay behind for work. It made me feel like I was saying goodbye to all three of them again, just like the day I was admitted to the rehabilitation centre."*

In 2019, Theo turned 40. Forty – that dreaded age for men stared him squarely in the face. It forced him to his knees again with the question in his heart, "What have I achieved?"

"The meaning of 40 was huge for me, because it implied the halfway mark. Halfway through my life. It was scary because I thought that the previous 40 years of my life were not significant enough to make me feel like I could be proud of myself."

It was the inexplicable uncertainty about who he was as a person and man, his calling, missed opportunities, wasted time, and the constant wondering about "what if" that occupied Theo's mind. During this uncertain time, he was requested to fulfil a supporting role for a fellow member of Narcotics Anonymous (NA). Theo was on step five of a twelve-year programme and had been clean for five years. By the programme's standards, he was fully equipped to provide the necessary support. Yet, constant questions and uncertainty overwhelmed him. How could he act as a role model and pillar of support? *"Even though I discovered the Ironman competitions and used them to recover while following the NA programme, I still felt like I was not being held accountable for my mistakes."* The only answer was that He had to surrender, because without surrendering his will to God, he would fail again and again. Theo's misconceptions about himself caught up with him; despair, isolation, denial, and powerlessness began to consume his soul. *"Surrendering saved me; I was finally able to identify the obsessive forms of behaviour that even in the 'programme' manifested in so many ways in my life. I could just surrender. Not give up."*

"Do not waste any more light."

These were the words – a clear message from God to him. On that day, Theo's heart and mindset changed. His actual recovery process was in God's hands. He could not and did not want to tackle it alone anymore! For the next twelve months, Theo's journey would begin with a yearning for personal development, obedience to God, and the beginning of a career in coaching.

Theo is now celebrating his ninth year of freedom from addiction. He has found new ways to live and to give back by living the principles of recovery, vulnerability, and accountability.

"I now live with God-given tools to make sure that despair does not blow me to pieces when obstacles fall on me like missiles: I just take one step at a time with God. This way, I am not swept off my feet. Walking with Jesus one step at a time means that I am steadfast in my core values so that I do not get emotionally overwhelmed. It also means that I have clarity about my 'why' and my one big focal point that drives me forward, regardless of what lies ahead."

Theo also had to learn to forgive himself and love himself again. A walk of being vulnerable before God, in intimacy with Him and in faith, followed.

Psalm 19:14,
"Let the words of my mouth and the
meditation of my heart be acceptable in Your sight,
O Lord, my strength and my Redeemer."

"If there was ever one verse that sums up what it means to have a heart that seeks after God, it would be this one. For me, this is the blueprint of who I want to be for God. When I begin to question myself and the value I add to life, when I reach an abyss of uncertainty, when I encounter hardship and I falter in my ability to discern what God expects, I read this verse. I can apply this to any situation in my life, and in the blink of an eye, I calm down. There could be no simpler guideline to live by. And as a former addict, it is like the oxygen I breathe."

How does a 44-year-old man like Theo get through 452 km of swimming, cycling, and running in 48 hours? By realising that we do not have to do anything alone. *"I do not run alone, and I do not recover alone. I do not do life alone. God is, was, and will always be with me, one step at a time. One decision at a time. Day by day"*

Theo during Ironman 2022 in Gqeberha

What do you think is the biggest obstacle in men's lives?

There is a complete lack of self-love in men. It is about understanding how we attribute value to ourselves as men; therefore, to have a deeper insight into what gives us a sense of self-worth. It is recognising that, as men, we sabotage ourselves and prevent our own progress. Then there is the ever-elusive confidence; we must learn how to cultivate a good self-esteem. Sometimes we have to admit that we are stunting our own growth.

As men, we often ignore our own needs and deny what is going on inside of us. We bottle up our feelings, do not process them, and build up resentment – this becomes our default behaviour. Before we know it, we are on a path where bad thought patterns give rise to bad decisions – "stinking thinking". How many times has an unfulfilled man not stood laughing amongst a group of friends around a braai, hiding the pain and emotions inside that could be healed, if he would only admit to them... We all show pain in different ways and, therefore, we process it in different ways.

We must learn to put God first and listen to Him – then the focus is on Him and not on our weaknesses and failures. I was a man who had unrealistic goals, things that were not connected to my "one big thing". I had to learn how to set goals that were achievable and break them down into daily, achievable tasks. It is okay to be held accountable for these goals and to know that success is not measured by our ability, but by the journey to the end goal.

How would you like to be remembered?

I would like to be remembered as:

- A successfully recovered addict who never relapsed.
- A man who always said what he did and did what he said.
- A man who was always honest with his wife, and never again put his "mask" on.
- A man who was always present and devoted to his children – as children and as adults.
- A man who served with zero ego, with vulnerability, and proudly.
- A man who fulfilled his purpose and carried out God's will to its fullest.

"My help comes from the Lord who made the heaven and the earth."

Your message to South Africa

It is important to highlight how circumstances from our past can cause us to create stories that we grow up with and that shape us as adults. These are stories that limit us, that reinforce limiting beliefs about ourselves. Pain is passed down from one generation to the next, until someone is willing to feel it (acknowledge it) and do something about it. Our healing saves the next generation. However, the healing cannot begin unless we are willing to feel pain. If you are someone who is simply lost and needs to regain control of your life, then accept responsibility, and when you do, do not shy away from your vulnerability. You also do not have to be an addict to recover, you may simply be someone who is just lost and needs to find your way to recover.

If you want to be in charge of your new life, take responsibility for your health and exercise, for your fitness, but even more importantly, take responsibility for your emotional well-being and make Jesus the centre of it all.

Theo Bierman
Exclusive interview
Scan the code to watch

Day 3 of the The Paige Project Back-to-Back

"A special moment in my life. A new beginning"

Wenda Nel

Wenda Nel (née Theron), born on the 30th July 1988, is a two-time Olympic athlete. Early in her life, this daughter of Worcester's name became synonymous with the 400 m hurdles event. She won her first senior national title in 2010 and dominated the discipline until 2022. She was only beaten in 2013 and in 2019. Wenda's career highlights include the 2011 World Championships, African Championships in 2014, 2016, 2018, and 2019; the Commonwealth Games in Australia in 2018, and the Olympic Games in Rio de Janeiro, Brazil (2016), as well as Japan (2021). Her personal best time in the 400 m hurdles is 54.37 in 2015, and 52.03 in the 400 m sprint in 2017. From 2014 to 2018, Wenda counted among the 20 fastest athletes in the world – in 2018 she was the ninth fastest.

During the 12 years she has been running hurdles, this University of Pretoria athlete has won a bronze medal at the 2018 Commonwealth Games, two African titles (in 2014 and 2016 she was the African champion in the 400 m hurdles), and won nine South African titles.

In 2022, at the end of her 13th season and at the age of 35, Wenda announced her retirement from athletics and put away her spikes for good.

My love for sport began... *I have been running since I can remember! I was extra privileged to grow up in an active and sporty family. I was able to explore my love for sport freely and this developed my passion for athletics. From a young age, I was exposed to opportunities and never felt undue pressure to perform. I was able to experience the joy of participation on my own terms and, therefore, fully enjoy it. I also learnt quickly about all the good qualities that sport develops in a person. Being sporty was a talent that I received as a gift from God and I wanted to develop it to the fullest to glorify Him.*

If I was not a sports star, I would... *I realised from a young age that I would like to do something relating to sports. I developed an interest in becoming a physiotherapist, but then life took a different turn for me. I have also always enjoyed a good meal and was interested in sports nutrition; hence my choice to study and become a qualified dietitian. I suppose I would have started it much earlier in my life if professional sport had not been my destiny.*

I am incredibly grateful for... *my husband, family, and friends' love, care, and support in my life's journey. Gratitude has a high priority in my life. Breathing is a privilege and*

I often remind myself to not take anything I am or have for granted; to choose joy, regardless of my circumstances. I am truly grateful for all the life lessons I have learnt. I strive, on a daily basis, to be a better person who can make a positive difference, no matter how small it is.

If I could edit my life, I would... Hindsight is a perfect science – this is something I had to learn and understand. I am truly grateful for all the life lessons. I tried to teach myself from an early age to, "Live with no regrets." Yes, we all make mistakes, but it only remains a mistake if we choose to not learn something from it. So, my journey is full of life lessons, not mistakes. The choices I made in life were based on the information I had at my disposal at that stage of the game, and I believed and trusted that I would make the best decision with what I had. Yes, when one looks back, you often think that you should have made different choices ... but that is exactly my point – with more information, you probably would have decided differently. That is why I choose not to walk around with regret, because we will always wish that our lives were different. Find the joy in your circumstances and be the best person you can be with what you have. So, I do not think I would change anything. I am grateful for the highs and lows in my life. They helped me to develop into who I am today and I remain open-minded to keep on learning.

One of the biggest lessons I learnt this year... Nothing is guaranteed. Do not take anything for granted. Love your neighbour and your enemy even more so. Celebrate life and use every opportunity in the best way you can. Be grateful, love. Bitterness destroys your soul, so say "sorry" and learn to forgive.

My greatest achievement is... the bronze medal at the 2018 Commonwealth Games in Australia. It is not about the medal for me, but it is a reminder of extra appreciation for the build-up of my journey to the Games. It is an inexplicable feeling, but I believe the Lord sent me on a journey of transformation at the time. Even though I am always learning more about life, I still hold on to the qualities that I virtually mastered during that time. The fact that I had the opportunity to participate twice in the Olympic Games was also a great goal of mine that I attained.

The Bible verse that carries me...

Psalm 46:11 (NIV),
"Be still and know that I am God! I will be honoured
by the nations, exalted above all the earth."

I have many Bible verses like that, but I stick to this one because it gives me extra peace and keeps me calm in times of uncertainty. It reminds me of God's omnipotence and that I am never alone, no matter what pain I experience. He is always with me and I am in His hands.

MY STORY
Wenda Nel

"Life is full of storms and we are not immune to them. I have been through many storms, but while I had to choose again and again Who my lifeboat was, I only came out stronger on the other side."

Wenda Nel had to apply this approach from an early age, and found peace in her heart about who God was going to be in her life. For her, He is her lifeboat, the One to whom she swims when life's waves capsize her boat and the gales of life catch her off guard; the One who softens painful scars and allows character to be built ... because there will always be other people coming your way in the future, who also need a lifeline...

Wenda lost both her parents at a young age.

She was two years old when her mother died, and only six years old when her father passed away.

"My father remarried after my mother's death, he married a wonderful woman, but he died soon after. I was six years old. It certainly had an impact on my life. Even now. But at the time, I had to choose what I would allow to affect my life. I gained a new mother, who influenced my life so positively; therefore I could choose to see the silver lining around the dark cloud."

As a little girl, Wenda was raised in a Christian home and feels that she was introduced to the Christian faith in a healthy way. Later, during her student years, she wandered off on her own exploration of faith, which eventually brought her back to Jesus' feet. *"I had to explore things and get clarity for myself, because life was and will probably always be full of unanswered questions. I had to find out that life can be unfair and full of brokenness, but that there is also one promise to stand on – God's inexhaustible love. I had to learn that God plans good things for our lives, but that sadness and pain inevitably go hand in hand with life on earth. However, this does not diminish God's goodness and love at all ... we just have to be a little more sensitive to His Spirit and voice."*

When newspapers report crime stories and news channels mention crime statistics, the general reaction of the South African public is to shake their heads and feel a familiar

Commonwealth games 2018

anxiety, because it remains one of the biggest fears in every household: a home invasion and hold-up scenario. At the end of 2016, after an exciting athletics season, Wenda and the people closest to her experienced a terrifying evening that tested her faith in God to the limit. What was supposed to be a festive gathering for a family wedding, turned into a nightmare. Four of them were detained and robbed in their guesthouse that night. *"We were already asleep when I woke up after midnight with someone screaming in our little unit. Before I knew it, there was a man with a balaclava and a weapon next to my bed; he motioned that I should go with him to the other room where the others were already gathered. The whole thing felt like it took a lifetime. Four men forced us to sit on the beds while they nonchalantly riffled through all our belongings and took what they wanted."*

> **"I was frozen to the bed and could not move, with terror gripping my heart."**

"For a moment you think, 'This is it … my life is coming to an end'. When that thought came to me, I experienced the greatest peace, and knew that the Lord was sitting right there with us. The men gave us final instructions and then locked us in the bathroom. When we could no longer hear their voices in the house, one of us climbed through the bathroom window to raise the alarm."

As with any traumatic experience, no one comes through unscathed or unchanged. Wenda fooled herself for a few months by just going on with life as normal – until one day. She came to the realisation that she was living with a "numbness" and that the horrible feeling was keeping her from truly living life to the fullest. *"I purposely started to sit at the Lord's feet more to regain my joy in life. I had to learn to let my ship sail on without fear, knowing that God is the captain at the helm. Through my journey that next year, I discovered again how good He is to me. Nothing can separate us from His love … no anxiety, fear, uncertainty, or emotion can drive us away from Him, or is greater than His love and mercy. I gained a new appreciation for life. But I also could let go of my fear of death.* As Paul says in Philippians 1:21,

> ### *"…for to me, to live is Christ, and to die is gain."*

Wenda lives by *"even if not…"* – a statement that taught her that even if none of her plans work out in her favour, and even if things happen to her that were totally outside of her plans and control, even then she would still believe in God's goodness. God's love remains the only unchanging aspect in her life; the one thing that stays with her no matter how bad the storms are. *"I am not a Jesus follower for the earthly happiness that I can gain from Him. I am a Jesus follower for what He has already done for me on the cross. This belief is the foundation on which I base everything in my life. We are human, we are not perfect, but it is my belief that God loves me infinitely with all my imperfections, which helps me to be able to live life to the fullest."*

On the sports field is precisely where she experiences God the most; when she can live out her talent with joy. Wenda was created in God's image and she believes that He wants every person to enjoy what they do, regardless of disappointments and setbacks, *"…because it is not just about us as people. It is not about me. I believe we are God's instruments and each one has a playground where we can use what has been given to us to glorify Him."* With an emphasis on humility, the sports field was her playground and mission field for years – the arena where the world's eyes are fixed on status, medals, and records. *"It was definitely enjoyable and satisfying to win and have the medals around my neck, especially when I worked hard to achieve a specific goal. However, I knew that it was a temporary playground and that part of my life would also come to an end one day…"*

> ### *"I submitted to the pruning process, again and again, so that I would not find my value and identity in a win, because what we have can be taken away so easily, and what remains is who we are."*

"I was able to find joy in who I am in the Lord, and the rest is a result of that."

She had her fair share of pruning sessions with every injury and every setback with illness. When her body was weak, she had no choice but to fall back on her mental and emotional strength. This is when prayer became as natural as breathing and she had to use her well-trained and conditioned mind to lift her out of the dark void. Looking back at the past few years of her life, it is adaptability that has been her salvation. *"The COVID pandemic and lockdown taught me to be more adaptable; I learnt how to change my goals. We may have a plan, but life can change it for us very quickly. It was also a big mental challenge for me. Various emotions resurfaced and forced me to face them. I definitely became aware of the fact that my identity should not be in my sport and that I am more than just an athlete. Through the process of renewed self-discovery, God also showed me, once again, that I am never alone. Who I am and what I have is lent to me. I am made in His image and must be an example of that to my fellow man."*

Hebrews 12:1 remains an anchor for her, "Therefore we also, since we are surrounded by so great a cloud of witnesses, let us lay aside every weight, and the sin which so easily ensnares us, and let us run with endurance the race that is set before us…"

"In my life, God has often made me aware of the fact that we should not compare ourselves to others. We are each running our own race, and only through His strength will we reach the finish line. It may seem that other people's challenges are easier, but God has taught me that I should celebrate my joys and disappointments and not compare them to the road that others may have to walk."

After thirteen hard seasons on the sports field, a new one lies ahead for Wenda. Her spikes have been packed away forever and, at 35, she has turned her lifeboat towards the open sea. The well-known singer Jo Black, in his Afrikaans song, *Skepe* (ships), sings about ships that look beautiful and peaceful in the harbour, but that is not their purpose. They were made to face the rough seas and conquer the waves.

'n Skip word in 'n hawe gebou
'n Skip lyk in 'n hawe baie mooi vir my en jou
Maar dis nie waarvoor skepe gemaak word nie

Die storms en die winde sal waai
Hys jou seile hoog
Want een of ander tyd moet die tyding draai

Laat die kompas van jou siel weer jou hart bepaal
Kry jou maste reg
Haal die anker uit, in die rigting van die Suiderkruis

Wenda with her husband, Jacques

Ons is gemaak om uit te gaan
Op die golwe van die diepste oseaan
Ons vind ons rigting in die sterre en die helder maan
Ons is gemaak in hoop se naam
Ons is gemaak om uit te gaan

Die lewe sal jou gooi en jou rondruk
Soms voel dit of jy sink
Maar jy moet net jou voete soos Petrus vind
En dalk net weer glo soos 'n kind

Hou net koers, want soms kom die twyfel
Dit gaan meer oor hoe jy opstaan en
minder oor hoe jy struikel
Moenie vrees as die waters rof raak nie
Tel jou skouers op
Voel jou hart weer klop

Ons is gemaak om uit te gaan
Op die golwe van die diepste oseaan
Ons vind ons rigting in die sterre en die helder maan
Ons is gemaak in hoop se naam
Ons is gemaak om uit te gaan

Stuur jou skip nou deur die poorte
Ons hoop is meer as net leë woorde
Jy's in beheer van jou bestemming
Hoe jy daar uitkom is jou eie besluit

"My love"

Love for nature

This is exactly how Wenda is facing her new season of life, with hope and faith in her heart.

"I have learnt anew to be patient, to have faith in the unknown, and to pay more attention to the type of person I would like to be. I do not want to focus just on what I have achieved on the sports field. With only the confirmation of God's Word that He is in my future, I choose life now and celebrate the small victories of day-to-day life. As long as I have breath, I can make a positive difference wherever I go and that is what I would like to do ... to give others hope."

What do you think is the biggest obstacle in women's lives?

A woman's self-esteem. We are easily judged by our appearance. I believe we still struggle with the fact that in the eyes of the world, most things / professions are dominated by men. This causes women to act much more tentatively. We must begin to believe that we are made in God's image, and live with confidence in that truth.

How would you like to be remembered?

I would like to be remembered as a woman who was a living example of God's love, compassion, and care towards her fellow human beings – one who inspired other people

through my example as a sportswoman. I would hope others could experience certain qualities in me that I exhibited on and off the sports field. I would hope I could teach the younger generation about grit – the type of endurance and persistence that is becoming increasingly rare. I would like people to realise that you do not have to give up after one disappointment in life, but that you can discover a type of fight in yourself that will make it worthwhile for you. I would hope people learnt something from my example of getting back up from setbacks and trying again. To be able to do most things in life well requires discipline and perseverance. I would hope people witnessed that despite disappointments, sacrifices, sadness, and anger, I still enjoyed what I did and honoured my Father with my talents.

Your message to South Africa

Never think that your dreams are too big. Choose life and remember that comparison is the greatest killer of passion. Write your story without comparing it to others, find joy in what you do, and be happy for others' success stories, but at the same time stay motivated to keep writing your story. We were made for a much greater purpose than our achievements, may the hunger continue to grow in all of us to understand that purpose. My prayer for South Africa is that everyone may live in such a way that we choose to build each other up and not tear each other down; to let the fruit of the Spirit flow from our lives. Choose to live with more joy instead of bitterness. Don't be bitter, be better. There is someone out there every day who just needs your smile – share it with them.

Wenda Nel
Exclusive interview
Scan the code to watch

Rio Olympics support system

Tokyo Olympics coach and agents (Newton Agency)

Marco Labuschagne

Marco Labuschagne, born on the 30th of January 1998, is a native of Winterton in KwaZulu-Natal, and a former pupil of Bethlehem Voortrekker High School where he matriculated in 2016. Known for his agility, he often wore the number 15 rugby jersey and played alongside the likes of Kwagga Smit, Seabelo Senatla, and Werner Kok. He played for the Griffons from 2014-2016, and then for Western Province (2017-2019). On 22nd of May 2017, at 19 years old, Marco made his debut at Twickenham as a sevens player for the South African national team. With the guidance of coach Neil Powell, they triumphed in 2017 and lifted the trophy as the winners after the Dubai sevens tournament – one of the highlights in Marco's life.

My love for sports began... *with my parents. They are both very fond of various sports and this spilled over into my life. Rugby, tennis, any sport that the school offered, I participated in – but rugby was always the great love of my life. My father was the captain of the town's club team, and I was the "ball boy". Sport has a way of developing good friendships and bringing different cultures together. I cannot imagine my life without sports.*

If I was not a sports star, I would... *be a physiotherapist. Actually, any profession where I could have the opportunity to get to know people, work with them, and make a difference.*

I am incredibly grateful for... *my parents. I can count on my one hand the sporting events, tours, and meets that they did not attend. They were always there, always supportive, and they stood by me through the highs and the lows. I am also grateful for the coaches throughout my career and life – our high school's first team coach, Mr Petrus du Plessis, as well as Braam van Straaten and Ryno Combrinck were all influential in my life. They were the people who summed up my personality and understood how to bring out the best in me. They saw the potential and believed in me when others did not want to give me a chance. Coach Neil Powell is the type of person who inspired me to give my all – on and off the field.*

If I could edit my life, I would... *follow the advice that coach Neil gave me the day my contract with the Blitzboks came to an end. He said to never follow the money, but rather opportunity. I can clearly see the hand of the Lord in my life. I would never be the man I am today if it was not for everything that has happened to me. I am incredibly grateful for all my injuries, all the politics, as well as all the pain and rough times I have* experienced. It has built character in me and transformed me into the man God created me to be.

One of the biggest lessons I learnt this year... *It was a decisive year for my sports and spiritual life. I spent a lot of time in Portugal and learnt lessons about evangelism. We should rather remind people how much God loves them; not how lost they are. I also decided to hang up my rugby boots and go into ministry. I believe this is what I was called to do and the joy I experience is a clear confirmation that I am on the right path.*

My biggest achievement is... *being able to make my debut as a 19-year-old for the Blitzboks at Twickenham. The legendary Rosko Specman and I ran onto the field together as substitutes. It was also a great honour for me to be part of a group of Sevens players who won the Dubai tournament in 2017. After the Sevens, I retired and achieved great success in fifteen-man rugby.*

The Bible verse that carries me...

Judges 6:12,
"When the angel of the Lord appeared to Gideon,
he said, 'The Lord is with you, mighty warrior.'"
This verse is linked to an amazing testimony in my life. Three different people, independently from one another, have confirmed this verse over my life. I hold on to it with my whole heart.

Marco – one of Evangelist Angus Buchan's spiritual sons

MY STORY
Marco Labuschagne

It was after the first team's third league match that Marco had to process the damning news. His ankle would have to undergo an eight-week recovery process, even after a series of blood plasma injections – a medical procedure when white blood cells are injected into a torn muscle, speeding up healing.

He might have had to miss the upcoming SA Schools rugby tournament and forgo his dream of donning the green and gold. Hours turned into days and, on the 26th of May 2016, after many pleading prayers, Marco's mother, Riëtte, sent him a video of the preacher and evangelist, Angus Buchan. It was in this very sermon that Uncle Angus mentioned that one should not have self-centred prayers, but rather God-centred prayers. In the middle of his sentence Uncle Angus stopped suddenly and mentioned that he felt there was a rugby player watching the video, one who was struggling to play provincially, and he wanted to tell this player that if he believed he could do anything with and through God's help, he would not only play provincially, but also nationally!

The 18-year-old Marco took those words and promise to heart in the hope that this would be his year. Where he would initially have been out of action for eight weeks, he ended up playing his first game after only five weeks and had an exceptional Craven Week. Since the majority of the sports experts were of the opinion that Marco's rugby career seemed to be on the highway to success, there was great disappointment when the team selections were announced, and his name was not there.

Dr Martin Luther King wrote, "We must accept finite disappointment, but never lose infinite hope." The truth of this was also proven in Marco's life, because in 2016 – his matric year – he signed a contract with the SAS Rugby Sevens Academy and WP Rugby. It was also in that year that the national prayer day, "It's Time", was held on the 22nd of April 2017 in Bloemfontein – the day Marco Labuschagne gave his heart to the Lord. *"I have done this many times before, but on that day the Lord pulled me out of all my old habits and religious traditions into the realisation that He wants a relationship with me. In an instant, my life changed forever."* Matthew 16:24 reads, "Then Jesus said to His disciples: 'If anyone wants to come after me, he must deny himself, take up his cross, and follow me.'" *"Before I could always give everything to the Lord, but never my rugby ... because I found my identity in rugby."* It was two weeks after Marco gave his heart to the Lord, and two weeks after he gave his rugby to the Lord, that God took control. *"One morning I was sitting at the sports academy in Stellenbosch, eating breakfast, when a coach approached me and informed me that I had to pack my bags, because that*

Marco with coach Neil Powell on the day before his debut in 2017

evening I would be flying out to London to possibly make my debut for the Blitzboks." On the 22nd of May 2017, Marco made his debut in the green and gold on the field at Twickenham. He gives all the glory to God – not only for the achievement, but because God is able to do so much more with those things that we are willing to hand over to Him, than we could ever do in our own strength.

When Marco looks back on an illustrious rugby career, he realises all too well that there are still stormy seasons within the grace of God's hand. The three years from 2019-2021 were some of the most difficult times in Marco's sporting career. Politics, team selections, and injuries hit him hard and there were also challenges in his family life. The periods before, in the midst of, and after COVID sometimes felt like a continuous storm. This was the season that he realised how important it is to find your identity in Christ. *"As children of God, we can hold on to His promises and know that He will come through for us in His own way. God remains good, no matter what the circumstances look like, no matter how impossible something seems, and how difficult things are going. If you stay focused on God, your eyes fixed on Jesus, it is possible to continue to shine wherever you go."*

God's character never changes, even if your season or circumstances change, He remains constant. Marco remembers a conversation with a coach in Pretoria. He wanted to know how Marco stayed so positive despite not being considered for the team, to which Marco replied:

> *"Coach, I'm going to be honest, whether you pick me or not, nothing is going to stop me from getting where God wants me to be. In the end, I will achieve what God wants me to achieve, as long as I keep working hard. Even if I never achieve anything again with sports, I am at peace; even if I am called to do something else."*

Like Peter kept his eyes fixed on Jesus and was able to walk on water, Marco tries to keep his eyes on Jesus every day, because the moment we look at our circumstances and lose hope, we sink. It is a hole that many people struggle to get out of.

What do you think is the biggest obstacle in men's lives?

Men stumble easily because they do not find their identity in the right place. Society says that money, possessions, and performance determine your worth and thus men lose themselves in the pressure of what society says one must be or do to be successful. One of the biggest obstacles, if not the biggest, is that men are too proud to talk about their problems and ask for help. Men think that they must not cry and are not allowed to be weak. I believe true power and strength comes from admitting, raising your hand, and saying, "I'm struggling. I do not have everything under control; there are things that worry me". Nowadays, men are expected to keep silent and try to sort everything out themselves, but a stronger man will raise his hand and ask for help. Men should realise they could have therapy or ministry in their life. This is why the Lord made counsellors and psychologists. Men must learn how to voice what is going on inside.

What are the words and messages from God's heart for you over these last couple of years? What has He shared with you about your life, character, and being you, away from the sports field?

The past few years have been a whirlwind of highs and lows with one constant – God. The realisation that life involves so much more than achievements, medals, and earthly things changed my life in 2020. It was during the lockdown period that I decided I wanted to get involved in full-time ministry and turn people back to Jesus. When you choose God, it means you have to die to yourself. Your own desires are no longer greater than God's desires for you. This is how, since the day I met God, I started living my life. That choice led to a moment in 2022 where, after my last injury, I realised that I was done with rugby and was ready for another season; one where God would use everything, I had experienced so far to prepare me for what He has called me to do. The past few years have ingrained in me that you cannot take anything for granted. The Lord began to challenge me about my prayer life. I no longer ask God to take me out of difficult seasons and change my circumstances, but rather that He will change my heart in those seasons to mould me more into the man He has destined me to be. Uncle Angus Buchan always says, "Show me your friends and I will show you your future." I went through a season where I had to change some friendships and today, I surround myself with people who draw me closer to the purpose for which I am here on earth. I have never in my life experienced the joy that I am experiencing right now. I realise that it may seem, to some people, that my life has gone downhill – from Blitzboks to hanging up my "toks". I know that I am exactly where I need to be – focused on God. Opinions and circumstances have no influence on my joy because my joy is found in Him, the Prince of peace.

How would you like to be remembered?

I would like to be remembered as a man of God, someone who never held back from sharing my love for Jesus and telling what Jesus has done and is still doing in my life. According to my own definition, a man of God understands that it is not the end product of a few actions, but rather an eternal, persistent pursuit of obedience that leads to holiness, and so, becoming more and more like Jesus every day.

Your message to South Africa

It is important to remember that you are not alone, God loves you. It is time for us to turn back to the One who gives true peace and joy. He is the answer to all our problems and darkness, He is the light, and He is faithful. It is easier said than done, until you do it and realise how simple it really is.

Marco Labuschagne
Exclusive interview
Scan the code to watch

Marco with mother Riëtte and father Natie at the Blitzboks' year-end function where he received his green and gold jacket

Leon Schuster

Leon Ernest "Schucks" Schuster, born on the 21st of May 1951, is a South African filmmaker, comedian, actor, prankster, and singer. Mr "Hie' Kommie Bokke!" is not only a sports fanatic but is also a keen sportsman himself. The former Wilgehof Primary School learner excelled in athletics and rugby and, until recently, could boast of holding the record for the 75 m. At the time, Leon was awarded the Victor Ludorum of his primary school for outstanding sporting achievements. After his high school years at Jim Fouché High School in Bloemfontein, he continued his studies and obtained a BA degree at the University of the Free State. There he also played for the first rugby team. This son of Vereeniging returned to his alma mater as a qualified high school teacher before starting his career in broadcasting behind the microphone at the South African Broadcasting Corporation (SABC).

This is where Leon Schuster or "Schucks" took shape. Under the guiding hand of experienced broadcaster Fanus Rautenbach, the radio series, *Die Vrypostige Mikrofoon* (the cheeky microphone), saw the light. During inserts, Leon disguised his voice and pranked unsuspecting victims with the fake phone calls being broadcast. It was during this time in 1982 that Leon approached Decibel Records to put together a series of sports songs which resulted in his first record, *Leon Schuster*, selling 10 000 units. His second album, *Broekskeur*, sold more than 40 000 units, followed by *Briekdans* and *Leon Schuster – 20 Treffers*, which sold more than 270 000 copies. His hit CD, *Hie' Kommie Bokke!*, sold more than 235 000 copies during the 1995 Rugby World Cup and won an FNB South African Music Award for Biggest Selling CD of 1995. Leon's music and films include *You Must Be Joking* (1986), *You Must Be Joking! Too* (1987), *Oh Schucks.... It's Schuster!* (1989), *Oh Schucks...! Here Comes UNTAG* (1990), *Sweet 'n Short* (1991) and 13 other well-known films that often left international films and Hollywood blockbusters in the dust at the South African box office. These films were candid camera-type prank movies and slapstick comedy films, including *Mr Bones*, his most successful film, which earned over R33 million at the South African box office. Leon can also add 23 complete music albums to his resume (1981-2008) and a successful single in 2019.

Leon Schuster is currently a writer, speaker, and father of four children (and a whole commotion of grandchildren). And to complete the CV – he is a cornerstone of South African culture and friend of every South African!

My love for sport began... *with my late father. He was a gifted sportsman and had lots of talent. My older brother, Johann, and I inherited it. In my primary school days, I was a lad with a lot of speed. At the end of my primary school career at Wilgehof Laer in Bloemfontein, I won the Victor Ludorum award for outstanding sports achievement. My greatest achievement is that I held the Free State record for the 75 m sprints for u12 boys. My record stood for a long time. Unfortunately, in high school I "stood still" in terms of my growth. I was short and had to compete against guys much taller than me. It was a setback, so I just concentrated on rugby – in the lower ranking teams. My parents played an important role in my interest in sports and were always there to encourage my brother and me.*

If I was not a film producer and singer, I would... *have become a commercial fisherman. It was also thanks to my father that us two boys developed a great love for fishing. I acquired my first boat in 1992 after I bought a small holiday home for our family at Brenton-on-Sea. Those were wonderful days, and I became a skipper of note, I could steer my boat through the dangerous "heads" in Knysna with great ease. Unfortunately, there are no more fish in that part of the world because the big Japanese trawlers with their massive nets have ruined marine life. I fell into a total depression because my hobby was utterly and completely ruined!*

I am incredibly grateful... *that the Lord has given me four beautiful children – as can be seen on my WhatsApp profile picture! Our times together in Knysna were extremely precious. There, I taught my only son, Ernest, to fish. I am grateful to the Lord for second chances in my life in so many instances. No one will ever be perfect, but the fact that He is willing to give me a second chance is a privilege and an honour.*

If I could edit my life, I would... *quite possibly change a few things. I was a man's man and spent a lot of time with my friends and wasted it on drinking. I was always the "clown" and often had to "perform" for my friends. In Brenton-on-Sea, we all spent many*

Leon and (then) Prince Charles

nights together, into the early hours of the mornings. I serenaded the whole community well into the nights – to my great regret today. It was precious time that I could have spent with my family, but I squandered it.

One of the biggest lessons I learnt this year... *is to share your love for your fellow man! Tell your children and buddies or whoever every day: "I love you!" There is no substitute for those three words!*

My greatest achievement is... *my "Hie' kommie Bokke!" album, specifically that song. I have heard from many sources that I helped to spur the Springboks on to a World Cup victory in 1995! During the Rugby World Cup, there was a group of spectators in the open pavilion who waved a giant banner, "Schuster for president!" I think Madiba was "worried" there for a while...*

That was probably my greatest achievement – apart from the day I gave my heart to the Lord.

The best advice I have ever received... *If you are standing, stand on your knees! The good Lord has made many miracles happen in my life, and I have a particularly close relationship with Him. I remain a sinful person, but I can now run to Him and ask for help, or just thank Him!*

The Bible verse that carries me...

Romans 8:31, "If God is for us, who can be against us?"

Leon's four children: twins Shelley and Ernest (34), Leande (40), and Lelani (42)

MY STORY
Leon Schuster

The words of Romans 8:31 still stick in his memory. They took root in his heart, because every time little Leon was afraid and his legs trembled, his father quoted this passage, *"If God is for us..."* and then waited for Leon to complete the sentence *"...who can be against us?"* Armed with these words, like chainmail around his small shoulders, Leon would then take on the task before him – whether it was as bugler in the brass band, playing the last note, or to run out on the rugby field as the smallest player. He believed in these words.

"I grew up in a strict, loving, yet conservative home. Principles and discipline from my father's rule book were our criteria, and my mother's religion was the guideline and foundation of our household. For us, as children, she was the anchor rope that connected us to a living God, and He was her anchor. Who was God to me? The Man we referred to every night when we had family devotions around the dinner table. I did not realise it as a child, I only paid attention to it much later as an adult, almost too late in my life. I connected the spiritual dots that my mother left for me between the pages of her used Bible like a pilgrimage – God was her everything. He was the One who would hear the secret petitions and prayers from a mother's heart. The One who came to meet with her on her knees and through the pages of her Bible. The One she turned to in the prime of her life and also when, at the end of her life's story, she could barely open her eyes ... She always knew Him.

In contrast, I would constantly and stubbornly stick to what I wanted to believe and how I wanted to live ... and I had more questions than answers for the most part of my life."

Leon became interested in filmmaking at an early age. As a child, he and his brother played pranks on their family and filmed it. For example, he poured tomato sauce over his foot and, yelping with his air rifle in hand, showed up at his grandmother's house. He would run down the aisle of the Ritz Theatre playing cowboys and crooks, impersonating Laurel and Hardy, Charlie Chaplin, and the Three Stooges ... always plotting how to elicit the next shock, laugh, or apoplectic fit of rage. Leon thrived on people's emotions and reactions. He was the clown, but brainy and one with a high EQ (emotional intelligence). The one who understood emotions well and was able to draw out reactions with remarkable success and unite people under the banner of laughter and humour.

"For many years I believed that humour was the weapon of unarmed people. However, looking back on my life now, I know that the first weapon of unarmed people is in the spiritual dimension with God. Humour actually comes second and the rest after that. For most of my life, my armour was my own skill and ability to read people. Humour served me, but I knew that somewhere I would have to face the truth; that I would have to make life-changing choices and show people another side of myself ... the side I have kept hidden for too long, fearing that I would miss out on 'something' if I did..."

That other side was his relatively strong personal relationship with God. However shaky it was in his own eyes or according to public opinion, it was always part of his life.

Watershed experiences in his life would repeatedly push Leon in God's direction. The first incident was a freak accident on an athletic field. A discus throwing accident led to the death of one of Leon's close friends. It happened right in front of him and the other high school learners. The second incident, his divorce, forced his four children to live with the consequences of his choices. The third incident was his health, with a nagging back injury and a terrifying back operation that awaited him. The fourth incident, the breakdown of a 25-year relationship with his life partner. The fifth and most recent incident, when the pillar in his life passed away – the final goodbye to his mother when she, as a 100-year-old wife, mother, grandmother, and great-grandmother, died on the 5th of May 2022.

"My life fell apart a little bit at a time with each life-changing event. Because I was so small in stature, I was a nervous young man. After the freak accident and the death of my friend, Oupatjie van Heerden, depression, and anxiety soon followed. I wanted to make sense of the pain in life, but the answers always eluded me. Although I managed to survive several years in a certain sense with learnt behavioural patterns, the backlash of a failed marriage dented my identity as a man and left my fatherly heart in tatters, because I so desperately wanted to spare my children this pain. The third, fourth, and fifth setbacks were the breaking points in my life. It was these three that finally brought met to a place where I broke into pieces before God."

At the age of 70, for the very first time ever, Leon did not have a wisecrack, the answer, or a plan to avoid or numb the pain. On the contrary, the pain would emphasise the depression, all the other shortcomings, and "sin" in his life; he felt he could no longer control it. He could not just give up, he had to surrender, because the pressure of loneliness, an aching heart, constant longing, unanswered questions, depression, and despondency left him anxious and without zest for life.

Leon would face a huge decision. The choice that had followed him around for years and, every now and again, knocked on the door of his heart and asked with the quiet, soft voice: Are you ready for Me yet?

"I could not run away any longer. I did not want to hide anymore. That is why I decided to leave everything. I started cutting out the booze, cigars, and bad habits out of my life.

I had to start taking care of myself physically; to start filtering what I was watching to heal my soul and start focusing on my spiritual well-being. I lost my zeal for life, hid my laughter under a bushel, and no longer saw the light. For weeks on end, I forced myself out of bed in the morning, tried to finish a gym session, sat quietly in my sunroom, and opened my mother's Bible. After that I would sit down in front of the computer, try to write again and be creative. I had to believe that I still had a purpose, that God still had a mission for my life."

It was during those weeks of routine that Leon found God again. God already knew his name and started calling it long ago, but Leon had to open his ears and hear it.

"At the ripe old age of 71, I have taken hold of God and I am not prepared to let go of Him. Not again. I read His Word and believe one hundred percent what it says. I believe like a child again, even if it sounds like a fairy tale to some. Through His Word I found a comforter and protector in God. I can have a conversation with Him, pray to Him, and see His presence in small miracles in my life. He is more important to me than anything else in my life. My children and my heavenly Father are my everything. The devil has held my attention long enough, it is time for me to start living in obedience to my other mission in life."

That mission is to win souls for God; in Leon's unique way and with his way of speaking because God made only one Leon Schuster. Unconventional, a rough diamond, but someone who will most likely go to places and talk to people who will never set foot in a church.

"I speak from my own experiences and mistakes. I say it like it is and speak from the heart. I cannot, will not, and do not want to be someone else. I just want to be Leon, walking hand in hand with God. I look forward to the next chapter of my life, because I know God has a plan for me..."

Leon Schuster is a national treasure. His name is unanimous with Mrs Balls Chutney, droë wors, biltong, Marmite, koeksisters, and milk tart. He needs little to no introduction. He does not mince his words and he calls a spade a spade. He is willing to take a "klap" for what he believes in.

"And this time, I believe in something bigger than myself. It is time that we all welcome the Holy Spirit into our lives. One will never feel fulfilled and be happy without Him in your life. There will always be a void and a longing for something. My challenge to you is, choose Him, leave the nonsense and wrong things behind. Then make a point of it to start reading your favourite chapter in the Bible. A spiritually deeper dimension is needed to get to know God. I promise you, when you really give Him a chance in your life and get to know Him, you will never walk away again. Trust me. I know what I am talking about."

What do you think is the biggest obstacle in men's lives?

If you were to put this question to most men, they would probably readily admit – women. But that is not the truth. No, us men need good women in our lives. When we first understand and admit to ourselves that we are each individually responsible for our own choices, thoughts, and actions, the temptations (in all forms) will be less problematic. Yes, we struggle with many obstacles and every man has a weakness – whether it is the bar, the stadium, pornography, or thoughts you struggle with – it is your responsibility to not suppress the problem and turn to another bad habit behind closed doors. No, somewhere the problem and bad habit must be faced and then you must choose to let that habit go or sort it out ... even if it takes time and help. It takes a man to make a tough decision, see it through, stick with it, and adopt better habits.

How would you like to be remembered?

I would like to be remembered as someone who was given a gift to make people laugh, but in the same breath I want to be remembered as a man who dedicated his heart to God ... even though I only chose later in life to walk closely with the Lord. I want to be known as a man who never hesitated to talk about God and who understood the value of the full armour of God and put it on daily. It is now my only salvation.

Leon singing for his favourite team, the Cheetahs!

Your message to South Africa

Die to the old nature and become a new person. Make a decision to, again, bow your knee before our heavenly Father. Become a born-again Christian and strengthen your relationship with God. Make an effort to spend time in His Word. Read His Word as the only truth and do not question what He shows you. Get to know Him personally and, if you do not have a relationship with Him, start one. And when you get to know Him, hold on to Him.

Pray this short prayer with me: "Lord, I am a sinner. I choose to call on Your name. Please help me, have mercy on me, and forgive my sins. I ask that You will come and fill my heart and life with Your presence. Protect my thoughts, manage my actions, put a guard before my mouth, and embrace me as my heavenly Father. Lord, thank you that I can be called your child. I love You. Amen."

Leon with his only son, Ernest

Hie' Kommie Bokke!